Cloud Computing

Technologies and Strategies
of the Ubiquitous Data Center

Cloud Computing

Technologies and Strategies of the Ubiquitous Data Center

Brian J.S. Chee and Curtis Franklin, Jr.

CRC Press
Taylor & Francis Group
Boca Raton London New York

CRC Press is an imprint of the
Taylor & Francis Group, an **informa** business
AN AUERBACH BOOK

CRC Press
Taylor & Francis Group
6000 Broken Sound Parkway NW, Suite 300
Boca Raton, FL 33487-2742

© 2010 by Taylor and Francis Group, LLC
CRC Press is an imprint of Taylor & Francis Group, an Informa business

No claim to original U.S. Government works

Printed in the United States of America on acid-free paper
10 9 8 7 6 5 4 3 2

International Standard Book Number: 978-1-4398-0612-8 (Hardback)

Visit the Taylor & Francis Web site at
http://www.taylorandfrancis.com

and the CRC Press Web site at
http://www.crcpress.com

Contents

Preface

This book looks at cloud computing from a manager's perspective, and it provides information that a manager can use to engage those who want to talk about the mechanics of application design or the intricacies of finance. There are certainly many subject-matter experts on various middleware frameworks or the return on investment of virtualized environments who could take the discussion much farther than this book will be able to go. That's fine. If you can begin the discussion, ask intelligent questions, and follow along as the conversation begins to go into detail in one direction or another, then this book will have done the job we intended.

What is it about cloud computing that demands that a book be written (and, more important, read)? One of the most important reasons is that cloud computing is a major trend in information processing today. Consumers and enterprises alike are embracing the notion that they need computing *services*—something that happens—rather than computing *devices*—something that sits in the corner. The basic realization that one can have access to a critical service without having to find room for a box that sits in the corner is at the heart of cloud computing.

Of course, if that realization were all there was to cloud computing, then this would be a very thin book indeed. Unfortunately, one of the key qualities of clouds is that they are confusing. What are they? How are clouds different than virtualization? Should my organization use a cloud (or multiple clouds)? Can both clouds and virtualization play significant roles in my organization at the same time? These are just four of the questions that come to mind about the topic that might just be the biggest thing in computing in a generation (or, possibly, might be a passing fad that we'll all laugh about in the future). Just as meteorological clouds can appear to look like different animals or historical scenes depending on the point of view and imagination of the viewer, computing clouds can take many forms depending on the needs and philosophies of the users.

We decided to write this book because we wanted to begin to look for answers for these questions and many more. We spent many hours listening to discussions and arguments about whether clouds were an appropriate answer for given computing problems, and how they might best be understood as part of a comprehensive enterprise computing solution. We found that there was a great deal of disagreement among experienced, intelligent professionals about just how cloud computing could best be incorporated into an enterprise network, and even about whether cloud computing was a legitimate technology framework for enterprise application delivery.

Being able to take part in that discussion is what we hope you will take away from most of this book. We begin by looking at where clouds come from—going back into the history of time-share computing and into the parallel present of virtualization and clusters. If you understand what came before clouds, and all the technology pieces that go into building a cloud, then it is much easier to place clouds into the proper context within the overall enterprise information technology universe. When you understand where clouds came from and what they can do, in a strategic sense, for an organization, then it's much easier to think about how a cloud might answer specific computing questions you might have.

Speaking of answers, we'll share one with you right now: Cloud computing isn't a fad. As with many new technologies, the terminology will likely change with time, but the concept will be around for some time to come. The reason clouds will be around is quite simple: They solve real problems at compelling price levels. Users and organizations will continue to need nearly ubiquitous access to data and services, and they'll be able to count on wide availability of high-speed Internet access. That combination both enables clouds and makes them almost necessary as a technology framework. The middle part of this book is intended to let you begin the process of understanding whether your organization is one for which cloud computing might work. We'll show you some specific use cases and walk through some of the specific issues that particular organizations might have to deal with. We'll also introduce you to the concepts behind different types of clouds. Just as the world of meteorological clouds encompasses everything from high-flying cirrus clouds to fog, computing clouds include public, private, and hybrid clouds; clouds for storage, CPU time, and application delivery; and clouds that mix any and all of these types. After you've finished the middle third of the book, you should have a much better basis on which to have strategic discussions around clouds in your own organization.

The final portion of the book is intended to do a couple of things. The first is to provide some cautionary notes for the discussion. It's not that we were suddenly stricken with cold feet after writing the first part of the book, but that we want the conversation about clouds to be realistic. In any realistic discussion you have to consider issues such as security, application integration, and structural limitations, and we go into some of those as we move through the latter chapters.

Of course, we can't just leave things on a cautionary note, so the final chapter of this book is our look into the future of clouds. Some of the things we'll talk about are right on the horizon, while others are, well, a bit more forward-looking, but all represent realistic (we think) possibilities for future development in the cloud.

Information technology managers and executives who deal with corporate IT should be able to read this book and understand the major issues surrounding cloud computing and its place in the enterprise IT world. From the basics of virtualization and clusters to more advanced strategic considerations of security and return on investment, we provide essential information for readers to be able to join in the discussions that are already in progress at many organizations, and that are coming soon to many, many more.

If you want more information, we will provide pointers and links at the website we're developing to support this book. Professional Cloud Computing, at www.professionalcloudcomputing.com, will help you find information to go deeper into the discussion in any of a number of directions. Once you've read the book, head over there if you want to learn more about any aspect of cloud computing or read other opinions on any of the subject areas we've addressed.

It's also important to understand that it's possible for technology to move faster than the process of writing a book. Several of the topics that started out in the "we think this will happen" category turned into "this is what's happening" during the writing of the book. While this gave us a pleasant glow in the prognostication department, it was inconvenient from a practical perspective. It's possible that it has happened again since these words were written and, well, there's just no solution for the problem. We can only hope that the evolution of the industry will follow our ideas, and that we'll look quite brilliant when you get to those chapters. We're not counting on that, of course, but it would be nice. . . .

Brian J. S. Chee
Curtis Franklin, Jr.

Acknowledgments

As with any large project, no one person is responsible for 100% of the effort, and in our case the road to clouds has been a long and cumulative effort. I'd first like to thank Admiral Grace Hopper, who was most responsible for one of the first computing abstraction layers in the form of COBOL, without which we'd all still be writing in Assembler. Admiral Hopper gave my entire class a short piece of copper wire and told us that it was a nanosecond, or, more accurately, how far an electron would travel in a single nanosecond. I'd also like to thank Norman Abramson, PhD, for his efforts on the AlohaNET project that made Ethernet possible. I was only a gofer, but it was still an honor to be part of history. To my mentors Jeremy Jones and Ward Hayward at Chaminade University, I give my thanks for dragging me into the world of electronics and teaching me about thinking outside the box. My parents, and the Iolani School (K–12), taught me about human networks, cooperative efforts, and the role that education plays in forming long-lasting connections. Wayne Rash and Oliver Rist made superhuman efforts in helping me to form the Advanced Network Computing Laboratory at the University of Hawaii, and helped in setting the standards for large-scale enterprise networking product comparisons.

Most important, I thank the InteropNOC team, which has never failed to humble me before the amazing collection of talent that has built the world's largest networking trade show and the world's largest temporary network. It is this unique collection of talent that has taught me the value of being a generalist instead of a specialist. It is this skill that has taught me how to see a bigger picture.

Lastly, my wife Kathleen has put up with the amazing amount of grief during the writing of this book, and also as I've kept trying to convince folks that Hawaii isn't really a technological backwater.

Brian J. S. Chee

This book has been, in ways far more profound than usual, a team effort. I must therefore offer my thanks to those who have made it possible.

My co-author, great friend, and general partner in crime, Brian drove the project forward when I could not. I can't imagine a better writing partner or friend, and this book quite literally would not exist without his efforts.

My dear wife and partner in life, Carol is the reason I'm here to write this note. An exhaustive list of the reasons for my gratitude would be longer than this book, so I'll have to go with "Thank you for everything," and hope it's enough.

My son Daniel cheered me when I was down, was my window into the computing life of young adults, and made me want to write the best book possible.

Scores of friends around the world offered prayers, good wishes, and general support. My special thanks go to Kathy, Iñigo, Renzo, Brigham, and Marta, each of whom showered me with far more love and support than a reasonable man could expect.

Curtis Franklin, Jr.

About the Authors

Brian J. S. Chee has seen the networking industry grow almost from its first days, working first as a student helping on the AlohaNET project and then as sales support for the early network offerings from Xerox. As one of the first 10 Certified Netware Instructors outside of Novell, Inc., Brian has seen networking evolve from the ground up from the viewpoints of a manufacturer, a distributor, a reseller, a computer scientist at the U.S. General Service Administration Office of Information Security (GSA-OIS), and now at the University of Hawaii School of Ocean and Earth Sciences and Technology (SOEST) as a researcher. As a Senior Contributing Editor to *InfoWorld* magazine and a long-time member of the Interop NOC team, Brian has a unique insight into networking trends and the emergence of new technology.

Curtis Franklin, Jr., has been writing about technologies and products in computing and networking since the early 1980s. A Senior Writer at NetWitness, he also contributes to a number of technology-industry publications including *InfoWorld, Dark Reading,* and *ITWorld.com* on subjects ranging from mobile enterprise computing to enterprise security and wireless networking. He is also online community manager for the Interop conference. Curtis is the author of hundreds of magazine articles, the co-author of three books, and has been a frequent speaker at computer and networking industry conferences across North America and Europe. When he's not writing, Curt is a painter, photographer, cook, and multi-instrumentalist musician, and is active in amateur radio (KG4GWA), scuba diving, and the Florida Master Naturalist program.

Chapter 1

What Is a Cloud?

Nature is a mutable cloud which is always and never the same.
— Ralph Waldo Emerson

In This Chapter

Clouds are, if anything, a moving target of misunderstood buzz words that seem to have caught the attention of industry journalists. Like its namesake, the concept of a cloud is nebulous and at the moment is changing faster than most of us can keep up. However, like rain clouds, cloud computing has the promise of providing a massive surge of growth in an industry that is struggling to grow up. This chapter provides some historical background for the development of cloud technology, because today's (and tomorrow's) cloud environments are built on the shoulders of the giants that came before them.

In this chapter, you'll learn about:

- History, or the mainframe revisited—It's amazing just how cyclical the IT world is. We draw comparisons to how our experience with mainframes is helping to shape the emerging cloud marketplace.
- Abstraction layers and how they hide the gory details—They say that great works are built on the shoulders of giants, and the road to Cloud

City is the same. Abstraction layers have been developing and maturing over the years into a platform fit for the denizens of Olympus.

- Why scientific clusters, also known as high-performance computers or HPCs, are both similar to and different from clouds—Clouds may have started as scientific computing tools, but the overall architecture has diverged to create a whole new technology. We take a hard look at what came before and how it has set the stage for Cloud City.
- Connections to the world and to data all have to happen seamlessly— If clouds are to be accepted, access to the clouds must be reliable and ubiquitous enough to drop off the radar of users. We discuss some of the changes happening that seem tailor-made for clouds.

In the Beginning

In the beginning was the mainframe and it was, if not good, at least straightforward. Users and staff alike knew precisely where input, output, and processing all happened. Think of the mainframe as the dense, hot core of what would become the computing universe we know now. In the (computing) moments just after the "Big Bang," time-share and remote terminal services divorced input and output from processing, but it was still possible to walk down a hall, open a door, and point to the box doing the work. As early as 1960, though, computer scientists such as John McCarthy foresaw computing services that would be treated as a public utility. A decade later, networks and the Internet continued to make processing a more abstract piece of the computing pie.

Abstraction and a move toward computing as a public utility took a great step forward when the concept of Software as a Service (SaaS) was developed in the early 2000s. As the link between applications (or application components) and specific pieces of hardware continued to weaken, information technology professionals searched for new ways to describe systems that resulted of disparate components coming together with no regard to the location of any single piece. The Internet has long been referred to as a "cloud"—named for the symbol used to represent the Internet in network diagrams—and has come now to encompass the trend toward SaaS and Web 2.0 as computing continues toward a disconnect from computing at physical locations. Cloud computing is, in many ways, a return to the centrally coordinated integration of the mainframe time-share era: The personal computer gave users the opportunity to strike back against the "glass house" and the elitism common to that day instead of allowing more cooperative integration of the new resource. Cloud computing is a counterreformation that brings with it the possibility of some very real performance wins for users and their organizations.

Cloud resources can also be described as the latest in a long line of technology advances that have further distanced us from the details of running a data center. Science fiction author Arthur C. Clarke wrote about a global computing facility without shape and form—his characters simply used the "network" to communicate, play games, and do many other things, all without regard to what the operating system or CPU was behind the scenes. People used only what they needed and paid only for what they used. It didn't matter where in the world (or the solar system, as Clarke proposed) you were; you could access your stored information regardless of whether you were using a private or a public terminal. This network was also ubiquitous, since even the monks at the top of a mountain mentioned in *Fountains of Paradise* had a terminal.

So what, precisely, is cloud computing? According to Carl Hewitt, in a paper published in 2008 by the IEEE, cloud computing "is a paradigm in which information is permanently stored in servers on the Internet and cached temporarily on clients that include desktops, entertainment centers, table computers, notebooks, wall computers, handhelds, sensors, monitors, etc." That's a pretty thorough definition, but it may still be incomplete for our purposes, because it doesn't mention management, efficiency, delivery mechanisms, or the concept of abstraction. A more complete definition might be

> Cloud computing is an information-processing model in which centrally administered computing capabilities are delivered as services, on an as-needed basis, across the network to a variety of user-facing devices.

This is the definition on which we will be basing the discussions in this book. We will expand on some of the terms, but this is where we will begin.

For us to get to computing in a cloud, we first have to understand what, precisely, we are talking about. We will start with a discussion of key concepts that underlie cloud computing, then proceed to look at the specifics of cloud computing—and what it is that separates cloud computing from virtualization, clustering, and other forms of computing that separate processing from processors. Along the way, we'll be defining terms used in cloud computing discussions and looking at how and why organizations are using cloud computing for their critical applications.

Computer Services Become Abstract

A computer system's functions and interactions with other systems can be visualized as a set of children's interlocking building blocks. A system architect starts with an imaginary pile of blocks of various colors and sizes, each color representing a different function or process. The expectation is that pieces will lock together from bottom to top, and that they are of compatible sizes so they will form a solid wall when they are fitted into a structure. The concept of an abstraction layer is similar: It provides a way to connect two systems together without radically changing either. As a pleasant (and productive) side effect, abstraction layers can also be described as a way to hide architectural and programming details on either side of the interface.

Abstraction is a critical foundation concept for cloud computing because it allows us to think of a particular service—an application, a particular communication protocol, processing cycles within a CPU, or storage capacity on a hard disk—without thinking about a particular piece of hardware that will provide that service. Let's imagine abstraction applied to a task that has nothing to do with computers; we'll discuss the abstraction of going to the grocery store.

Pretend, for a moment, that you don't own any vehicles for transportation. Instead, you contract with service providers for transportation services. When you're ready to go to the grocery store, you pick up the telephone, dial a number, and tell the operator who picks up where you want to go. The operator, in turn, tells you when transportation will show up at your door. The telephone, telephone number, and the messages sent and received can be thought of as the program interface between you and the transportation service—they are part of a standard, consistent way of requesting transportation. Now, you wait the stated length of time and open your door to find a portal that leads you into a passenger compartment. Every time you request transportation, the portal and the passenger compartment look the same, but you'll never know whether the compartment sits inside an automobile, a bus, a luxury RV, or a yak-pulled cart. The fact is that the vehicle doesn't matter, because the passenger compartment, and transportation to your chosen destination, is all that's important.

When you reach the grocery store (within a time limit specified in the service-level agreement you have with the transportation company sign), the portal opens and you walk out into the store. When you've finished shopping, you place another call, and the same sort of transportation takes you back home (or to your next errand). For each trip, the transportation company is free to send whichever vehicle is available and can make the trip most efficiently, and you're never faced with the inefficiency of having an unused vehicle sitting around while you're doing things at home. Divorcing the transportation from the vehicle is what abstraction is all about. We'll come back to this abstract transportation example later on, but first let's look at just how abstraction has been applied to some common computing and network situations.

The ISO-OSI Model: Seven Layers of Abstraction

The most commonly used abstraction layers in the computing world are found in the Open Systems Interconnection (OSI) seven-layer networking Basic Reference Model. This application of abstraction layers means that network equipment manufacturers (NEMs) no longer have to write software for specific pieces of equipment. In practice, this means that network adapter cards made by, say, 3Com, can connect via a standard cable to an Ethernet switch made by, say, Cisco. It also means that common communication applications such as email and the World Wide Web can operate without having to be aware of which vendor made the network they are communicating across. The International Standards Organization (ISO) developed this seven-layer model, with each subsequent layer fitting into the next in a well-defined, standardized fashion. Very much like Russian *matryoshka* nesting dolls, the ISO seven-layer model separates the network communications path into layers that allow the NEMs to leverage a body of standardized work (see Figure 1.1). This separation of roles has also led to the creation of an entirely new industry that concentrates their work on the manipulation of those middle layers for new and previously unknown services. These nested layers provide a way for

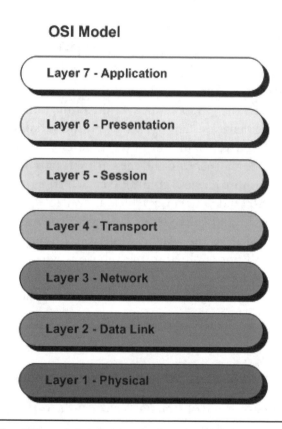

OSI Model

Figure 1.1.   The OSI model defines specific roles for hardware, software, and services that fall into seven distinct layers.

specialization to work toward accomplishing a significantly more complex outcome by eliminating the need to constantly reinvent the wheel whenever a new network services is designed.

The OSI model provides for distinct roles for devices, services, and protocols that lie within each layer, and for specific ways in which the components in one layer interact with components in other layers. These carefully engineered roles and interactions not only make today's open networking possible, they provide a model for the kind of open yet highly structured architecture required for cloud computing to be possible. While the networking model is critical, however, it isn't the only sort of abstraction model required before we can understand cloud computing. Let's look next at the way in which Web servers and databases talk to one another to build popular applications on the Web.

ODBC: The Abstract Database

Another common abstraction model describes the way that Web servers connect to databases. The original database-to-Web connection wasn't developed by a standard committee, but by two programmers searching for a solution to a problem. Richard Chan and Jim Laurel owned a Honolulu-based computer equipment distribution firm called Aspect Computing. Their problem was how to leverage the new World Wide Web to allow customers to check stocking levels for their products. What they came up with became the foundation for the set of protocols that Microsoft and the standards committee would eventually name the Open DataBase Connection (ODBC) at some point after they purchased the technology from Aspect Computing. Originally called WebDB, this fundamental abstraction layer paved the way for many of the cloud services we will discuss later in this book. Basically, instead of having to modify the web server directly through extensive CGI calls specific to each data source, Richard and Jim utilized a set of functions to query various types of databases simply by changing a few configuration items (see Figure 1.2).

Let's take a moment to think about the importance of what ODBC provides. In traditional database applications, the programmer writes an application in language that is specific to the database management software. The piece of the application that makes it specific to a particular database is, in other words, an intrinsic part of the application. If the database manager is changed, the application has to be rewritten in order to remain functional. In the ODBC model, a common query language is used, and an external file provides the configuration information required to make the application work with a specific database. If the database management system changes, no modification is made to the application—all the change happens in the external configuration file. It is, to be sure, an additional component for the overall application, but it is an additional component that makes programming easier and far more efficient for application developers.

OpenGL: Abstract Images

For a number of years the prevailing wisdom was that the additional components required for an open application model such as ODBC exacted a significant cost on the computing system—a cost so heavy that those

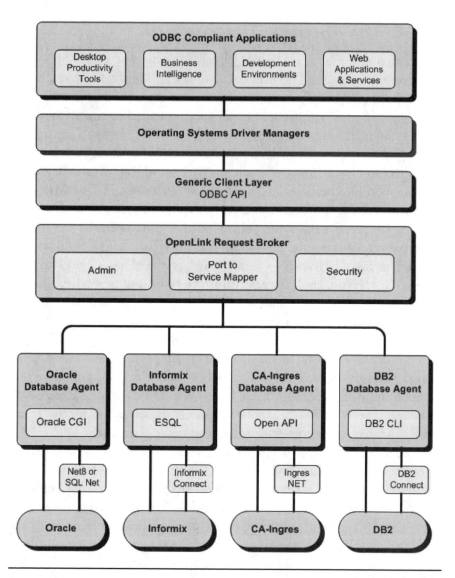

Figure 1.2. ODBC defines a specific set of queries and actions that provide a standard method for an application to make use of any database (or set of databases) without requiring code customized for the individual database language.

applications requiring the highest performance weren't suitable for development on such a model. This wisdom was overturned by the rise of an abstraction model that enables some of the most critically high-performance computing around: graphics display processing (see Figure 1.3).

OpenGL is a library of abstract layers that allows application and operating system programmers to write code for a standards graphics abstract layer, rather than for each new display adapter that might be released to

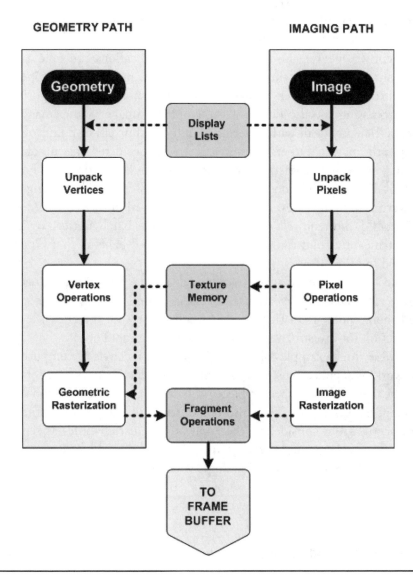

Figure 1.3. OpenGL proved that an abstraction model can be fast enough to service the most performance-intensive parts of a computing platform—the graphic display components.

the market. OpenGL is an important development for the computing industry because of the rapid pace at which new display adapters are brought to market and the critical importance of graphical interfaces to the modern computer user experience.

OpenGL has been well accepted for several reasons. First, it has helped insulate application developers from a very rapidly changing marketplace. New graphics processors, and cards based on them, are brought to market frequently. OpenGL ensures that existing applications can take advantage of the latest hardware as soon as it reaches market. Next, OpenGL is written in a way that allows it to use the most efficient algorithms for processing specific pieces of the graphical image. Some images are most efficiently dealt with in terms of individual pixels, or points of light within the picture. Others are more effectively considered in terms of lines, points, and other geometric components. OpenGL can do both. Finally, OpenGL began to be adopted as graphics processors were becoming more powerful, in many cases, than the basic CPU used in the computer. Even if OpenGL did require a processing tariff, it was barely noticed by users, and it meant a solid trade-off for the substantial benefits that OpenGL offered in other areas.

In OpenGL, we see an abstract model that has been accepted because it lowers the cost of applications, makes those applications available sooner and more widely than they might be otherwise, and provides a level of protection for investments against the horrors of rapid obsolescence.

These three examples of abstraction at various levels of computing—networking, applications, and user interface—demonstrate how software can be divorced from specific pieces of hardware when application development is in question. They also demonstrate the range of benefits that can accrue from considering the application a user handles as separate from the hardware and software infrastructure on which it runs. This abstraction from the computing angle is one side of the equation needed to get to cloud computing. The other side of the equation is abstraction of user demand, and that's what we'll look at next.

Demand Abstraction

In order to visualize demand abstraction, we need to travel back in time a bit and learn from the systems created to support the "glass houses" of the mainframe elite. In those days, computing time was so expensive that systems administrators started charging a premium to users who wanted to go to the front of the line.

In the era when computing meant buying CPU time on a mainframe, users were forced to balance the health of their budgets versus actually being able to run programs within a reasonable amount of time. The balancing of low-priority and high-priority users was done through management services such as the Houston Automatic Spooling Priority (HASP), with faster queues costing more and slower queues costing less. Using Job Control Language (JCL) statements, users could tell the mainframe what kinds of resources their jobs needed, estimated time, libraries, and other parameters. Users with special project needs could go a bit further and, in some advanced cases, blow a ton of money to request a job queue that had its own initiator (each mainframe "CPU" had multiple initiators, which today would be called a virtual CPU core). To put this into perspective, the entire time-sharing option (TSO) system, which at that time supported up to 32 simultaneous users, had a single initiator assigned to it. In those days the infrastructure necessary to support time sharing was expensive enough that a whole market for data PBXs (think of these as phone systems for terminals) sprang up to allow hundreds or thousands of terminals to share the 32 "real" connections on the mainframe communications processor. A side benefit was the ability to switch between various time-share systems at each terminal, just like dialing a telephone.

The next, and most important, function of JCL was to allow users to request system resources in terms of memory, both temporary and permanent disk storage, print queues, punch queues, tape archiving, and dataset merging. If you had enough money and authority, you could even request access to specialized virtual machines that normally ran jobs of exceptionally high priority.

Why the emphasis on JCL? JCL was a very concise language set up to request resources from a computing facility when users had no knowledge of the resource's exact configuration. Users just made requests to this nebulous facility and ran their jobs. If this sounds familiar, it should: We've just reviewed one popular definition of a cloud. Demand abstraction in a cloud is exactly what users were doing with JCL back in the 1970s.

What are the differences, then, between the mainframe time-share computing of the 1970s and today's cloud computing? Some differences are trivial—XML and middleware frameworks have replaced JCL on punchcards. Other differences are far more substantial: Today's clouds may be physically spread across the globe rather than just spread across a couple of IBM mainframes. One of the most important differences is that cloud computing uses the Internet, rather than private leased lines, for communications.

Why is that important? Well, in one sense, it's yet another layer of abstraction, since, without performing a series of trace-route operations, you have no way of knowing how the commands get from your workstation to the computer doing all the work (wherever that is). We should also point out that by treating the Internet as an abstraction layer, cloud computing can take place anywhere you have connectivity. Regardless of whether you're in your office, at home, or going mobile; you're now free to leverage cloud resources in a nearly constant fashion. So perhaps the change isn't the computing paradigm but rather the usage paradigm.

The point behind bringing this up is not to claim that there's nothing new in cloud computing, but to point out that some strategic, deployment, and management practices developed for mainframes may find new currency in the cloud environment. It's not that everything old is new again, but that the old can guide the new by lending their past elegance.

What Can You Do with a Cloud?

One of the great difficulties in having short discussions about cloud computing is that clouds can look like so many different systems and do so many different things. Ultimately, the question, "What can you do with a cloud?" can only be answered with the question, "What can you imagine?" We'll talk about a number of things that individuals and companies are doing with clouds, but those examples will make a bit more sense if you start with some knowledge of where clouds got their start. Earlier, we said that clouds have a great deal in common with the mainframe time sharing of the 1960s and 1970s. That's quite true, but most of today's cloud infrastructures owe a great deal of their essential architecture to computer clusters.

The original clusters were a knee-jerk reaction by researchers starving for supercomputer time, but who were either too low on the priority list or too poor to actually get as much time as they needed. In their most basic sense, these clusters were systems that tied a number of inexpensive computers together into a single computing environment. They took advantage of the rapidly increasing power of small computers and promised researchers and technical computing customers near-supercomputing performance at near-personal computer prices. We see great similarities between the PC revolution, in how many sought out the PC as a less expensive way to ask business questions of their data, and the ways that scientists sought ways to ask the really hard computing questions of their data. The problem is that some of the problems in science are so computing-intensive that science has created massively parallel and expensive computing engines that have been out of the reach of all but the best-funded projects. The necessity for large amounts of computing for less well funded projects became the engine of creativity. One of the first successful projects in this direction was Beowulf.

Beowulf

In late 1993, Donald Becker and Thomas Sterling began sketching the outline of a commodity-based cluster system which they envisioned as a cost-effective alternative to large supercomputers. In early 1994, while working at the Center of Excellence in Space Data and Information Sciences (CESDIS) under the sponsorship of the High Performance Computing & Communications for Earth & Space Sciences (HPCC/ESS) project, they began work on Beowulf.

The initial prototype was a cluster computer consisting of 16 DX4 processors connected by channel-bonded Ethernet links. The machine was an instant success, and the idea of providing off-the-shelf commodity systems to satisfy specific computational requirements spread quickly through NASA and into the academic and research communities.

Although Beowulf took off like wildfire, it was still a long way from being a cloud. Beowulf laid the foundation for clustering a large number of inexpensive, off-the-shelf computers to provide high-performance computing cooperatively, but it was still a complex environment in which users had to write or rewrite their applications in terms of "parent" and "children" nodes, with the problem split into lots of smaller questions that were worked on as "children" and the results compiled at the "parent" node. Quite a bit of skill was required in a variety of disciplines to break up larger questions into lots of little questions that could be handled by the commodity processors. Computing questions that could be solved nicely on traditional supercomputers didn't work anywhere near so well on the smaller PC platforms.

Invention being the mother of invention, however, the developers leveraged their experience with traditional supercomputers and applied it to the smaller PC-based clusters. Key to their success was extension of the Message Passing Interface (MPI) abstraction layer that allowed the massively parallel applications to talk to each other effectively, effectively providing the ability to have a master application spin off and control other applications and then aggregate the results. Key to the success of the MPI abstraction layer is that it removed much of the complexity of writing for large-scale computing problems involved with passing data back and forth between parent and child nodes in the computing cluster.

Still to come were the abstraction of applications and hardware that is such an intrinsic part of true cloud computing, but these developments provided the foundation for a larger idea that was still years away. And what came next extended the idea even further.

Grid Computing

The basic concepts developed in Beowulf were taken much further by the folks at the SETI (Search for ExtraTerrestrial Intelligence) project, who needed massive amounts of computing power to process their radio telescope data (to separate background noise from what they hoped would be a real signal of intelligent life). Their approach took advantage of the concept of *grid computing* and relied on legions of volunteers donating their screen saver time to help look for life "out there."

According to Wikipedia, the free online encyclopedia:

> Grid computing is a form of distributed computing whereby a "super and virtual computer" is composed of a cluster of networked, loosely-coupled computers, acting in concert to perform very large tasks. This technology has been applied to computationally-intensive scientific, mathematical, and academic problems through volunteer computing, and it is used in commercial enterprises for such diverse applications as drug discovery, economic forecasting, seismic analysis, and back-office data processing in support of e-commerce and web services.
>
> What distinguishes grid computing from typical cluster computing systems is that grids tend to be more loosely coupled,

heterogeneous, and geographically dispersed. Also, while a computing grid may be dedicated to a specialized application, it is often constructed with the aid of general purpose grid software libraries and middleware.

In the evolution of distributed computing systems (and cloud computing is, to this point, the ultimate expression of distributed computing), grid computing marks a middle step between clusters and clouds. Grids are far more widely dispersed than clusters, and the hardware tends to be somewhat more abstract (since the user doesn't know where the computer running the software is located). They also require a certain level of computing redundancy to be built in. The most famous grids have been built on the generosity of users around the world donating unused CPU cycles while their computers are idling on screen savers. It all sounds great, of course, but the programming techniques are radically different from other forms of programming, and both application developers and users must still be acutely aware that the application is running on a grid.

Virtualization

Another key piece in the march toward cloud computing has come with greater adoption of virtualized PC operating systems, starting with work done in the Linux community and leading to commercial versions by VMWare, Microsoft, and others. Taking a cue from the mainframe world, PC operating system architects applied those history lessons to allow full server systems to exist inside a virtual container on a host, thus allowing for more complete utilization of host system resources while maintaining control. Think of this as putting a house inside a big warehouse: It's complete, it's a full house, but it's connected to the outside world via the utility connections owned by the warehouse. Now, for the first time, an entire operating system, applications, and accessories can be packaged into a set of files that can be run in any compatible virtualized environment—an environment that for all intents and purposes looks and feels just like a nonvirtualized environment. And these virtualized environments may house multiple virtualized machines to utilize hardware more efficiently and dramatically increase potential returns.

What Would You Like in Your Cloud?

So far we have seen why the abstraction (or separation) of function and system is the critical concept that underlies cloud computing, and that system design took several steps, from mainframes, to clusters, to grids, and finally to clouds. We'll look at several concepts in more detail as we move through the coming chapters, but now it's time to start answering the truly important question: What can you do with a cloud? We asked the question at the beginning of the section, then stepped aside and looked at history. No more teasing: Let's look at the practical side of clouds.

We've begun to define what a cloud is, but we haven't yet approached the question of what a cloud can do. This is in some ways a much more difficult question, because the answer can vary so widely from one cloud computing application to another. Do you need a word processing application to run on a workstation that is underpowered for today's most popular personal productivity software? A cloud application such as Google Docs could be your answer. Do you need a system that will allow a workgroup to collaborate on a project even though they're in different locations using different operating systems on their computers? Zoho has cloud applications to help make it happen. Does your start-up application provider business need to make an application available to an unknown number of customers without being forced to make an investment in massive start-up hardware costs? Amazon's cloud platform might be just the ticket. Does your company's business continuity plan call for off-site backup of critical data? You have a wide variety of storage cloud options to choose from. Each of these examples is different from the other, and yet each is a solid example of a cloud computer application. As we move forward, we'll look at the different types of applications and the consequences of choosing a particular one. First, however, let's consider the conditions that might lead a company or an individual to choose a cloud computing platform for a given application.

For some organizations, the decisions to move toward cloud computing starts with the most pedestrian sort of practical statement. "My IT staff is overextended, but I can't afford more staff and I still need to provide more services" is a common starting point, as are "The power bill for my data center is killing me" and "I can't afford the colocation charges to provide globally load-balanced applications—why can't I let someone else pay for the data centers around the globe?" Each of these is a good reason to explore options for new computing solutions, and they are just three of hundreds of reasons why cloud computing has become such a hot topic in the IT world.

Cloud computing's flexibility in service delivery (and, generally, billing) make it an ideal solution for companies faced with highly variable service demand or an uncertain financial environment. Let's look at a couple of examples of decisions to embrace different aspects of cloud computing from both large and small organizations.

Honolulu, Hawaii, is home to some of the most beautiful beaches and some of the most expensive electricity in the United States (as an example, the University of Hawaii paid something like $0.26/kilowatt-hour as of September 2009), and the university research community's thirst for supercomputer time is never-ending. Now, add to expensive electricity a growing push to make both new and existing facilities as "green" as possible. The trend toward building "green data centers" is no longer limited just to using better lighting or more efficient air conditioning, but extends to locating facilities in areas where both power and cooling have dramatically less impact on our world.

Rather than building a new series of data centers to meet research demand, the university began looking at cloud computing options for providing computing services to faculty and research staff. Microsoft has started opening a series of "green data centers" around the world to provide globally load-balanced services to both itself and to its customers. These centers are located in areas where inexpensive (and carbon-friendly) power sources are available, and they are usually situated where environmentally friendly cooling options are also available. One such Microsoft facility is located high in the mountains, where the year-round air temperature is cool enough to provide inexpensive cooling to the racks of computers housed there, and the center gets hydroelectric power directly from a nearby dam. Given the opportunity to save money, protect the environment, and still provide necessary computing services, the decision to move to the cloud was easy.

In another case, a small consulting firm based in Florida decided that it needed to look at options for a widely distributed group of employees and contractors to collaborate on projects. The owners looked at the cost of deploying and managing server-based systems based on Microsoft Windows and on Linux. The owners realized that maintaining the server required would demand either a dedicated employee or a substantial (for the consulting firm) contract with a service organization, and they decided to use Zoho as the firm's personal productivity and collaboration platform. For the firm's employees and contractors, the choice allowed the freedom of choosing the personal computing platform that suited them best (or, in some cases, that they already owned), and the security of knowing that work was stored on a managed remote cloud-based server. Zoho's use of Google Gears (a cloud computing service from a competing service provider) allowed employees to use personal productivity tools (such as a word processor) even where no connection to the Internet was availabile. For the firm's management, costs were contained while information security and organizational interaction were achieved.

As a third example, suppose a small company wanted to offer a set of services to Washington, D.C.–area visitors around the time of the presidential inauguration. The owner recognized that if her company was successful, there would be a surge in traffic, data storage, and compute activity in the days leading up to the inauguration, with a drop-off following the event. While she felt she could be successful with the service, she didn't have the resources to purchase a server and software, deploy and maintain them, and then figure out what to do with it after the event—all for a project with a finite life span. Instead, she chose to deploy the service on the Amazon Elastic Compute Cloud (EC2) of Amazon Web Services (AWS).

Using AWS allowed the owner to spend a small fraction of the money that would have been required to purchase and deploy hardware and software, and was thus able to concentrate all her resources on developing and marketing the service itself. While a successful service-based business might or might not stem from the inaugural project, the cloud-computing limit on capital expenses allowed her to proceed with a plan that might have remained simply a promising idea in an environment without clouds.

The Anytime, Anyplace Cloud

Now that "my server" can be anywhere in the world, can be managed from anywhere in the world, and can expand or contract on demand, why do we even think in terms of a server anymore? Once you've thought to ask this question, you've finally crossed the bridge into "Cloud City."

While there are still legitimate strategic and tactical concerns that can make a self-hosted server and application the best solution for a particular organization, the fact is that in many cases you don't need to care about where you application lives or what your application is running on. In the rest of this book we'll look at the considerations that will come into play as you try to decide whether a cloud computing platform is the best solution for you and your organization, and the options that are available as you begin your research into clouds. We'll also talk about key factors to keep in mind as you begin to think in terms of clouds, rather than servers, as the host for your applications.

For example, it might have been years since you last thought in hard-dollar terms about *when* a job should run. This was a common consideration back in the days when mainframe computing was the only game in town, but it fell by the wayside as personal computers and PC-based servers came to the fore. Now, you might agree to a service-level agreement that has your application running off-shore in a lower-cost cloud farm up to a certain level of demand, and then automatically moves your application to higher-performance on-shore systems once demand crosses a certain threshold. The agreement might also include allowance for demand spikes exceeding your performance or bandwidth cap for a certain amount of time, with the expectation that the demand will shrink within a reasonable amount of time. These spikes might include surges in volume, memory, CPU time, and storage, with resources being determined by a formula instead of having specific limits. The best part of the cloud formula from your CFO's perspective? The odds are good that the agreement will mean you only pay for the higher performance for the period of time in which it is being used.

Abstraction, connection, and well-defined interfaces are the three components that combine to make cloud computing a viable option for a growing number of individuals and organizations. Now, let's learn more about precisely how you can plan and deploy your cloud.

Clouds Flight Path for Chapter 1

- *A historical perspective on what has led up to clouds.* We're standing on the shoulders of giants as the technology building blocks are created. We've looked at some of the key blocks and how they fit into the world that will be clouds. Technologies such as HPC clusters and grids have all contributed to the foundation on which Cloud City is built. So, though it's still under construction, the historical perspectives of past technology trends are paving our way to Cloud City.

- *The growth of the abstraction layer.* The world has grown more and more specialized, and we've talked about how abstraction layers are the key to amazingly complex systems and also the key to the explosion that is now call the Internet. As each layer is created, implemented, and understood, it also provides the foundation on which to build new technology. Layers such as Ruby on Rails, Python, OpenGP, ODBC, and others will pave the way for the construction of Cloud City.

- *Networking models and their impact.* With the advent of abstraction layers, the networking world has embraced modularization in order to create some truly massive software projects. The key to the explosion of networking technology is a concept that is best conceptualized by the Lego child's toy. Modularity freed developers from constantly having to reinvent the wheel each time they wrote a networking application. It was this kind of freedom that really made the World Wide Web a reality.

- *Networking databases and how they changed the world.* Plug compatibility and the ability to change a data storage system quickly and easily are key features of why the Internet has grown from a static bulletin board–like feature to an amazingly complex and dynamic way to access data. Like the changes to the networking industry, database designers sought a way to avoid the constant cycle of customized programming for each new project.

- *Demand abstraction—Just how do we formulate the question?* It's all about abstraction layers, and without the ability to ask questions across a myriad of data sources, the Internet would be dramatically less dynamic in nature. Programmers have long sought efficient ways to reuse code so that they can concentrate on exciting new technology. The ultimate reusable codes are abstraction layers, and for those we must thank people like Admiral Grace Hopper, who developed COBOL, the original abstraction layer for the IT industry.

- *A wish list for clouds.* Where should we go, and how can we get there? We began to talk about our view of the cloud worldscape: how computing might very well be heading for appliance status, and how clouds and ubiquitous communications are quickly getting us there.

Chapter 2

Grids, HPCs, and Clouds

If I have seen a little further it is by standing on the shoulders of Giants.
— Sir Isaac Newton

In This Chapter

In this chapter you'll learn about computing grids and high-performance computing (HPC) clusters—two critical precursors to cloud computing. You'll learn about the challenges in scheduling resources in each of these group computing situations, and how solving those problems laid the foundation for developing fully-functional cloud computing.

In this chapter, you'll learn about:

- Grids versus high-performance computing versus clouds—We talk about how grids are potentially less expensive but can also be dramatically less reliable than a traditional HPC. Both have their place in the world of scientific computing. Balancing the differences could mean the difference between a massive in-house investment or just leveraging corporate screen savers.
- Software differences in each platform—Just because you can do similar things on a grid and a traditional HPC doesn't mean the same applications will run on both right out of the box. Tweaks and tuning are a way of life for both, and you need to take into account those differences when writing for each.

- Examples of grids and HPC systems—We look at some of the success stories of both grids and HPCs, and we provide a bit more insight into which system is capable of doing various types of tasks.
- Job schedulers in HPCs as the beginning of a cloud description language, and why we should take a page from history—Managing job flow and shoehorning it into the available hardware resources is what it's all about. From mainframes to grids, to HPCs, making the most of your expensive hardware has always been the name of the game.

Scientific Computing and Its Contribution to Clouds

Grids, high-performance computers, and clouds often seem to be mentioned all in the same breath, they're all quite different and one size does *not* fit all. In this chapter, we're going to take some time to look closely at what each of these technology families are, and the sort of applications to which each may best be applied. There will be times when it seems we're diving rather deeply into one technology or another, but understanding the technology that underlies each of these terms, and learning the lessons to be gathered from deploying and managing grids and HPCs, will pay dividends when you start thinking about the best way to make cloud computing work for you and your organization.

Defining Terms: Grids and HPCs

Let's start by defining some key terms we'll be using in this chapter. First, what is grid computing (or, to come at it from another direction, what is a computing grid)? We can begin by saying that a computing grid is the application of multiple computers working on a single problem at the same time. That's fine, as far as it goes, but that definition could apply to many things that aren't grids. What makes this computing collective a grid? Three terms fill in the necessary details: loosely coupled, geographically dispersed, and heterogenous.

When computers are joined together for an application, they can be tightly coupled or loosely coupled. Tightly coupled systems generally share memory and other system resources, with the processors often linked through a system bus or some other high-speed, short-distance network.

Think of tightly coupled computers as conjoined twins: One can't get very far without the other. Loosely coupled systems, on the other hand, are separate, autonomous computers that take directions from a central controller that breaks the problem into single-computer-sized packages, parcels the individual pieces out to members of the grid, then accepts results and assembles them into answers. Loosely coupled computers are like fraternal twins that lead their own separate lives but can come together to work toward a single goal when asked nicely.

Grid computers are loosely coupled. They can be used for separate tasks until they are called on to act as part of the grid—and they can often continue fulfilling their stand-alone responsibilities even when they are occupied with grid applications. This loose coupling allows for the next quality of the computing grid: geographic dispersal.

Since the members of a computing grid communicate through standard networks (or, most commonly today, the Internet), it doesn't really matter where the constituent computers are located. It's as easy to have a computing grid that spans the globe as it is to have a grid in a single room. The dispersed grid is easier, in many ways; the electric power requirements are dispersed to many different power grids, and infrastructure problems that might take down a particular data center will usually affect only a small piece of the overall grid. With grid applications often designed to take advantage of unused CPU cycles available on each constituent computer, grid computing tends to leave a shallow resource footprint across a very broad swath of a computing environment.

The computing environment that makes up a grid can be dispersed across more than just geography—it can cover multiple operating systems, as well. The heterogenous nature of many grids increases both the performance and the robustness of the grid. Now, it must be noted that heterogeneity is an architectural possibility of a computing grid, not a requirement. Plenty of grids make use of only a single type of computer. Whether the grid is made up of a single type of computer or a veritable "United Nations" of machines, the software that brings it together is a suite of resource controllers, data assemblers, client-computer applications, and a special class of software called "middleware" that glues it all together. We'll come back to middleware in just a bit, but first let's look at high-performance computers and how they do their work.

High-performance computers (HPCs) are similar to grids in that they are loosely coupled computing environments, though they tend to be not quite so loosely coupled as grids. The reason for the difference in coupling "tightness" has to do with the nature of the communication between the different elements of the computing environment, and particularly between the central controller and the remote nodes that actually process data. Widely dispersed grids make extensive use of asynchronous communications, in which a computer sends out a message knowing that it will see a response eventually. It tends not to matter whether that response comes back in 200 milliseconds or 3 days. HPCs, given their emphasis on the best possible performance, are much more reliant on synchronous communication, in which messages are sent back and forth between two or more systems with each computer waiting on a necessary response from another before it can continue processing.

The need for accurate synchronous communication means that HPCs tend to be centrally located, rather than highly dispersed, and connected via 10-gigabit GB Ethernet, Infiniband, or some other high-speed computer interconnection network rather than the Internet. Because of the nature of the communication requirement and the work that is done, HPCs are almost always made up of clusters of homogenous computers, in which each constituent is precisely the same as every other constituent in the system.

All this performance tends to add up to some hefty numbers not only in performance but also in infrastructure costs. When the University of Texas at Abilene entered into a project in 2008 with Sun Microsystems to take the record for the world's largest supercomputer, the project ended up with $30 million in hardware costs alone. Some of the numbers were 62,976 CPU cores, 125 terabytes of memory, 1.7 petabytes of disk space, and 504 teraflops of performance, sucking down 3 megawatts of power and costing nearly a million dollars per year to run—not to mention the human resource costs to run this extremely specialized piece of equipment. And all this just to hold the record for a few short years. Rick Stevens, the associate director of the lab, has predicted that the system will be considered only moderate-sized system within just five years. He has, however, drawn an analogy to having a time machine that lets you look five to ten years into the future of general-purpose computing.

Software for Grids and HPCs

The differences in software architecture make writing applications for grids and HPCs dramatically different. Learning to architect for this difference has been one of the many reasons why HPC/grid applications have tended to remain in the domain of research.

One of the key concepts in writing applications for grids, HPCs, or any other distributed computing systems is the idea of parent and child processes. In briefest terms, when a particular task has to be accomplished, it is analyzed to see whether it might fruitfully be broken up into smaller tasks. If breakup is possible, the distributed computing environment's controller breaks it up and sends each of the new, smaller tasks to another computer to be performed. The original task (the "parent") then waits for data to be returned from each of the smaller tasks (the "children") before it continues processing. The most important skill in writing effective code for a grid or an HPC is the ability to tell code how to break up larger tasks into smaller tasks so that parents are completed (and therefore report their results) as quickly as possible.

While traditional programming methods still apply, the change in writing for a parent and child environment can be likened to the learning curve a programmer had to go through when moving from stand-alone to networked applications. There's a whole new set of rules and a whole new set of tricks to learn as you optimize your code.

The biggest challenge is the overall architecture, for which you need to be prepared to think in terms of parent processes spawning children on what may be physically separate computing nodes, which may in turn spawn grandchildren under certain conditions. So now, instead of just worrying about endless loops, you have to wonder if your app will spawn too many children during its run and empty the resource hopper.

It may seem that grids and HPCs are the same thing from a programming point of view, but grids have wrinkles that tend to make life interesting for application developers. As we mentioned before, grids utilize asynchronous communications that now have to also learn about each individual node's resources and perhaps even figure out whether a given portion of the problem can actually be shoehorned onto a small node. Not only that, the communications pathways can be extremely variable and may have periods of no communications at all when a traveling node (such as a laptop computer) is offline for a while. As a result, grids usually need to work on smaller portions of a problem in which all of the data for a given process is downloaded to the individual node when the process is assigned to the node. In addition, the program needs to have the ability to be suspended cleanly as the grid client returns control back to the user.

Keep in mind that many grid node systems are installed as screen savers, enabling those "idle" CPU's to become part of the overall grid cluster, so giving the machine back to the user is an important part of "playing nicely" in the grid world.

Overall, the problems that HPC and grid computing systems are designed to solve tend to be huge, but can be broken up into smaller, more manageable pieces. These problems also tend to be of high value in order to justify the huge amount of human resources necessary to create the complex application to take advantage of the environment. Problems such as weather modeling, processing echo-return information for petrology surveys (looking for oil), gene folding, and ship or aircraft drag calculations are all excellent examples of HPC and grid cluster uses.

Examples of Grid Applications

It's one thing to talk about the way a system works. To get a better understanding of the differences between the platforms, let's look at some examples of the problems each is used to solve, and the ways in which each is deployed. We'll look first at a couple of applications of grid computing.

A Grid for the Stars

In 1999, at the University of California Berkeley, the SETI (Search for Extra-Terrestrial Intelligence) project folks took a good hard look at their computing needs and then looked at the budget they had and heaved a collective sigh of frustration. Scheduling time on existing high-performance computing clusters was prohibitively expensive, and the waiting list was sometimes measured in weeks or months. Another frustration they faced, as many academic projects did, was that many of their best students were foreign nationals, who couldn't use many supercomputer facilities because of their military funding. (Any sort of mixed-classification computing system in which classified materials are potentially processed is restricted to U.S.-cleared personnel only, even if the unclassified machine is physically separate from the system the foreign nationals want to use.) So with all these roadblocks in their way, what were the SETI people to do? The answer was to turn the HPC world on its head by changing the paradigm.

The SETI@home team published this overview on their blog:

> The UC Berkeley SETI team has discovered that there are already thousands of computers that might be available for use. Most of these computers sit around most of the time with toasters flying across their screens accomplishing absolutely nothing and wasting electricity to boot. This is where SETI@home (and you!) come into the picture. The SETI@home project hopes to convince you to allow us to borrow your computer when you aren't using it and to help us ". . . search out new life and new civilizations." We'll do this with a screen saver that can go get a chunk of data from us over the Internet, analyze that data, and then report the results back to us. When you need your computer back, our screen saver instantly gets out of the way and only continues its analysis when you are finished with your work.
>
> It's an interesting and difficult task. There's so much data to analyze that it seems impossible! Fortunately, the data analysis task can be easily broken up into little pieces that can all be worked on separately and in parallel. None of the pieces depends on the other pieces. Also, there is only a finite amount of sky that can be seen from Arecibo. In the next two years the entire sky as seen from the telescope will be scanned three times. We feel that this will be enough for this project. By the time we've looked at the sky three times, there will be new telescopes, new experiments, and new approaches to SETI. We hope that you will be able to participate in them too!

Translation: We can't afford to schedule a 2,000-processor HPC cluster for a couple of years, so why not try to shoot for 100,000 nodes where we might lose 70% of the nodes over time? Let's make it hugely redundant to make up for the node loss. We then make it a screen saver with some cool eye candy (see Figure 2.1) and voilá, nearly free supercomputer time for research. The idea worked well enough that Stanford and many others have all jumped on the bandwagon.

A Grid for Proteins

Medical researchers are investigating the effects on children of their parents' age and race at the time of their birth in order to better understand

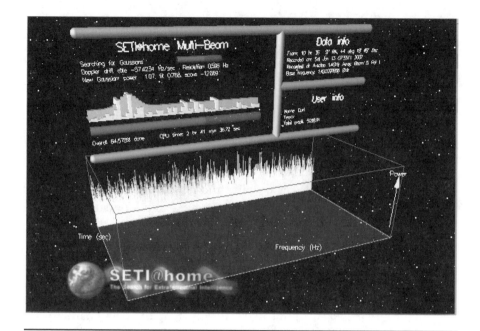

Figure 2.1.   While the grid computing goes on in the background, the screen saver displays the radio signal patterns that are currently being worked on.

the proteins at work behind genetic disorders such as Huntington and Alzheimer's diseases. In order to understand the disorder, they need to simulate the protein folding process that occurs naturally in the body. Stanford University and associated project members have created a system called Folding@home, in which large numbers of volunteers install Folding@home screen savers. Each screen saver then downloads a small piece of the puzzle and works on a single portion of the huge dataset that the project is currently working on. When the screen saver is running, it chugs away on its small piece and then uploads the results to a master server. It should be noted that because of the variable availability of these "nodes," just about all grid projects have multiple nodes working on the same piece of the puzzle. That way, if a machine is turned off for a long weekend or is out for repair, they don't lose that little piece.

In the case of Folding@home, the total size of the dataset is known, as is the scope of the anticipated result. The problem for researchers was to get access to enough CPU time to crunch through the data that existed. According to the project's website, as of the first of January 2009, there were over a quarter-million CPUs working on the project. Folding@home is extremely heterogenous grid architecture, with client software for Microsoft Windows, Linux, Apple's Mac OS X, and the Sony Playstation 3 now available.

An example of the kind of problem being tackled by Folding@home is the following research as described by the team at Stanford University:

Combining Molecular Dynamics with Bayesian Analysis to Predict and Evaluate Ligand-Binding Mutations in Influenza Hemagglutinin
P. M. Kasson, D. L. Ensign, and V. S. Pande. *Journal of the American Chemical Society* (2009). Published online July 28, 2009.

Summary. The influenza virus infects people and animals by binding to complex sugar molecules on the surface of the respiratory tract. Bird viruses bind most strongly to bird cell-surface sugars and human viruses bind most strongly to human cell-surface sugars. As the recent swine-origin influenza virus has demonstrated, there is considerable overlap between the binding ability of human and pig viruses to cells of the other host. Changes to this binding affinity are one key component for viruses to make a jump between species, and it is difficult to predict the necessary mutations ahead of time. We would like to predict high-risk mutations to enable better surveillance and early control of potential inter-species transmission events. This work represents a first step in that direction, as we examine mutations to H5N1 avian influenza that alter ligand binding. We use Folding@Home as a powerful computational screen to evaluate mutations that will eventually require experimental testing to verify.

First launched in 2000, Folding@home is the most powerful distributed computing cluster in the world, and one of the world's largest distributed computing projects. Like all grid computing projects, however, the "secret sauce" involves breaking up the problem into a great many little pieces, which is also why such solutions aren't very useful for most "normal" business applications.

High-Performance Computing in *Blue Hawaii*

In the world of high-performance academic research computing, the researcher uploads an application written specifically for a clustered/ HPC environment. Each application consists of at least three pieces: the parent process that handles coordination of all the processes, the child applications that work on individual pieces, and a scheduler that allocates resources on a job-by-job basis. The real key to a successful HPC is a scheduler that "fits" the jobs into available resources to maximize the utilization of the cluster according to resource requests as each job is submitted to the system. If the scheduler is written properly, and the HPC environment is configured correctly, the clusters can be spread out over a geographic area among several cluster members controlled by the scheduler system. Now, at this point you may be thinking that the environment has just moved from a HPC to a grid. While HPCs share much in common with grids, a major difference is that HPCs tend to be more homogeneous in makeup and child processes tend *not* to be duplicated, since HPCs tend to be dedicated to the purpose.

A very good example of HPC computing was the IBM SP2 called *Blue Hawaii,* which, architecturally, was the grandchild of the famous chess-playing *Deep Blue.* It was in learning this system that programmers experienced just how different HPC was from writing an application for a monolithic machine. With supercomputer time being horribly expensive and with long waiting lists for time, HPC programmers were and are motivated to wring as much performance as possible out of each CPU cycle. A common "Aha!" experience involved learning that looping was "unrolled" instead of nested. (Nested loops are like the Russian dolls that fit one inside another.) This technique was developed to open up the outer loop into multiple stacked single loops so that more statements could be shoved into the CPU cache at a time. Similar to "pipelining" in the PC platform, programmers strove to learn additional details about the processor platform to "tune" their applications to fit more into the super-high-speed CPU cache and reduce the number of requests for instructions from the slower main RAM.

Let's stop to think about this for a moment. Programming for multiple stacks, and unrolling rather than nesting loops, are all about maximizing system resource utilization. This is a theme we'll see repeated in virtually every technique and architecture we look at. Where HPCs are concerned, the reason for the optimization is speed, pure and simple. When we begin to look at cloud computing, the need for system optimization will be just as great, but the reason is based on economics rather than performance: System administrators want each piece of hardware to be utilized as close to 100% of the time as possible. Regardless of the motivation, the operating principles are the same: Build the architecture on a scheduling base that is able to optimize resource utilization without requiring users who are submitting jobs for processing to have any knowledge of the system.

In addition to optimizing CPU cache performance, programmers on *Blue Hawaii* took advantage of the way in which the CPU handles floating-point calculations. The SP2 was able to handle two calculations per cycle, so formula lines were tinkered with to make sure that exactly two floating-point requests were made per line. This is a solid illustration of the fact that a single optimization is rarely enough to ensure that computing resources are being used at top efficiency. Developers of schedulers, controllers, and middleware components must study, understand, and program for every system component their software touches in order to make the system perform efficiently.

Scheduling Grids and HPCs

Both grids and HPCs have at their heart a job scheduler to control how the individual programs will run and best fit into the available resources. This scheduler must not only have knowledge of the program to be run, with algorithms for managing the way in which child and grandchild processes are spawned, it must also have deep insight into the resources available on each member system of the computing environment. Obviously, there are many different ways of creating a piece of software with a set of functions as complex as those encapsulated in a scheduler. You need to think of a scheduler as a proxy for dozens, hundreds, or thousands of computing nodes. It has to handle authentication, resource allocation, and the actual run of the software.

There is an old saying about reinventing the wheel every time you need to make a trip, and that certainly applies to schedulers for both HPCs and grids. Two of the more commonly seen examples include one most often used in the grid computing world and another that's frequently seen in high-performance computing. The efforts by the Job Submission Description Language Working Group (JSDL-WG) are popular in the grid world, and the Maui Scheduler has become popular in the HPC world. JSDL-WG is a grid-oriented job control language that's independent of any programming language that might be used to create the jobs. JSDL can use XML to define different aspects of the job request, making it an open standard built on other open standards. This notion of open access will come to be a critical component of the move beyond grids to cloud computing.

The Maui Scheduler was developed in the 1990s as an open-source scheduling engine for high-performance computing clusters. Written to join groups of Unix computers together into cohesive high-performance systems, Maui allows administrators to set schedules and priorities, reserve resources for particular applications or pieces of applications, and perform other tasks that make systems more functional in a world where multiple simultaneous applications and competing priorities are the rule rather than the exception. Since the release of the Maui Scheduler, a commercial version of the software—Moab—has been developed, with support for additional operating systems (including Linux, Mac OS X, and Windows), a workload manager, cluster manager, and access portal, and resource management capabilities that aren't available in Maui. This pattern, of taking open-source software and building additional capabilities and components on it, is another direction that we'll see again in cloud computing. The Moab scheduler developed by the University of Utah Center for High Performance Computing built on the success of the Maui Scheduler to create Moab:

CHPC Software: Moab Scheduler

The Moab Scheduler is a software tool designed to allow flexible and near-optimal scheduling in a multi-resource high-performance computing environment. Jobs are screened through a large number of administrator-configurable fairness policies and then prioritized based on factors such as job queue time, job expansion factor, and user CPU usage history. The Moab Scheduler maximizes control of system resources by allowing certain nodes to be reserved for specific users, groups, accounts, or projects and minimizes the amount of wasted computer resources by permitting anticipated downtime to be scheduled.

The Moab Scheduler is also a analysis/research tool. The Moab Scheduler collects a large number of statistics and can analyze this information to determine the effectiveness of the scheduling approach being used by Moab and the utilization of the resources available.

(*Source:* www.chpc.utah.edu/docs/manuals/software/moab.html.)

How Grid Scheduling Works

It should be obvious by now that the scheduler for either a computing grid or a high-performance computing cluster is a complex piece of software. When the software is moved to a cloud environment, it gets no simpler. As the software moves away from the cluster into larger grids and clouds, some people stop referring to it as a scheduler and begin to call it a broker, a reasonable label when the product is dealing with components that have their own intelligence and ability to make relatively simple decisions.

Let's take a look at the process of scheduling tasks in a computing grid as we set the stage for moving beyond clusters and grids into the computing cloud. Grid scheduling can be divided into three phases, consisting of 11 steps. The descriptions that follow are the authors', but the steps and phases seem to be common to many scheduler efforts.

It should also be noted that the Open Grid Forum on environments such as the Open Grid Services Architecture (OGSA) has made a significant contribution toward creation of tools and standards for a common job management standard. Furthermore, IBM has been in the HPC game for a very long time, early on making a huge splash with their chess-playing HPC called *Deep Blue*. Much of IBM's work on scheduling and HPC job description languages are documented in a collection of documents called the Red Book series (www.redbooks.ibm.com).

Phase I: Resource Discovery

Step 1: Authorization Filtering

Consider that the collection of nodes that make up a grid isn't too different from a hacker's botnet. (*Botnet* is short for *robot network;* in this case, the network consists of computers infected by hackers for the purpose of executing nefarious applications.) So it's probably for the best that modern grids include authentication before anyone can submit a job into the grid. It also makes sense that user profiles describe just what resources any authorized user is allowed to use. The approved resources may or may not include some sort of billing information if this isn't a volunteer grid. Billing information is often belittled by technical and scientific users as an unnecessary crutch for the "bean counters," but properly allocating costs and allowing for capital recovery is a very real issue for most business (and many nonprofit) organizations.

Since some sort of dataset access is also normally needed, the user profile might also include some credentials for one or more network-attached resources. An element of identity federation, or single sign-on capability, is generally covered by the initial authorization filtering stage, allowing the user credentials presented for one computer within the cluster to serve as authenticating documents for every computer and application within the cluster.

Step 2: Application Definition

In this step the user specifies a minimum set of resources for consideration by the scheduler. It would be counterproductive if, for instance, a job required nodes that could handle 64-bit word lengths but the scheduler kept trying to shove it onto older 32-bit nodes. This is where values such as RAM, scratch space (temporary disk storage), specialized libraries, etc., are described in a job submission script supported by the scheduler. The rise of XML as a widely supported open standard for data interchange has made application definition a much more open and standards-based process for most clusters and grids. And although we speak of application definition in terms of user specification, in many cases the definition is generated by the application automatically, as it tells the environment what it needs in order to function successfully.

Step 3: Minimum Requirement Filtering

Based on the resources an authenticated user is allowed to use (see step 1), the scheduler attempts to find the first open slot that will fulfill the need. In small systems this might be a pad and pencil, but in much larger systems it could involve nodes checking in periodically to update available resources. Regardless of the job and cluster size, it's all about matching needs to resources in such a way as to accommodate the needs of the users in a timely fashion.

Phase II: System Selection
Step 4: Information Gathering

This stage is where politics can rear its ugly head. While the "best fit" for resources might exist on a particular set of hardware assets, business rules may force users into an alternate set of resources instead. This happens frequently in organizations such as universities, in which multiple departments have "contributed" to an institution-wide grid. In theory, all departments that contribute to the grid have equal access to its resources. However, the "string" that many departments have attached to their participation in the grid is that during certain hours, researchers in that particular department *must* have priority over a particular subset of nodes. It should be pointed out that there exists a potential for resource changes by the time a job is actually submitted. A considerable amount of research is being done on predictive methods for resource allocation to create some sort of tuning feedback loop that will increase the accuracy of a predictive model over time, making gross time-block priority locks unnecessary to protect a department's authority over its own systems.

Step 5: System Selection

The decision as to which nodes to use for a specific job varies in complexity, but a common thread has appeared in many scheduler development projects. Some methodologies that are commonly tossed around include Condor matchmaking, computational economies, and many others.

Condor matchmaking bases its operation on a classic scheme—the classified ad. Computing resources—the "sellers" in the analogy—advertise their services and capabilities through ClassAds, where they can also list the asking price for the resource. Users and applications—the "buyers" of the scheme—create their own ClassAds listing their requirements and preferences along with what they're willing to pay to have their requirements met. Condor matchmaking then goes through the ClassAds from buyers and sellers and makes the best matches based on the specifications given. The matchmaking is a one-time, static process though, as Condor continues to scan the environment to determine whether a better match might become available at any time.

Computational economies include a variety of techniques used to decide which processes will run on which resources. The techniques bring the principles of classic economics to bear on the problem in an attempt to get around the fact that both application-based methods and resource-based methods can lead to significant levels of system instability under certain circumstances. Using computational economies, resources and application pieces can constantly revalue themselves based on demand for their services and demand for their results, while the central scheduler constantly makes application deployment decisions based on the latest valuations. An economics-based system with constant review should mean that, at any given moment, the resources are being used most efficiently, while the application itself is operating at peak effectiveness.

Phase III: Job Execution

Step 6: Advance Reservation

Reserving grid resources in advance may be as simple as blocking a collection of nodes within a particular department or as complex as an agent application watching and then placing holds on resources as they become available. Unfortunately, for most users, most long-term holds are the result of departments or managers blocking access to certain assets for significant lengths of time, "just in case." While the desire to make sure that our scientists or our engineers can have unfettered access to resources that came from our budget, the truth is that the computational grid as a whole will operate far more efficiently (and most researchers and engineers will have far more productive encounters) if the scheduler is allowed to make decisions based on resource allocations and expenses.

Step 7: Job Submission

If any of the steps we are discussing needs additional work, this is it. It's our opinion that if the Free and Open Source Software (FOSS) movement has an Achilles' heel, it is the attitude of rolling your own if you don't like how someone else does it. Just look at the number and variety of Linux distributions and you can begin to see why commercial (and closed) operating systems command the lion's share of the marketplace. This lack of standardization in the open-source grid world is where open source will again be left behind, as narrowly focused commercial efforts become a standard due to the lack of anything better.

Step 8: Preparation Tasks

This step is where the rubber meets the road. As the job execution kicks off, resources such as datasets are moved into temporary storage and the parent process starts to populate information for each child to work on. As with anything, variety in temporary datasets may involve anything from little snippets of audio (a là SETI@home) to massive genomics databases. So, while most of us think of BitTorrent as a method for downloading illegal movies, it also happens to be a very efficient way of moving large files to a collection of hosts very quickly. FTP (File Transfer Protocol), scp (secure copy), and sFTP (secure file transfer protocol) seem to be the current favorites, but Torrent is certainly being experimented with for large dataset distribution on grids.

Step 9: Monitoring Progress

All good programmers build in error checking, and high-performance computing is no exception. Since HPC is typically carried out in an asynchronous environment, there is great potential for a "child" to run out of data and sit idle unless the programmer has anticipated such a possibility and built in some sort of interrupt facility to notify the "parent" process that the "child" is now idle due to lack of data. Another good example is an application that *must* have all the pieces of the problem done in order to have valid results. So, if a child process should crash, it is better to end the entire run instead of having the rest of the processes continue running, in the end producing a worthless run because one node is missing results.

Step 10: Job Completion

What happens when the job is done? Do you ring a bell, send an email, or do a file transfer of the results to a file in Timbuktu? This might also be where the program will need to write result codes into a file someplace.

The important thing to remember is that the application *must* end and produce results of some sort—otherwise, it's not an algorithm, and therefore not a useful application at all.

Step 11: Cleanup

Do you trash the temporary datasets, or do you write them out to something more permanent? Where do the results go? Do you need to send a "close" transaction to an accounting system? It may not be very glamorous, but a good cleanup process means that your application cleanly closes down the use of a resource, rather than the system merely waiting for some sort of timeout to happen. The ideas and concepts in the material above are drawn from J. M. Schopf's paper: July 2001 "GFD-1.4 Scheduling Working Group, Category: Ten Actions When Super Scheduling."

Grid Versus HPC Versus Cloud

There are many reasons why you might choose to run an application on a grid rather than an HPC. Quite a few revolve around money, some revolve around availability, but both types of solution require massive amounts of computing power. Quite a few problems in this world just don't fit onto a monolithic computer system (one or more CPUs in a single computer) at a particular point in time. Moore's law ("The number of transistors that can be put on a chip doubles every 24 months") keeps us on our toes, since what didn't fit a year ago may fit today. However, we're talking about problems such as gene folding, analysis of seismic data for oil exploration, meteorology simulations, and so on—all applications that seemed out of reach for anyone just a few years ago, but that now are, through HPCs, grids, and computational clouds, within the reach of even the most underfunded research scientists.

To the frustration of many computer-industry historians, business clustering doesn't seem to have had a clear-cut inception, with a whole lot of people claiming the "first" or the "original" application. Let's just say that one or more folks must have looked at both grids and HPCs and saw an opportunity if they could be combined with the concept of a virtual machine.

When journalists first listened to a pitch by the folks in the Scyld Computing booth at the LinuxWorld 2003 Conference, their description of a business application cluster didn't sound very different from load balancing. However, the load balancing seen previously didn't have the ability to move applications from one physical machine to another. It also didn't have the ability to apply business rules to the process to allow lower-priority tasks to be suspended in order to let a higher-priority task to take over the physical machine. Scyld's example was of a company whose magnificent new widget is featured on CNN—suddenly, the traffic on their website explodes. Under normal circumstances the Web server would crash, but instead, lower-priority tasks are suspended so that the company website can take over multiple blades in the cluster. When the load subsides, the Web server shrinks back to its normal configuration and the lower-priority tasks are restarted. This was not unlike IBM's OS-VM and the way in which resources were allocated based on a complex set of business rules as demand and human intervention trigger dynamic reconfiguration of the systems. The difference, of course, was that Scyld could balance across huge numbers of individual computers, each running its own operating system and controlling its own resources.

Let's dissect the pieces and see why it is unlikely that this was a single "Aha!" moment for a single person. The key point is that all the technology had been around for a while and was now only being combined in novel ways to allow cloud computing to exist profitably within a corporate computing infrastructure. Because of this newness, the exact definition of cloud computing is a bit fuzzy as it and the industry develops. We provided a working definition of cloud computing in Chapter 1. If you need to go back and review it, feel free—we'll wait. Back? Good. It's our belief that cloud computing, like all emerging technology will most likely develop in stages.

Cloud Development Stage 1: Software as a Service and Web 2.0

Software as a Service (SaaS) and Web 2.0 trends set the stage for clouds. Today's users have started wondering why they really need to keep all their Web apps internal to the organization. As content management systems (CMS) made inroads toward replacing traditional websites, we saw an explosion of hosting sites catering to the latest craze. We really think that SaaS more than anything else got people saying "hmmmm. . . ." Imagine a situation in which a manager has key services for his or her people, but she's not paying for a data center to manage it. We also feel that the rapidly rising cost of energy has driven many a CFO to start asking if the organization really needs a data center, with all its inherent costs. If the programmers already use remote access instead of sitting at a physical computer, does it really matter where that server lives?

Cloud Development Stage 2: Hosted Virtualization

Hosted virtualization has become the "having your cake and eating it too" idea. Managers and system administrators have been using remote access to get to servers in the data center for years, so it sure isn't any different to point Microsoft's Remote Desktop Protocol (RDP) over a virtual private network (VPN) at a hosting site. As an indicator of just how fast virtualization has become mainstream, just recently, the way systems test engineers take systems out of a test drive changed radically. Instead of downloading just the application and then going through a full installation, now we can download a fully set up virtual machine, with all the OS tweaking already done. So why not take that idea a bit further by prototyping your new servers in-house, and then, when they're debugged, push the virtual machine image to the hosting service.

Cloud Development Stage 2.5: Playing the "Energy Savings" Card

Recent spikes in the cost of energy had a huge impact on the acceptance of virtualization. With everyone talking about recession punctuated by rising energy prices, suddenly maintaining your own datacenter isn't quite so cool anymore. Microsoft and Amazon apparently stumbled on a pretty good crystal ball, because they've been building data centers in areas with inexpensive green energy sources and cool-enough temperatures to reduce the cost of cooling these huge data centers. Remember, it doesn't matter where your data center is anymore.

It really hit home that virtualization is here to stay when we heard about an energy conservation program sponsored by Pacific Gas and Electric (PG&E) in northern California, under which PG&E offered dollar matching for consulting, purchase, and installation of virtualized environments (with a $2 million cap). The story we heard was that in some cases the company was able to shrink its server farm by a factor of 10, with electrical energy savings in the millions.

Cloud Development Stage 3: True Clouds

As with HPCs and grids, we'll soon be seeing a further level of abstraction in which the underlying operating system is no longer as important as being able to submit tasks into the cloud. Like HPCs and grids, clouds are going to need to be provisioned with some sort of job description language for resource requests and billing. It will be in the third stage that we'll most likely really start seeing things such as application rentals, or per-use licenses, appear on the market. We might even see application use billing become something like advertising click-through charges. We would even go as far as predicting that we might start seeing applications sold more along the line of those sold in the Apple iPhone AppStore.

Key to the development of a true cloud environment will be the lessons learned by people in the grid and HPC world, combined with the lessons learned as virtualization keeps growing, hopefully mixed in with some history lessons from the days of mainframe service bureaus. The job submission description systems have to mature and converge into some sort of industry standard; the development (or acceptance) of such as standard will be a critical moment in the development and survival of cloud centers.

Our vision for clouds is one in which the broker/agent/scheduler will shop for the best deal on a set of resources. As resource costs change over time (cheaper rates at night and on weekends, just like mobile phones), the cloud application agent will then move our tasks to the next cheapest set of resources, while continuing to shop for the best deal.

So is a grid a cloud? Is a cloud an HPC? We really think it's more a matter of standards. After all, a Web server, given the proper resources, could run on an HPC or a grid, and if the scheduler had the ability to detect load on, say, a Web server, it could react to that load and start up additional Web server nodes.

Our prediction is that cloud computing will, when the dust has fully settled, be made up of the best ideas of all its predecessors.

In the end it will be market pressures that force the competing technologies to standardize their efforts. It might in the end be a 1,000-lb gorilla that forces the change. On October 27, 2008, Microsoft unveiled its version of a cloud operating environment, and only time will tell whether Microsoft will do for cloud operating systems what it did for workstation operating systems.

In the upcoming chapters, we will look at tools and systems from Microsoft, Amazon, Google, and many others. The lessons learned from clusters and grids will stand us in good stead as we begin to understand what clouds can do for an organization and how they can best be deployed and managed within a corporate IT structure.

Clouds Flight Path for Chapter 2

- *Defining grids and high-performance computing clusters.* We looked at how the two similar but different technologies played their parts leading into the world of cloud computing. When was each appropriate, and what were some of the issues of using each? They both had their place, but that was in the world of scientific computing. Business clusters are different.
- *Why HPC and grid software is so different from stand-alone applications.* We just scratched the surface of why high-performance computing and grid computing programming is so radically different from something that runs on a PC or Mac. We could compare it to the change from thinking in two dimensions and then all of the sudden having to think in a third. Programming is considered an art by many, and tweaking and tuning those applications to take full advantage of the hardware platform has always been the name of the game in high-performance computing, regardless of whether it's on a huge cluster of identical machines or spread around the globe as screen savers.
- *Some grid and HPC examples.* We talked about who's using grids and HPC computing and laid down the foundations for why HPC has seen such an explosion over the last couple of years. The explosion really happened because of the ability to make some truly stupendous computing arrays out of inexpensive personal computers. Since the driving force was financial, it only made sense to try to figure out ways to squeeze performance out of even less expensive platforms. Clouds can easily be seen as an extension of the work done on both, but with a sprinkling of lessons learned over the years.

- *Why schedulers are so important as a foundation for a true cloud computing job description language.* We keep harping on how the industry stands on the shoulders of giants and how one technology leads to another. It's our opinion that a true cloud description language will look very similar to the work being done with HPC schedulers. After all, you're in business to make money, and not squeezing the most out of your expensive investment is just a shame. Schedulers are a step in the direction of shoehorning every last computing job into available resources by playing a complex game of resource matching. For clouds to be profitable, they'll have to do the same, and the answer will more than likely be based on the lessons learned while progressing from mainframes to HPCs to grids.

- *Reiterating the differences between an HPC and a grid.* They do similar things, but they are as different as night and day. They have radically similar programming issues, but each has some massive quirks of its own. We talked briefly about these issues. While the potentially low cost of a grid has immediate appeal, it's potential lack of reliability softens that appeal when deadlines loom. The lack of uniformity in grids also means that programmers don't have as many opportunities to tweak their code to take advantage of homogeneous hardware platforms. One isn't better than the other, just different.

Chapter 3

Virtualization and the Cloud: What's the Difference?

I don't pretend we have all the answers. But the questions are certainly worth thinking about.

– Arthur C. Clarke

In This Chapter

There are significant differences between simple virtualization and cloud computing. In this chapter, we'll examine how they differ, and the criteria for determining which is the better solution in any given business situation. In this chapter we will learn:

- What should be virtualized—There are some good fits and some not-so-good fits; it pays to do a bit of testing before you jump into the deep end.
- How to control cloud resources—There'll be no return on investment if you don't pay attention to maximizing cloud usage efficiently. It's going to be about learning from historical lessons.

- Virtualization as the key to building clouds—If clouds are to succeed, there will need to a level of operating system agnostics, and virtualization will be the key to meeting the migration needs of enterprise users on their way to true clouds.
- How to manage the virtual machine and the cloud—The move from virtualization into a cloud will be about moving the virtual servers around within your collection of physical servers in order to maximize efficiency. Front-end management pieces are quickly developing to the point where even energy consumption can be taken into account.
- How to make the cloud pay for itself—How do you bill for cloud services when you're in some sort of shared tenant arrangement? Here we take a page from the mainframe world and are finally seeing the back-office financial aspect of clouds appearing.
- Development issues in the cloud—As paradigm shifts occur in the industry, so do changes in the techniques and methodologies of writing code. The cloud advantage is years of abstraction-layer development, which removes the "ball and chain" of low-level programming details.

Virtualization as the Foundation for Clouds

Regardless of whether you're going to build a mini-cloud in an existing data center environment or put your applications into a full cloud, the environment the applications go into will be virtual. We've already seen how a virtual environment divorces the idea of computing resources from specific hardware (or instances of an operating system); now, we'll look at what that can mean to the IT operations for an organization. Next will come a set of questions that can be summarized as, "How virtual do you want to be?" It's one thing to create multiple virtual environments on a single piece of hardware in order to maximize the extent to which that hardware is used. It's quite another to spread a single virtual image across an undefined number of hardware resources in order to maximize the performance and availability of an application.

How do you know what to virtualize? The decision on which resources to virtualize generally comes down to a question of the resources already being used on various available servers, and where the organization needs to maximize return on investment and performance. If you were to look into the server closet of just about any medium-sized business, you'd find three or more physical machines running email, file services, and Web services. Each physical server is typically dedicated to a single task, and each spends the majority of its time "idling," running at between 10% and 20% CPU utilization, spinning its computational wheels while waiting for input or external processing to occur.

All those CPU cycles "going to waste" is probably an extravagance in modern business, and the hard-dollar costs associated with the servers can be a drag on a company's bottom line. Those physically separate machines have software and hardware maintenance costs along with the human resource costs of remaining independent. Server operating system software alone can become a significant expense when multiplied across an entire enterprise. In addition, the cost of the energy required to power and cool many separate servers has become considerable. When electricity was cheap, running multiple servers, each with twin 500-watt power supplies, wasn't a big deal. Today, however, as energy costs have skyrocketed, many companies have been forced to take a much harder look at overall company power loads.

Virtualization can provide cost savings on all fronts through upgrades to more efficient servers (some new servers have 95%-efficient power supplies, as compared to the 80%-efficient units common just a couple of generations ago), and in most cases easily combine all three of the servers mentioned above onto a single virtualized machine. The real icing on the cake is the ability to take a "snapshot" of virtual machines in any desired state and spin the image off to some kind of external storage.

The entire march from dedicated data centers to virtualizaton, external hosting, software as a service, and now clouds is just a series of steps toward the eventual commoditization of data processing. The questions of whether an organization is ready to treat its various information assets as commodities or considers them "crown jewels" is at the core of the decision-making process that must be followed if virtualization or cloud computing is to be used as a successful IT strategy.

If the logical steps from single-purpose servers to virtualized applications to cloud computing are so smooth and straightforward, why not simply go straight into the cloud for all an organization's needs? As we'll see, a number of ingredients keep the various computing types far more stratified in practice than they are in principle. While this is likely to change with time, for the foreseeable future, managers and architects will need to keep the differences firmly in mind as they build applications for their organizations.

Sir Isaac Newton's remark about "standing on the shoulders of giants," reproduced at the beginning of Chapter 2, is an apt description of how the computer industry works. A great example begins with Dr. Norman Abramson's DARPA-funded project called AlohaNET, which created a radio network that allowed students, faculty, and other staff at the University of Hawaii to connect to a time-share system on the university's BCC-500 central computer. It worked, but it had limitations in terms of congestion and collisions, which were later fixed by Robert Metcalf of the Xerox Palo Alto Research Center (PARC). This work led eventually, with the help of Intel and Digital Equipment Corporation, to Ethernet. Like a set of child's building blocks, ideas spawn new ideas to build something bigger and better over time. What made AlohaNET such a landmark technology was that it marked the first time that large numbers of users were connected by a single communications medium to a single large number computing system. It should also be noted that the Carrier Sense Multiple Access (CSMA) system proposed by Dr. Abramson was augmented with a collision detection system (CDMA/CD) by Xerox to increase the efficiency of the overall system and avoid many of the problems of collisions in the original DARPA project.

The Missing Link Between Virtualization and Clouds

One of the chief factors complicating the decision on virtualizing or moving to the cloud is the handful of missing pieces in an overall control suite that makes application movement seamless. The true equivalent of what existed in JCL (Job Control Language), the comma-delimited mainframe control system that filled the days (and nightmares) of people who ran applications using punched cards on large IBM systems, hasn't arrived on the scene. It's not the punched cards that are missing; it's the control wrapper where environmental requirements for the application can be reported to the host system automatically that hasn't yet appeared. What's missing is a control layer that can convey resource requests to each cloud implementation in lieu of a human conversation. The job submission automation process is still a collection of incompatible systems with no current method to move cloud jobs around automatically between clouds of varying flavors (Microsoft, Amazon, Google, etc.).

When users can submit applications to any system they have credentials for and not worry about installation issues, then we're at least in the neighborhood of a true cloud. It all needs to happen without human interaction. Something on this scale exists for desktop productivity applications, for which users can easily see data synchronized between desktop hard disks and storage located in the cloud through applications such as Dropbox and the Microsoft Mesh. On the server end, however, things are rather more complicated, and it's here that we'll focus our attention for most of the remainder of this chapter.

Virtualization: Abstraction in a Box

Virtualization, as we've seen, is all about abstraction. In practical terms, this means figuring out the boundaries of abstraction layers and just how specific a developer needs to be in writing a new application.

An abstraction layer is a way of formalizing the OSI seven-layer model (see Chapter 1) and choosing one of the layers (or even a slice from one of the layers) as the piece of the overall data processing puzzle that will be abstracted and virtualized. Make no mistake: Without abstraction (defining the services of a layer in terms of what they do and how they connect with the layers above and below them in the stack), virtualization (divorcing services from the hardware on which they run) just isn't possible. The ease and transparency with which this is possible play a huge role in determining the success of virtualization (and, ultimately, cloud computing) projects.

For example, for all its faults, Windows successfully removed a huge amount of effort previously required to develop network applications. Microsoft's .NET framework went a great way toward creating a *de facto* standard with applications that in theory could cross between servers, to desktops, and then to mobile platforms. However, .NET certainly wasn't the first and certainly isn't the only framework of its kind. An entire flood of new toolkits, such as PHP, Python, Ruby on Rails, and others, are all about hiding the layers below. The ability to have a single line of code, rather than dozens, open a dialog window enables additional consistency and capabilities that had previously been rarely touched by programmers.

These toolkits offer advanced capabilities to a wider design audience and provide a faster adoption curve because of their reduced learning curve. By eliminating the need for users or administrators to determine explicitly the machine on which a particular application (or piece of an application) will execute, these high-level toolkits made network service virtualization practical and widely accepted virtually overnight. What has been brought up time and again, however, is that these abstraction layers have almost become the flavor of the month. Conversion between systems obviously has to be taken into account as new systems are adopted.

Microsoft probably began the virtualization wars in earnest when their Virtual Server product was made a freely downloadable solution, a move that was closely followed by VMWare. While some observers focused on immediate product pricing and distribution strategies, what was really important was that both companies planted the seeds for much broader adoption of virtual machines when they made "type 2 hypervisor" products basically free.

A hypervisor (also called a virtual machine monitor, or VMM) is software/hardware platform virtualization software that allows multiple operating systems to run on a host computer at the same time.

- *Type 1 hypervisors* are installed onto bare metal or directly on the hardware platform. They run directly on the host's hardware to control it and also monitor guest operating systems. This type thus represents the classic implementation of virtual machine architecture. And, by essentially eliminating the general-use operating system, type 1 hypervisors actually offer better performance than the later type 2 systems.
- *Type 2 hypervisors* are software applications that run inside a conventional operating system environment as a user or system space application. The main difference from type 1 hypervisors is that type 2 hypervisors run as normal users rather than as privileged "super-users." A very common application is as a "safe" workstation environment that is protected from outside attack.

Type 1 hypervisors have been available for some time, but they require significant effort to install and configure properly. Types 2 hypervisors, by taking advantage of the additional layer of abstraction provided by the underlying operating system, are both less expensive and less labor-intensive to install, configure, and administer. Now that type 2 hypervisor systems are freely available, droves of users have rushed to develop virtual environments.

Why the rush? The widespread availability of type 2 hypervisors meant that system administrators and individual users could begin to experiment easily with virtualization. In many cases, the experiments led to acceptance of virtualization on at least a limited basis within the organization, as concerns about performance, administration costs, and stability were answered. The early experiments also sowed seeds for even greater virtualization acceptance as companies and users sought higher virtualized performance for lower costs.

Ironically, the search for higher performance drove the market back toward type 1 hypervisors, where now-experienced administrators could customize installations for optimal behavior, and software publishers such as VMWare, Citrix, and Microsoft could make some real profit. Some companies were able to import administration talent in order to begin their virtualization push with a type 1 hypervisor, and some organizations and users remained completely happy with a type 2 hypervisor. In most cases, however, organizations that will eventually make the move to a fully virtualized type 1 environment to maximize performance start off with a type 2 hypervisor environment first, to keep the cost of the learning curve down.

Interestingly enough, this mad rush to adoption has wedged open the licensing door at Microsoft with their Data Center Edition for Windows Server 2008. Lest we accidentally misinterpret Microsoft's "legalspeak," here's a paste from their website describing how the licensing works for this special version of Windows Server:

> Windows Server 2008 R2 Datacenter features Hyper-V, a flexible high-performance hypervisor-based virtualization technology.
>
> In addition, Windows Server 2008 R2 Datacenter licenses include unlimited virtualization rights, meaning that you have rights to run an unlimited number of Windows Server instances on servers licensed with Windows Server 2008 R2 Datacenter. This gives you the benefits of virtualization while helping to reduce license management headaches and costs, thus helping you:
>
> - Logically consolidate servers and streamline management.
> - Reduce the cost associated with power, cooling, and data center space.

- Increase the availability of your systems. (The quick migra-tion feature enables you to easily move running virtual machines between their physical hosts.)
- Reduce server sprawl by using multiple virtual machines hosted on a physical server.

(*Source:* www.microsoft.com/windowsserver2008/en/us/2008-dc. aspx.)

Instances

Before we go further, we need to introduce a key piece of jargon. An individual running copy of a particular operating system in a virtual environment is called an *instance.* On a single VMWare platform, for example, a company might have half a dozen instances of Windows Server running simultaneously, each instance hosting a separate set of applications. Regardless of whether you're running a type 1 or a type 2 virtual environment, all the instances of the operating system will be resident in a single box. The ability to move virtual instances from box to box depending on demand is where the idea that would become clouds first arose.

As a historical note, this trend toward putting key pieces of code into hardware for speed reasons has happened several times during the his-tory of computing. IBM had communications processors, network inter-face cards started adding intelligence to preprocess network packets, and graphic cards are now appearing with dozens of graphic processors. It just made sense for, first, VMWare and then Microsoft, to work directly with the CPU manufacturers to move some key virtualization code into hardware. Hyperthread-capable CPUs have become common, but for the most part they remain unused except on enterprise-grade servers. At this moment, most workstation operating systems are unable to take advan-tage of these additions, but it's only a matter of time. What's most likely to happen is the implementation of a toggle similar to how Parallels (vir-tualization for workstations, but currently a type 2 hypervisor) works on a Macintosh. Hit a key and the screen rotates like a cube to display the interface for a guest operating system, leaving the host running in the background. Will we see type 1 hypervisors at the workstation? Only the market can tell.

The concept of treating multiple servers as a single virtualized entity only became practical once bare-metal installations of virtualized operating systems became available and CPU manufacturers started adding hypervisor instructions directly to their base CPU code. The additional control over this high-wire balancing act was necessary to suspend an instance, and then move the entire program with state information to a new machine. In other words, a Web request could be stopped midway through and then continued on a new machine without anyone knowing. With this native hyperthreading support in place, a new instance of an operating system with its hosted application could be launched (or, in the language of virtualization, *spawned*) whenever the demand for an application's services became greater than a single instance could support. Virtualization technology could now be used for dynamic demand balancing, spawning new application instances when needed to meet short-term requirements, and then shutting them down when the temporary surge in demand was over—all without direct and immediate human intervention.

Another huge leap in virtualization technology occurred when vendors started providing for de-duplication of application code across machines. Shared OS kernels became part of the computing landscape early in the development of virtualization, but now vendors started providing the intelligence to share application code across virtual machines, further reducing overhead. Instead of a full version of the operating system for each virtual machine, portions were shared to cut down on the overhead for each virtual machine running. As the concept has continued to develop, storage virtualization is starting to offer de-duplication for common pieces (such as all the utilities in a typical OS install), further reducing the overall cost of the overhead for multiple instances of operating systems and applications. As the cost of multiple instances of operating systems went down (which happened as the knowledge of how to properly administer virtualized servers went up), companies became less reluctant to use virtualization as an alternative to reflexively buying new hardware every time a capacity crunch hit.

With these developments in common code sharing, mission-critical applications could move around in the virtual cluster and be assigned resources on the fly to respond to the massive surge of Web traffic caused by a product going viral because of unexpected success on You Tube or Oprah.

Managing Instances

Virtual machine management was the next hurdle to overcome. Since you no longer had a dedicated console for each server, nor did each machine have an optical drive, peripheral sharing for system generation and/or maintenance became necessary. Vendors such as Avocent, Raritan, Lantronix, Adder, and others that brought Internet Protocol keyboard/video/mouse sharing devices (IP KVMs) to market are now all bringing remotely mounted media to the datacenter. The ability to mount a disk image, spawning a new instance of an operating system from a virtual disk image stored on a hard drive rather than from a physical CD-ROM, appeared almost simultaneously in management systems for blade servers and in virtual machine console applications. This critical ability became an overnight hit for remote management and automated demand balancing.

At the same time, the ability to launch some sort of remote console for each virtual machine from a browser, eliminating the old "thick" console applications, allowed management to continue while operating system instances were spawned. The growing reliance on abstraction layers and rapidly spawning OS instances led to an ironic problem, however: While abstraction layers exist to physically detach one layer from another, the layers can't become *too* detached or the entire system won't work.

One of the most common examples is also one of the most frustrating for system administrators: The local cursor used to control actions on a screen can become disconnected from mouse movement in the remote console, with the local and remote cursors never quite meeting. This is a particular problem with "thin" console applications that use a Web browser to provide a logical window into the operating environment of a remote server. This has almost always been an issue with how the remote machine was set up, but the problem has arisen time and again. While it is seldom fatal to an administration effort, it is a frustrating example of why IT professionals are still looking for improvements in virtual system administration applications.

Another massive change in the way servers are controlled has been the development of the service processor, which is a small computer piggybacking inside the server that is intended for environmental control of the main server. Under most circumstances, when you press the power button on a server, you're not really turning on the power supply directly; you are sending a signal to the service processor asking it to send power to the main server equipment. The service processor is also responsible for monitoring temperature, fan speed, voltage levels, intrusion sensors, and other hardware-oriented functions. In the case of some Dell blade servers, this management goes as far as being able to track power usage by blade or chassis, providing the potential for submetering in collocation services. Overall complexity and capabilities depend on the platform; in most blade servers, the service processor is also responsible for remote access. For its blade servers, Dell has an agreement with Avocent for IP KVM services, and SuperMicro has an agreement with Raritan. In both cases, the service provides keyboard/video/mouse support to a remote computer over a network connection.

While remote console applications were being developed and deployed, network monitoring programs such as HP Open View, OpenNMS, Packet Trap, Nagios, and UniCenter started providing a deeper view into the virtualized environment. Instead of just monitoring to the physical host, they started providing views to the virtualized host and provided additional information specific to the virtualized environment. Now, in addition to spawning instances automatically as demand increased, virtualization systems could provide accurate, real-time information to system administrators so they could tell when hardware capacities were close to being exceeded or software license counts were dangerously close to being full. At last, the tools were in place to all enterprises to fully virtualize many aspects of their server farm, using rack-mounted servers or blade servers to pack hundreds or thousands of virtual operating systems into the space of a single 19-inch equipment rack. The use of blade servers has even started reaching into the medium-sized business realm with Hewlett-Packard's introduction of the C3000 series of blade server, nicknamed the "shorty." This smaller chassis can support four full-size blades or eight half-size blades. This branch office offering is typically configured with a storage blade and a couple of computing blades to handle branch office computing needs.

What happened when even virtual servers in the data center weren't enough to keep up with the rapidly growing demand for compute services? It was time; it seemed, to break out the clouds.

Beginning and Perfecting Cloud Computing

We've seen the growing movement toward abstraction in services and processes. We've seen the evolution of virtualization toward automatic spawning of instances when resource demand grows high. These have all been stepping-stones that have set the stage for the next step: cloud computing. What, precisely, differentiates cloud computing from virtualization? Originally, the difference involved the location of the servers involved. Virtualization involved virtual operating system instances on servers owned by (or provided through dedicated hosting agreements to) the organization. Cloud computing, on the other hand, was provided on servers located "in the cloud" of the Internet, at locations that weren't owned by, or even known by, the organization. In other words, computing resources don't have a specific location, but they're not in the organization data center.

We can begin with this definition of cloud computing: a set of services provided solely as a service, with no responsibility for or even knowledge of a server required by the service consumer. As enterprises have begun to explore cloud computing, the definition has broadened a bit, but we'll cover some of the variations in Chapter 6. For now, let's take a look at cloud computing and the providers who make it happen.

What might a cloud service provider (CSP) look like? First, the cloud provider will want to stay well out of the "operating system wars" that have consumed so many megabytes of blog and discussion group bandwidth over the last decade. In reality, the battle between Linux and Microsoft will continue for the foreseeable future, and the CSP will most likely need to have nodes for both operating systems available to their customers. In some cases, the CSP will make certain operating system-specific applications available to customers. In others, the CSP will make applications or functions available without ever letting the customer know which operating system lies underneath the service provided. As we move toward true cloud providers, it will be irrelevant what the base operating system is, since cloud applications should be able to move freely between different providers.

In order to keep their customers from being casualties in the operating system wars, the CSP will need to have the equivalent of the scheduler in grids and high-performance computing to determine which base operating system and resources are required for a particular job. This piece is not yet available from CSPs, though some are talking about putting it in place in the foreseeable future. The scheduler piece that is still missing is composed of two parts, which we'll call the *broker* and the *agent*. This idea for a path to better cloud computing is adapted from a description of HPC/

grid scheduling in a paper by Jennifer M. Schopf of the Mathematics and Computer Science Division, Argonne National Laboratory.

A *broker* provides a public interface for external processes to talk to a cloud application, and an *agent* is a piece of code that goes shopping through the cloud for services or goods that the user application needs. Together, these two scheduler pieces reconcile the abstraction between layers and components that allows cloud computing to work in the first place. Successful scheduling as discussed here would allow for greater component abstraction, which means that it would be easier for an application to be created from a large number of disparate pieces published by different CSPs.

Another missing piece in just about everything currently published on public grids and clouds, and the key to successfully building complete applications from a large number of cloud-provided pieces, is the concept of *identity federation*. In identity federation, a user or enterprise provides its verified identity to the first organization providing a piece of the application chain. Other publishers and providers accept the verified identity from the first organization so the customer needs to log in only once to satisfy the identity requirements of many different software or service providers. Simply put, it answers the question of how you set up and use trust relationships between foreign organizations that are only loosely connected. How you can set up business rules for automatic transactions and how you define a level of qualified trust for business partners are questions that still need to be answered. Web consumers today are using an early version at sites such as Amazon and UnitedMall. Credentials identifying individuals are passed from the umbrella site (Amazon or UnitedMall) to each partner online store providing discounts and special offers to UnitedMall or Amazon shoppers. Another example is how payment authorization is handled by PayPal, where payment requests are passed from the online store to PayPal and, once authorization is accomplished, payment credentials are passed back to the store.

Utopian Clouds?

This may sound a bit utopian, but it's easy to look forward to a day when "agents" and "brokers" utilize something like a credit bureau to set up a level of financial trust. This financial trust would be used like a credit limit to set up boundaries on just how large a resource request an agent could make of a broker. In principle, and perhaps in practice, this sounds very much like what telephone companies do millions of times per second with calls transiting from one telco to another. With a business model and billing software already in place (and the billing software is truly the most difficult piece of the puzzle to fit into place), it's quite possible to imagine a telco morphing into a "cloud dating service" or perhaps a "cloud matchmaker" handling third-party agent and broker services. This third-party validation facility would be very similar to what happens when you use a protected website. The user starts a connection to a website, which in turn starts the negotiation to establish a secure connection. The website has a set of credentials that is sent to the user's Web browser. The browser in turn sends those credentials to a third-party server called a *certificate authority*. The browser has already been sent a list of legitimate certificate authorities during its periodic updates, and all this happens via an encrypted conversation. If the website checks out against the certificate authority, the use gets an "All clear" to proceed with the encrypted conversation. It should be noted that while the most common use of certificate authorities is for SSL (secure socket layer) Web conversations, the same certificate authority is used for a great number of encryption methodologies and technologies that require some sort of third-party validation of identity.

Did that sound too simple? It was. Did that sound too definitive? You bet. The rub is that cloud computing today is as nebulous as the name implies. At this moment, most cloud services don't sound much different from regular old Software as a Service (SaaS), but marketing departments are using cloudlike buzzwords to describe future directions. True cloud computing is going to require a whole lot of new standards and lots of thinking outside the virtualized box. The crystal ball we're peering into has a massive collection of applications that might not necessarily have a single purchase price. Instead the cloud would handle usage billing, with the final bill consisting of CPU time, storage, application usage fee, and network transit fees. Late 2009 saw VMWare announce back-office cloud management coming out from behind the curtain. Instead of just market monsters such as Amazon and Google running clouds, it will be possible to handle the charge-backs necessary for something akin to "joint tenancy" billing for mini-clouds—the perfect role for small to medium-size Internet service providers as they morph to meet the changing market.

Accounting for Clouds

In a fully federated cloud, associated with every "cloud session" would be background accounting information, restrictions, a crypto key ring, and general preferences the user wants applied to the environment. There might also be different pricing for permanent prescience (always-available provisioning) covering specialized apps such as agents and brokers, which might very well morph into something like a company telephone number. Perhaps we'll see business cards with a new information line that might read: "cloud://cheebert.honolulu.hi.us," which might then broker different information depending on who you are. If you're a friend who has previously been defined in the system, it might give you my home phone number, but Joe Shmoe off the street would get routed to my general company information page. The public cloud broker might eventually be where Voice-over-IP, Web, instant messaging, etc., all combine for truly unified communications, where the broker would handle a much larger set of business rules to provide for automatic escalation of communications paths across multiple enterprises.

Security could potentially be high enough so that the line between public and private data would be simply a matter of credentials on a crypto key ring. After all, the world of classified processing has long had well-understood rules; for example, the National Industrial Security Program Operating Manual (NISPOM) has well-defined procedures on how to mix users with different "need to know" and different classification levels, all separated into various "protection levels." If the Department of Defense can mix protection levels, why can't corporate clouds? Especially if the cloud vendor has done a reasonable amount of due diligence to comply with whatever regulations may apply in a particular industry (i.e., Sarbanes-Oxley for publically traded corporations, or HIPAA for the medical world).

Could this be a case of too many eggs in a single basket? Sure, but when we first connected corporations to the public Internet, we were also balancing risk against benefit. Clouds have the potential to allow IT groups to concentrate more on the bottom line instead of being slaves to the system update dance. Vendors such as Coyote Point and F5 have gone to great lengths to address this need, with global load-balancing systems now able to start and stop virtual machines in geographically separated data centers.

A Matter of Trust

If brokers become proxies for foreign trust relationships, clouds will be instigators for changing ideas of trust in the overall system as well. Historically, the Wang VS minicomputer system provided assigned credentials not only to users but also to programs. There was, for example, an application that presented users with totals of students in various class sections, their ethnicity, etc. An individual user, however, might not be allowed to see any specific information on individuals because of student confidentiality rules. The Wang VS program was given enough credentials to access to the student information database, but would only present the user with totals, not the contents of individual records. None of the reports that the user had access to would give any type of student details. The registrar who used the same program would present a different set of credentials and be able to get to an additional set of reports that would allow him to print class lists with names and student ID numbers.

The next step in the iterative growth process occurred when network credentials began to catch up to what users had available on the Wang computer. At a 1995 InfoWorld Identity Management System bake-off, IBM displayed an IBM Thinkpad that was running a virtualized mainframe and demonstrated how a gateway application provided a proxy into the "mainframe" so that an employee could have proxied access to mainframe information. In the identity management systems, templates were defined for roles, and in almost every case, the proxies were assigned to the roles rather than the individual. So, while back in August 2005, federation was only just being hinted at, today it needs to rise out of the stagnant waters of the standards committee backrooms if clouds are truly to fulfill their destiny.

Self-Provisioned Virtual Servers

Before we leave the topic of virtual servers, clouds, and the differences between them, we should take a brief look at some of the ideas that engineers are talking about in relation to virtual servers. The concept of self-provisioning virtual machines is being mentioned with increasing frequency by engineers at both VMWare and Microsoft. While it is, at the time of this writing, vaporware from both, it's unlikely to be far away. How might these self-provisioning servers work? The basic premise is a simple expansion of an ability we've already discussed for virtual machines. Sets of business rules would be set up to extend the basic ability to spawn new instances previously available in products such as VMotion from VMWare.

Previously, Vmotion could pause a noncritical server in order to reallocate resources when required to handle load spikes. This "contraction" of services left CPU and memory resources available to handle the surge in demand for another service or component. An ability to expand on demand, adding instances on additional hardware resources when surges hit, meets user need without starving, even temporarily, other applications or services. This step moves virtual machines one step closer to the "agents" and "brokers" just discussed as an important feature in future clouds.

Why can't a broker application in the virtualized system wait for requests and only when, say, a call center opens for the day, cause the start-up of the customer relationship management (CRM) virtual server? Maybe there will be something like a Web proxy, where the very first user of the day will have to wait longer for the Web request to populate the cache. Then each subsequent user no longer has to go out to the wide-area network for that particular Web page, since it can now come from local cache. The same concept could be used for a self-provisioning VM as long as business rules are intelligently set up to prevent a flip-flop effect as the VM pages in and out of the main system. We can do a portion of this using outside influences such as load balancers from F5 and Coyote Point. We can also script the provisioning according to predetermined scenarios, but it all has to be planned out in advance.

An early example is now available from both Microsoft in their System Center Virtual Machine Manager and from VMWare in their Virtual Center system. Both allow the extended application of business rules beyond just shifting resources, to automatically starting VMs upon detect of certain load conditions. Both vendors have also gone further into backup and restore, by allowing for failed servers to reappear automatically on other clusters through the application of restore rules that are set up beforehand. The gist is that consumers want to pay only for applications they're actually using, and if the call center isn't open for a third shift, then shut it down and save energy. Or, better yet, pay only for when you actually use the CRM, since on-demand computing seems to be something that the people at SalesForce are hinting at for potential new pricing and usage models.

From Virtual Computing to the Cloud

We've said throughout this chapter that both virtual machines and cloud computing are all about abstraction layers. It's still virtualization if you can see details about the operating system, especially if you still need to make accommodations for which operating system is under it all. Once the OS details fade into the background, then that swirling mist around your ankles might now be a cloud.

Users should be able to write or configure an application, test it on local resources, and then have an agent submit it to the cloud service providers. The great benefit of the cloud includes the ability to "rent" applications developed by others in order to meet rapidly changing needs. As an example, a rapidly growing company might find it advantageous to rent, say, a payroll application, submitting an "agent request" that would also include temporary credentials to a human resources cloud app so that they could access payroll data. In this case, the list of cloud service providers might include any of a number of financial clouds the company has vetted, with something like PayPal providing a financial proxy to actually transfer the funds for payroll. As the company grows, it could either expand its reliance on Web computing or develop custom applications to meet its unique needs exactly. In the most likely scenario, though, the company's future will include a hybrid approach, with basic services provided through cloud facilities and certain very specific components hosted on dedicated virtual machines that are very tightly integrated with the cloud service providers.

There has been a vision floating around in the world of science fiction about data processing facilities handled just like a utility: You rent the applications you need only for the time you use them. You might have some in-house computing capability, but usage spikes could be off-loaded to the cloud as needed. This type of service is already being provided by a number of vendors, including Amazon, Google, and IBM. As the tools to integrate expansion capabilities into locally hosted applications improve and grow, it's not unreasonable to assume that overflow into the cloud will become a standard part of business continuity planning for most companies.

Our opinion is that the missing link is some sort of multiplatform computing abstraction layer that provides an identical development environment regardless of which platform or operating system lies underneath.

It might be on just such a development system that we will start seeing something akin to the iPhone apps store, but for clouds.

Developing into the Cloud

An early example of what a cloud development environment might look like is the Adobe Integrated Runtime (AIR) environment. AIR has the pieces that a cloud development environment needs to have, including:

- XML-based resource requirement descriptors
- Ability to support multiple high-level object-oriented Web development systems (Java and Flash in AIR's case)
- Ability to support Internet, database, and hardware interfaces, all within an environment that doesn't seem to care if it's on a Windows or Linux environment (not included in first versions, but a publically stated goal of Adobe for the AIR environment)

This is not to say that AIR is already a fully realized cloud environment. Missing at the moment are cloud versions of the schedulers now found on HPCs and grids. The brokers need to be able to handle accounting proxies, data access proxies, auditing proxies, and financial proxies. We'll most likely see the cloud environment start with all the pieces in a single cloud service provider; but as the environment matures, we'll begin seeing specialized cloud service providers offering additional options.

Clouds: Minimum Commitments and Maximum Limits

Cloud computing will have tiered pricing as never before. This is already beginning to be put in place by many cloud service providers. Just as the service broker model could easily be based on existing telephone company business models, cloud computing pricing is going to start resembling mobile phone contracts, but with utilization spike allowances that will sound just like collocation facility bandwidth service agreements.

As cloud applications mature and cloud operating systems migrate to more platforms, applications will be migrated from service provider to service provider by agent software, searching for the best rates for the amount of resources. There may be broker nodes that will be the primary public point of contact, with agent nodes shopping around the globe as brokers change their rates over the workday. In an interesting "back to the future" way, this sounds just like what the old model used in dealing with service bureaus. Companies once had regular IT business models that included a requirement to shop around for some IT functions rather than upgrading just to handle occasional load spikes.

There are now PayPal accounts that can be used in hundreds of e-commerce sites all over the globe, and it's not a stretch to see provider such as PayPal adding cloud information as part of the customer profile. As this model grows, perhaps eBay will provide "agent" applications for hire, using its internal cloud as the basis for a cloud service provider business. These agents would definitely have some of their heritage from Web crawlers (a key component in the primary business model of cloud provider Google) but will also a significant heritage component from a firm like PayPal, with its expertise in secure small transactions. This basis in existing well-understood technology and business models means that broker services will become as commonplace as mobile telephone carriers—and as competitive.

In fact, service providers may be forced to demand minimum usage commitments just to stay profitable in light of "shoppers." Just as mobile phone providers often demand a minimum 2-year commitment if you want the latest and greatest phone for free, cloud service providers could easily build their tier model on the notion of customer commitment. Do we predict that cloud computing may become the next supercommodity, like mobile phones? It's quite possible that the march of computing to commodity will drive the market to look very similar to this very familiar commodity market. Especially in light of the high cost of IT specialists, the high cost of energy, and the rapidly rising cost of collocation space driving the enterprise to look for new ways of doing business, cloud computing has benefits that we'll now explore in light of evolving business needs and models.

Clouds Flight Path for Chapter 3

- *Some things shouldn't be done in the cloud; virtualization isn't for everyone.* Do you really need a cloud, or just a more flexible data center? Sometimes, regulatory restrictions may make cloud computing impossible, but in any case you need to make sure you look at how you do business before you take the plunge.

- *We should learn from the lessons of the old mainframe JCL as we build automation for cloud job control.* We have talked about paying attention to history, because if you don't, you are destined to repeat it. As clouds provide for more and more job submission automation, we feel that the lessons learned from the old mainframe days are still worth looking at as we move into the future.

- *What types of virtualization are available, and what are the differences?* Since virtualization will be the foundation for most clouds, it is important to have a good understanding of those foundation stones.

- *Management tools for the cloud.* We have taken a look at how clouds will be controlled, and at some of the "gotcha's" we'll probably see along the way.

- *Accounting and its role in the cloud.* It all has to be paid for somehow, and the backroom accounting is just as important as the technology.

- *Autoprovisioning and why a cloud job control language will be important.* It needs to be automatic if we're to fulfill the full promise of cloud computing. We look at where we're at now, so that we can imagine the future.

- *Development issues.* Just as we saw in high-performance and grid computing, there are some "gotcha's" for programmers. We have touched on this subject and have provided some warnings about things you might trip over.

Chapter 4

Applications for Clouds

The first rule of any technology used in a business is that automation applied to an efficient operation will magnify the efficiency. The second is that automation applied to an inefficient operation will magnify the inefficiency.

– Bill Gates

In This Chapter

Cloud applications can take many forms and can be created using many development systems. In this chapter we'll learn about the tools available to build cloud applications and the variety of applications, from personal productivity to enterprise back-end support, that are available in the cloud. In this chapter we'll learn:

- The development environment's path to clouds—Just how are coding systems changing to take advantage of the new environment? What kinds of changes are happening that will help programmers "bootstrap" themselves into the clouds?
- The role of Software Development Kits (SDKs) and Applications Programming Interfaces (APIs) in rapid development—As development systems change, just how much help are cloud providers giving us in making changes?

- How abstraction is starting to leave the browser behind—Software as a Service (SaaS) started us on the road to clouds, but the browser by itself couldn't break us of the "thick application" habit until "rich Internet applications" burst onto the scene, bringing us the world the best of both worlds.
- How far we have come with higher and higher-level languages and the beginnings of abstraction—We now have an unparalleled choice of development systems, which has become a dual-edged sword and led to some unintended consequences.
- Commercial off-the-shelf, government off-the-shelf versus stove-pipes—Users are much less willing to pay for ultracustomized applications that perform only a single function. Just how are the new collections of systems meeting our needs?
- Storage clouds—How are cloud storage systems luring users? Thinly veiled storage clouds are being used to connect mobile users to cloud providers, and storage might very well be the way many corporations dip their toes into the world of clouds.
- Is Google getting closer to a "true cloud"?—Google and its amazingly close tie to the Android phone system leads us to believe that we might start seeing clouds that will become even less specific and might be paving the way for cloud computing to become more of a commodity.

Introduction

Just what does a cloud application look like, and what makes it different from the applications running on your desktop PC? With grids and HPC clusters in their lineage, cloud applications also need to have their functions split in several pieces; in the case of clouds, however, the user interface is typically the portion closest to the user, and some sort of back-end process makes up the bulk of the heavy-lifting component. A common misconception is that cloud applications must be very general in function and closely resemble traditional websites in form. How did these ideas arise? They came from the early days of Web-based applications, when active user interface tools were limited and most database applications were simple screen-scraping versions of green-screen applications (basic monochrome terminal applications ported to the Web with minimal enhancements to the user interface).

As an extension of the opinions about green-screen computing, some feeling about early cloud apps was based on response to the thin-versus-thick application debates. However, as new development environments such as Adobe AIR started appearing, the traditional line between thick and thin applications became blurred. The new trend is that Web-based applications neither have to be limited to the boundaries of a Web browser nor do they necessarily mean a compromise in the user interface. Much of the sense of what is possible in cloud applications is based on newer developments in the tools used to build those applications.

Browser Versus Desktop (aka Thick Versus Thin)

The browser has become the preferred way for delivering many applications because it allows easy deployment across operating systems and simplified application maintenance. Plus, the modern programming languages used in the browser enable rapid application design and development.

The Adobe® AIR™ runtime complements the browser by providing the same application development and deployment benefits while adding desktop integration, local data access, and enhanced branding opportunities. An emerging design pattern for Rich Internet Applications (RIAs) is to deliver a browser-based version of an RIA in the browser for all users and an RIA on the desktop for more active users.

(*Source:* www.adobe.com/products/air/comparison.)

Not long ago there was a great debate in the Java programming world about whether it was possible to have contextual information brought up simply by having a cursor hover over a spot on a Web page. Although we're all very familiar with this feature now, it wasn't long ago that Java didn't directly support this feature. Frustratingly, it took several years to get Java to the point where it could rival traditional programming environments for functionality. Now, however, with the browser so tightly integrated into the operating system (be it PC or Mac or Linux), the language capability to extend through to the base hardware makes even applications that demand services from a number of different hardware-based systems possible. Applications such as Web-based video confer-encing are now commonly used, and Web-based application sharing like that from Adobe (Enterprise Connect), WebEx, or Microsoft's Live Meeting is now regularly accepted as a key component in collaboration in distributed organizations.

Access to services both complex and simple is gained through the archi-tectural structure of browser plug-ins. These sub-applications connect to and extend the functionality of the browser in known, well-defined ways. This regular architecture carries a number of benefits and a couple of sig-nificant risks. Among the benefits are simple installation, small memory and CPU footprint, and rapid function extension. The drawbacks tend to be security-related, since users can often add a browser helper or plug-in without understanding the full ramifications of the act. Just look at how many users have Yahoo, Google, and MSN toolbars in their browser and can't explain how they got there!

Plug-ins and Code Generators

The behavior and impact of plug-ins is complicated by the fact that some plug-in code will act without user intervention to make rather profound actions. For example, choosing certain toolbar plug-ins has been known to change home pages, choice of video players, choice of music/MP3 players, etc. Too many users don't really read what the plug-in is for and in some rare cases have unknowingly shared some very private informa-tion. Simpler plug-ins are often installed on demand as an alternative to the huge overhead of a full installer session for traditional applications. Moreover, some complex plug-ins are much better behaved, such as the NetExtender SSL-VPN application from SonicWall, which will remove themselves and their history upon log-out. This makes the plug-in a way to deliver functionality with very close to zero footprint.

Add to this the revolution represented by systems such as Ruby on Rails, Flex, and Ajax, which all serve as programming abstraction layers, and you have a dramatic shift in the essential nature of the chunk of code we call an application. Anything these systems can do can also be done in a lower-level language (i.e., PERL or PHP instead of Ruby on Rails), but you also also spend considerably more time to develop and debug such a program. Another hidden advantage of programming abstraction layers is that these systems tend to force some standardization, which also increases the possibility of reusing code. You lose a bit of control, but the payback is increased development speed and increased standardization.

What we do lose is operating speed. In order to accommodate any potential situation, systems like this must have libraries and functions to cover most situations. This extra baggage is a big contributor to "code creep" or "code bloating." So, while putting up a message onto a screen could be done in a few lines of a high-level language like Python, those few lines of code can potentially expand to several hundred or even thousands of lines of code as various libraries are brought into memory to handle housekeeping. All of this extra overhead happens because the higher-level language will insert extra code just to handle any type of eventuality, regardless of whether it will be used or not. Our view is that although abstraction layers do provide quite a few benefits, the code bloat (larger and larger applications) is one of the major reasons why Moore's law exists. Every time computing capabilities take a jump, applications tend to fill the empty space. From a philosophical code-development point of view, an example from the other end of the spectrum are small-code purists such as Drew Majors, author of Novell Netware.

The Advantages of Low-Level Languages

It was the four gentlemen called the "SuperSet," with Drew Majors at its head, who developed the kernel of Novell Netware. Netware got its amazing speed in part because the "SuperSet" wrote the kernel in Assembler instead of a much higher-level language. In fact, some of the fastest code on the planet is still written in low-level languages, simply because a low-level language doesn't need to accommodate any possible eventuality. It's much easier to tune a program into a speed demon when there is less "stuff" to sift through.

Assembler and C are still among the most popular computer languages for writing machine control systems and device drivers, because of their extremely concise nature. The downside is that such concise programs also tend to be *very* difficult to write and in some cases are considered an art form. These time- and talent-intensive systems are almost always reserved for systems that are timing-sensitive, such as those in video encoding/decoding systems, flight control systems, or any application that has ramifications if things get out of sync. Programmers capable of writing such low-level code are rare and extremely expensive. It's no wonder that abstraction layers such as Ruby on Rails, Python, SPSS, SAS, etc., have been developed.

Also due to the smaller and more concise nature of the code, low-level languages like C are also popular for embedded computing. This type of concise code is also useful for extremely small processors such as the class of devices called PICs (peripheral interface computer), which are small enough and inexpensive enough that they're found in devices as small as watches and remote controls, as well as all the way up to automobiles. These stripped-down computers are also unique in that you can "burn" the program onto the PIC so that it can't possibly be erased. More advanced versions also have flash memory (just like the flash memory cards used in digital cameras), so that new, updated versions of the program can be swapped in.

So what those high-level abstraction layers give us is that the extra code makes building blocks easier to fit together. Similar in concept to the Lego™ child's toy, the blocks below have an expected pattern that's designed to fit into the block above. Many of the examples we've given thus far deal with individual systems and their applications, but the principles are identical when applied to cloud computing, and many of the application platforms we've discussed are used for both local applications and cloud-delivered apps.

With the massive surge in processor power available in a modern computer system, it's now possible to trade off speed of development and ease of maintainability versus tight, concise programming code. Maybe that's what "junk DNA" (http://en.wikipedia.org/wiki/Junk_dna) is all about: It may be Nature's programming code leftovers that are there to accommodate other situations.

We previously mentioned the Adobe AIR (Adobe Integrated Runtime) environment as an example of how far abstraction layers have progressed in the world of application development environments. AIR allows a developer to write for a single environment that is abstracted from the underlying operating system and hardware. What Adobe promises is a wrapper environment that allows both Java and Flash programmers to ignore whether they're writing for Microsoft Windows or the Apple Macintosh. AIR also gives the developer options to develop in HTML/AJAX, Adobe Flash, and Flex. While these languages were all intended to be Web-based, AIR has certainly been applied to all sorts of unique applications. We regularly use Klok (free software from mcgraphix) to keep track of time spent on various projects. Klok runs on several different platforms, limited only to which platform AIR is currently available for. Whether the Adobe team will fulfill AIR's destiny and extend it further in the Linux world and perhaps even the mobile world is yet to be seen.

Adobe's AIR isn't the only commercial abstraction layer in the market, but it is the first heavily supported platform that we've seen that works equally on the two major commercial operating systems. While the Microsoft .NET environment has done an amazing amount of reducing the work necessary to produce amazingly complex systems, it is limited to the Microsoft operating systems family, completely ignoring the fact that the bulk of the public Web servers in the world are Apache, with the bulk of them installed on Linux or a Unix derivative. The Microsoft Silverlight environment, while not as encompassing as AIR, has potential in how you can manipulate Web media and is capable of handling the complexities of digital rights management for video-on-demand systems such as NetFlix.

A Brief History of High-Level Languages

To understand better what these systems are providing and why their popularity has exploded, we need to go back in history a bit to some of the very first programming languages. The original assembler for the IBM 360/30 was very straightforward but tedious, requiring an intimate knowledge of the computing hardware and how instructions worked on data. Writing utilities in Assembler provided access to the most primitive instructions and capabilities of the tape and disk systems; at the same time, programmers had the ability to display messages and accept input from the console. However, every single piece of code had to be in each punched card deck, and code reuse meant literally lifting sections of cards out of one deck and placing them into another.

In the late 1970s, IBM released a new version of BAL (Basic Assembly Language), a macro assembler that allowed programmers to take advantage of a library of prewritten snippets of code (macros) to do certain repetitive tasks. Examples of the repetitive tasks that could be automated included rewinding a 9-track tape reel, skipping to the third dataset on the tape, etc. The ability to use tested and standardized code in programs immediately freed programmers from huge amounts of writing and debugging. Even though a program lost portability (unless the other system had the same Macro Assembler and version), what was gained was the ability to develop much more complex programs in a fraction of the time required by the earlier assembler.

It also meant that others on a programming team didn't have to adapt their code to reuse these functions. That alone had the effect of moving teams toward much more standardized coding. The macro assembler gained widespread use just in time to prepare programmers for a new programming language called COBOL (Common Business-Oriented Language), which in one "print format" line of code did what used to take hundreds of lines of assembler and days of debugging. At this point, you'll notice that we haven't discussed hardware abstraction. When everyone was using systems from a single large vendor, hardware abstraction was much less an issue, surfacing primarily when shifting code from one storage subsystem to another.

One of the authors (Brian Chee) heard a lecture in the mid-1970s by U.S. Navy Commander Grace Hopper (author of COBOL), in which she talked about things like cost analysis and how COBOL could potentially save the Navy hundreds of thousands of dollars in data processing costs and make data processing available to dramatically more people due to the reduced costs. Little did she know just how a big a leap we would make before she finally retired from the Navy as Rear Admiral Grace Hopper. As the computing world developed, new programming languages sprang up: FORTRAN (formula translator) for scientists, and a veritable Tower of Babel (BASIC, PL1, LISP, APL, SNOBOL and C were just a few). Each language reached out to a larger and larger and more specific audience by making it easier and easier to create more and more complex programs with less effort. SPSS, for instance, stands for "Statistics Package for the Social Sciences" and was initially targeted at the need for certain types of statistics in the social sciences; it eventually grew into one of the decade's most popular statistics system on mainframes and minicomputers, eventually reaching the PC. With IBM's recent purchase of SPSS, we predict that the SPSS suite of statistics modules will find their way into cloud modules in coming years.

SPSS had a huge impact on the scientific community because it was a very early example of a system that was nearly completely divorced from traditional programming languages. Instead of needing to write an extremely complex program to do standard deviation calculations, now all you had to do was feed it data and ask for it in a single instruction line. Nearly a 3000:1 reduction in coding effort was commonplace, and it allowed nonprogrammers to do complex statistical analysis without needing a degree in computer science. Philosophically, this was an important predecessor to the later cloud applications, because it allowed users to develop complex data analysis routines without having to learn the intricacies of a "real" programming language. At a certain level, this extended the concept of "abstraction layer" up the stack, to the point of allowing abstraction for the user, rather than simply for the computing system.

Database Abstraction and Putting the Database on the Web

Another huge step along the way to Cloud City happened quietly in the mid-1990s at a small Honolulu computer distributorship called Aspect Computing, where James Laurel and Richard Chan faced a dilemma: They wanted to have a home life, but their livelihood was linked to computer retailers that often needed to obtain information on equipment stock at some very odd hours. What they really wanted was a way to leverage this new thing called the World Wide Web so that these computer dealers could query the Aspect Computing inventory system even when the shop was closed. Jim also wanted to create an abstraction layer that would allow the system to have security but would be flexible enough that the system could be reused for new applications as yet unimagined.

The product they developed, WebDB, eventually became a commercial product that for the first time allowed Web hosts to provide a peek into databases from a Web client. To put this achievement into proper perspective, keep in mind that at this time it was very rare for any database application to be able to handle queries over a network, and those that could required that the network link appear as a mounted disk drive (i.e., through something like Novell Netware, the disk had to appear as a drive letter.) Networked database applications of this time all had to have access to files stored on this drive mount. No peer-to-peer or client-to-server database apps were available outside of development labs. Apparently, this technology was enough of a paradigm shift that Microsoft Corporation bought Aspect Computing in 1996.

Moving beyond drive letters was a critical piece of the overall puzzle in allowing virtual and cloud applications to be created. In a way, this was yet another abstraction layer, in that network database access became part of the "plumbing" of the Internet, allowing applications to perform queries and correlations across dozens or even hundreds of databases—far more than could be accommodated with the old "drive-mapped" methods—and leading eventually to true client server computing.

A standard way of programming database access was another vital link, as abstraction layers such as ODBC (Open DataBase Connectivity) became standardized across multiple operating systems. Another effort to develop the standard access method was begun in 1993, early in the Web's history, on a mailing list used to discuss Web programming projects. The result was the Common Gateway Interface (CGI), which became the basis for a great number of other programming efforts designed to create Web applications. It laid out a methodology to link programs outside the normal purview of the Web server, so that complex application results could be linked to the Web. This sideways step also allowed developers to extend the capabilities of Web applications in previously unforeseen ways.

Different Clouds for Different Applications

The definition that we're working with is that clouds are abstraction layers, hiding system details from the end users. The evolving goal that most cloud providers seem to be heading toward is an OS agnostic system, where users can choose applications from a vast library. A key element to be resolved is billing for these library items, but it's not hard to imagine a scenario in which billing would be handled like a mobile phone account, but with items like:

- Application use charges (since users don't buy apps anymore; perhaps this is what IBM had in mind when it bought SPSS?)
- Temporary and long-term storage charges
- Throughput (input/output) charges
- CPU or compute time
- Idle time (application in memory but suspended)

We all have to keep in mind that most users really don't care about where or even how their processing is done, just that they can do their task with the least amount of hassle. We've been around for a while and witnessed first-hand the transition from Hollerith cards to terminals, PCs, and now the Internet. Other than initial user resistance, each major technology change has swept through the business landscape and then has become part of the environment.

The direction of the evolution is all about computing turning from a world of customized solutions to the ubiquitous environment of a utility. The U.S. Department of Defense mandated that DoD systems move away from one-of-a-kind "stovepipe" systems to commercial off-the-shelf systems that can take advantage of the economies of scale. A new Navy submarine launched in 2009 is a good example of a "boat" that uses many commercial off-the-shelf components rather than custom-built systems (unlike the legendary $1000 toilet seat in the Air Force B1 bomber).

Processing Clouds

Jim Staten of Forrester Research provided an example of how the *New York Times* leverages the cloud. The *Times* wanted to makes its historic archives available for online access. They needed to process 11 million articles and turn them into .pdf files. Initial estimates outlined that hundreds of servers and about 4 Tb of storage would be necessary. The IT organization at the *Times* estimated a months-long delay before beginning, the need for a significant budget and highlighted the difficulty of locating the computing resources. The project manager gave Amazon Web Services a try and kicked off 100 EC2 instances and 4 terabytes of S3 storage. The job was finished the next day with a total cost of $240.

Another hard example comes from the *Washington Post.* Peter Harkins, a Senior Engineer at the *Washington Post,* used the Amazon Elastic Compute Cloud (Amazon EC2) to launch 200 server instances to process 17,481 pages of non-searchable PDF images into a searchable online library. With a processing speed of approximately 60 seconds per page, job was completed within nine hours and provided web portal access to the public 26 hours later. Harkins ruminates, "EC2 made it possible for this project to happen at the speed of breaking news. I used 1,407 hours of virtual machine time for a final expense of $144.62. The database of Hillary Clinton's 1993-2001 Schedule is publicly available at: http://projects.washingtonpost.com/2008/clinton-schedule/.

Examples like this show how cloud computing techniques can be used to revolutionize PED processes. By increasing the use of automation and focusing our analyst on higher level exploitation tasks, near-real time exploitation and dissemination of critical intelligence products may be enabled in the very near term with cloud computing.

(*Source:* http://kevinljackson.blogspot.com/2008/10/why-cloud-processing-exploitation-and.html.)

Amazon Web services (http://aws.amazon.com/what-is-aws) is just the tip of the proverbial iceberg when it comes to a cloud specifically purposed to bring on-demand computing cycles to organizations and users who need them. The trend we're starting to see is for companies to use cloud computing and storage to smooth out usage spikes and avoid upgrading data centers to size capacity for spikes rather than "normal" usage.

In the above-mentioned examples, those EC2 applications were still virtual machines that forced you to choose one operating system over another during the EC2 configuration phase. Some of the conditions for being a true cloud implementation were fulfilled, but not all: There was no sense of a seamless movement of processing from one platform to another, and no escape from a deep awareness of where the processing platform was located (in a virtual, if not physical, sense.)

To give a flavor of the variety of operating systems offered by Amazon and just how fast this list is growing; we thought we'd take a snapshot of what's offered, but also list where you can find the current listing.

Amazon Machine Images (AMIs) are preconfigured with an ever-growing list of operating systems. We work with our partners and community to provide you with the most choice possible. You are also empowered to use our bundling tools to upload your own operating systems. The operating systems currently available to use with your Amazon EC2 instances include:

Operating Systems

Red Hat Enterprise Linux   Windows Server 2003 Oracle

Windows Server 2008	Enterprise Linux
OpenSolaris	CentOS Linux
openSUSE Linux	Ubuntu Linux
Fedora Linux	Gentoo Linux
Debian Linux	

(*Source:* http://aws.amazon.com/ec2/#instance.)

Note: While it is rumored that the Apple Mac OSx will run under VMWare, there is still considerable debate whether such an action would put you in violation of the end-user license agreement.

A great amount of work still needs to be done on a job description language of some sort before cloud computing reaches the sort of state that the Web began to enter with the development of the Common Gateway Interface (CGI) in 1993. Reuven Cohen, co-founder and CTO of Enomily, Inc., is one of the people looking at the question of how to develop standards for cloud computing. He has approached everything from cloud resource description to cloud identity federation in his blog, "Elastic Vapor" (www.elasticvapor.com/2008/08/standardized-cloud.html).

We've said before that it's all about abstraction layers and whether can you see through the floor into the inner workings of the environment. Offerings are popping up everywhere in all the shades of gray. Some, such as Amazon's EC2, are close to the foundation hardware; some, such as AppNexus, only partially obscure the foundation; and a few, such as Google, fully obscure the foundation. What we really have today is a market in transition, with vendors feeling around in a speculatory arena trying to figure out what consumers really want.

Storage Clouds

Data storage space in any organization is like physical space in that nature abhors a vacuum. Anytime we've been involved with adding data storage space to an organization, we've been amazed at just how quickly it disappears. So therein lies the rub: Where do you find enough temporary storage to do huge projects? In the case of the *New York Times* PDF indexing project, they estimated that they needed 4 terabytes of storage; so, instead of trying to temporarily expand their data center, they turned to Amazon Web Services. This temporary boost in storage capacity is one of the leading applications for storage clouds for enterprise use. For personal use, cloud storage for off-site backup and remote access to critical files have led to acceptance of the idea of cloud-based storage.

For many individual users, the first experience with a storage cloud will come through an encounter with one of the remote storage or backup clouds. Commonly used storage clouds include Boxee, DropBox, Microsoft's Mesh, Apple's MobileMe, and Amazon S3. A frequent encounter with these might include using Amazon's S3 (Simple Storage Service) to back up traveling laptops.

While there is a single Amazon S3 service, and a single programmatic interface to the service, to say that there is a bit of variety in S3 backup tools is an understatement. With names like Jungle Disk, S3 Backup, Brackup, Duplicity, S3Sync, and others, Amazon S3-based backup tools are available for just about every desktop operating system available today.

However, backup is just scratching the surface:

> Amazon S3 provides a simple web services interface that can be used to store and retrieve any amount of data, at any time, from anywhere on the web. It gives any developer access to the same highly scalable, reliable, fast, inexpensive data storage infrastructure that Amazon uses to run its own global network of web sites. The service aims to maximize benefits of scale and to pass those benefits on to developers.

> (*Source:* http://aws.amazon.com/s3/#functionality)

It's all about developer support, and Amazon has poured a huge amount of money into creating a collection of developer support tools that we've not seen since the days of the IBM programmers' library collection. With examples, docs, best-practice guides, a knowledge base, and tools all freely downloadable, Amazon seems determined to make friends with the developer community instead of taxing it with fees as other systems do.

Another good move by Amazon has been its eclectic approach to programming library support. Instead of just going for the Microsoft "low-hanging fruit" and sticking with C# and the .NET environment, the Amazon SDK (Software Development Kit) collection is a smorgasbørd of languages and developer systems. Interestingly enough, Amazon also provides support for the OpenMPI interface in batch processing mode to attract Beowulf users. More information on Amazon's system and its programming can be found at http://developer.amazonwebservices.com/connect/kbcategory.jspa?categoryID=47.

On the flip side of this coin is Google's Web-minded approach. With a much more simplistic approach, Google has neatly sidestepped the huge support requirements that Amazon had to build. By concentrating primarily on Python for the development system, Google's approach gives unparalleled integration into the world of Google Services while also leveraging the huge number of Python programmers in the world. Instead of offering everything under the sun, as Amazon does, Google has been building its library of apps over the years as part of an all-encompassing Google environment. Instead of providing a simple storage facility, Google is concentrating on providing storage through the apps in the system. The world of Google is already tied together, already tightly integrated, and already well understood. Google seems to be saying to the market that not only have we built it, we're also making it inexpensive to play by pushing you into a single development environment while at the same time opening the entire Google world to you. What we're expecting to see is a collection of personal productivity tools to round out the office automation applications that are already part of the Google desktop.

In an effort to make their cloud solutions ubiquitous, all the major players are making inroads into blurring the line between mobile and desktop. In the past it was clearly computing power that separated the CPU-light mobile world from the bigger, faster computing capabilities of the desktop. Clouds place additional computing capability anywhere, allowing for CPU-hungry apps to run even on CPU-light mobile platforms by separating computing from the user interface. This "client-server" model has been used for years for network applications, where user interfaces on client machines communicate back to larger applications running on back-end servers to handle the heavy lifting. The key to this approach will be how fast and how far 3G and then 4G wireless networks provide Internet connectivity so that these new mobile platforms can keep the mobile platform connected to the back-end cloud computing environment.

An approach similar to Google's foray into the mobile world with Android has been used by Microsoft and Apple with their My.Phone and MobileMe services for mobile devices. The key differences are that the offerings from Microsoft and Apple are much more tightly tied to the operating system, making only minimal user interaction required after the initial relationships between desktop and cloud-based files are established. The downside of this tighter integration is that cross-platform performance is either not available or available only on a minimally functional basis. One of the great unknowns about Google's foray into a cloud-based operating system for mobile platforms is whether it will lead ultimately to wider availability on a variety of platforms or to tighter integration with (and therefore more exclusive ties to) Google's own products and services.

Users can hope that, as the market develops and more open definitions of cloud processes and procedures gain acceptance, it will be easier to find application, processor, and storage cloud services that are tightly integrated into operating environments and available on a greater number of platforms. There have been promising signs of this direction, but the market is, as of this writing, still too immature for users to know for sure which direction will predominate.

With a market in all the shades of gray, only time will tell which approach best represents the consumer.

Email Protection Clouds

It's funny how sometimes things happen so slowly over time that they slip by your notice. The world of anti-spam has become so cumbersome that almost no one handles his or her own "black list" maintenance anymore. Even if you're using a small firewall that has a check mark for anti-spam, you're almost certainly already using a cloud service. The number and variety of blacklisting services in the anti-spam world is varied, but the most successful anti-spam systems seem to use a combination of several blacklisting services and in some cases multiple technologies that filter for spam, fraud, phishing, and other email-based malware. We saw a product from CheckPoint around 2004 that provided this type of service in a cloudlike arrangement, but it wasn't until late 2009 that it reappeared in the firewall product line from vendors such as Cisco.

Strategies for Getting People into Clouds

In reality, many of your people are already using applications that have leanings into the cloud; perhaps a few well-placed memos and services could get your staff thinking about clouds and their potential benefits to the enterprise.

Let's start with a little of what's happening under the hood in the Apple MobileMe and the Microsoft My Phone services. The big selling point of both is the constant and convenient backup of your smart phone. With many people having upwards of 1000 contacts in their address book, the loss of the use of a smart phone could be devastating. As illustrated by an application from PocketMac Corporation, MobileMe can also be used as a DMZ for programs to transfer data back and forth in a secure way. In this example the PocketMac folks rely on the BlackBerry or Nokia phone to synchronize with MacMail and then upload to MobileMe. Now, with a database storing the address book information, they can harvest that data to synchronize with applications such as Sales Force, Meeting Maker, Lotus Notes, Entourage 2004/2008, and others. All in all, an interesting way to solve an address book synchronization problem, with the additional benefit of forcing the backup of the mobile device to a cloud storage service.

So, while backup of the Windows Mobile device is the primary selling point of Microsoft's My Phone service, this cloud storage solution will also more than likely morph into a similar service, especially considering how Microsoft has already added in several connectors to social networking services such as Facebook, Flickr, and MySpace. This type of service also gives us a hint as to how various platforms will leverage each other. In the case of the My Phone service, it's considerably easier to use a full keyboard to modify address book entries, or groom a music or picture collection. Use the cloud to do large modifications, while the mobile platform becomes the ubiquitous extension into the cloud. Not to mention it's a pretty handy way of moving that huge address book to your new phone.

We previously mentioned that the Amazon S3 service had a stealthy beginning, since some of the very first apps for it were automated backup systems for road warriors. Jungle Disk, Brackup, and Duplicity are a few that stand out, but backing up to the cloud has become a necessary task now being offered by ISPs all over the United States. The result is that being able to back up regardless of your location (as long as you have an Internet connection) has removed some of the pain of the task and seems to be getting more and more users to actually back up their systems. It's no wonder that traditional backup applications such as those from Paragon Software have shifted direction to embrace the cloud.

We've already mentioned SalesForce a couple of times, and while these folks certainly started in the customer relations management (CRM) game, they have recently tossed their hat into the world of clouds. So instead of just providing CRM, SalesForce is now providing the ability to host custom applications for its customers. The same applications can now take advantage of the direct (and secure) connections into their legacy CRM data store already in place.

Throwaway Clouds

Another strategy that was used by the people at the *New York Times* is to leverage the cloud for short-term or one-time projects. A good analogy is renting a car rather than buying one if you're only going to need it for a couple of weeks. Clouds can be very similar to a rental car agency, in that you can rent cloud service for a short period for specific projects. You could also use it to do a longer "test drive" of a model you're interested in. The analogy also works for variable-duration rentals in that longer duration normally means a lower cost per day. For instance, you negotiate to take a portion of SAP out for a test drive and you drop it into the cloud for the 90-day test drive. No fussing around losing several days while IT spins up a test machine for you, and if you don't like it, just let the cloud vendor blow it away when you're done. If you already have other modules in the cloud, connections become quite a bit easier, even on a temporary basis.

So why not take this concept a whole lot further? The VMWare folks have a repository on their site that has a truly staggering number of VMware appliances available for you to test drive. Think of a new-car lot open 24/7 with thousands of different models ready for you to take home and try out for a period. The big selling point is that you don't have to struggle setting up the environment just to find yourself with only a couple days left in the trial period. It's all ready to go: Just drop it into a cloud or a VMware system and turn it on. Everything is preconfigured and ready for you to explore the appliance.

Traveling Clouds

A fabulous example of "traveling clouds" arose when the Microsoft Unified Communications folks came over to show off their latest wares for the InfoWorld editors during the summer of 2007. Considering that the entire constellation of servers for this demo required five Windows servers, with one requiring a 64-bit OS, this was a pretty tall order to spin up on short notice. In this case the product manager hopped on a plane with a big USB hard drive and quickly spun up a preconfigured Microsoft UC constellation consisting of:

- Active Directory server with a certificate authority setup
- SQL server for storage
- Exchange Server for email
- Share Point Server
- File Server
- SIP Gateway (an appliance, so not a VM in this case)

Since the whole smash was set up to talk over the virtual network (i.e., isolated), we really only had to change a single IP address on the Exchange server for external connectivity. So what would have taken quite a few days to set up before we could even see the functionality instead became an afternoon install and a full demo the next day. It was especially useful when the Interop iLabs folks were able to use the "tweaked" virtual machines for a live demonstration at the Interop Las Vegas trade show. Keep firmly in mind that this trick only works if the external USB disk is formatted NTFS to get past the 4-gigabyte file-size limitations that come with the default FAT formatting typical of these drives. (Since many virtual machines are several gigabytes in size, Amazon's EC2 system [and other cloud vendors] allow for shipping of large USB drives to them for local mounting over their internal networks. This local mounting tends to have special pricing, making the setting up of custom virtual machines much more palatable.)

Occasional-Use Clouds

Virtual machine images also become a way to handle special projects that only see the light of day a couple of times a year. In the case of the Intero-pNET, those virtual machines are spun up twice a year (once for Las Vegas and another for New York), saving a massive amount of time during hot-stage setup that used to be taken up doing a fresh sysgen for each show. In this case the InteropNET team were also able to synchronize versions with the Global Data Vault's Cloud Hosting Service so that we could swap our VMs onto our blade servers during the show, while maintaining access between shows for data mining.

You also need to keep firmly in mind that you can download a free VMWare conversion tool that will allow you to prototype on a workstation version and then migrate to a full production system when appropriate. We regularly see engineers prototype servers under VMWare Fusion (Mac workstation), convert, and then SFTP up to the VMWare ESX server in the lab. You also need to be sure to spool off the images onto a disk first, to avoid the "oops" factor. And remember that on a Windows machine, the external disk needs to be formatted NTFS and on the Mac "MacOS extended file system" if you want to get those huge virtual disk files onto the external drive. Sorry, but FAT/DOS isn't going to cut it for those huge files.

We expect similar virtual appliance collections to start appearing as Microsoft kick-starts its Hyper-V community efforts. With the Advanced Network Computing Laboratory being InfoWorld's biggest testing facility, they're now spinning up both a VMware and Windows Hyper-V mini-cloud on a set of blade servers so that editors can drop in the VM of their choice for review infrastructure.

When you start talking about cloud storage heading out to the very edge, nothing gets closer than the tiny device called a PogoPlug. The University of Hawaii research community has been playing with the PogoPlug now for a while, and being able to mount a fairly eclectic collection of USB drives onto a NAS-like device without worries about format has been, to say the least, liberating. While traveling, one researcher had a 1.5-TB Lacie Mac OSextended drive, a Seagate 250-GB NTFS drive, and a couple of DOS thumb drives all mounted and available across the WAN with no firewall rules necessary. Since the entire authentication process is done in the cloud, the PogoPlug doesn't need that much CPU. Once the PogoPlug data center has finished providing users with a "dating service"-like approach, it gets out of the way, letting the conversations take place on a peer-to-peer basis. Yet all of this is still secure, because of the rigorous authentication over SSL that PogoPlug requires. Key to the success of this tiny device is how the creators have turned the network attached storage model on its head. Instead of expecting all the network conversations to start from the outside world and head inward, the PogoPlug keeps a heartbeat-style conversation going with the PogoPlug data center.

Authenticated users then ride back on the already-existing conversation. Since the conversation started from the inside going out, normal firewall rules don't apply, because of the assumption that conversations going outward are trusted. This device could be viewed in the same way that Skype has become an unwanted bug for IT. It's hard to control in that it starts as an outbound service, "tricking" the corporate firewall into trusting it. However, it should also be viewed as a superfast and easy way to replace the need for a departmental file server just to provide remote file access. It could also be used as a quick-and-dirty traveling project team server that would work even on some of those funky hotel networks. It's all about how you spin it, and knowing about it so you can work it to your benefit instead of letting it creep up on you.

Company in a Box

Some InfoWorld editors been toying with the concept of "a company in a box" ever since one of them mentioned a project that did some quick deploy networks for the Marine Expeditionary Force out of the back of a Humvee. Could this concept be used in the civilian world, and are there enough resources now that we can quickly spin up a company in a warehouse (or a tent) after a disaster? The gist is that there is a concept in the military called "shoot and scoot," where an entire artillery battalion regularly practice picking up and moving their mobile headquarters in a matter of minutes rather than hours. Quick-disconnect network trunks, gear in travel cases, and lots of documentation to handle the setup and tear-down all make for a system designed to move. This ability is not for everyone (not to mention that it can get pretty expensive), but it wouldn't hurt to consider at least some of the better ideas as part of your business continuity planning.

The answer to trying out this project has been a resounding yes they could, and yes they will. With the huge number of virtual appliances available now, we could easily see combining off-the-shelf VMs with a few roll-your-own VMs to bring us back from disaster quickly. Virtualization can be a massive boon to business continuity, far beyond the old concepts of hot sites, warm sites, and cold sites. The issue is that readiness costs lots of money, and the "hotter" the site ("hot site" means drive across town and you're running, warm means a bit of synchronization from storage, and cold means a full restore), the more it costs to keep everything running and up to date. Some banks have gone as far as completely duplicating their data processing facilities somewhere else, right down to empty cubicles, file cabinets, and office support equipment—simply a breath-taking cost item for business continuity insurance. What clouds provide is a middle ground, where someone else keeps all your virtual machines warm *and* duplicated in multiple locations, all without the massive expense of a physically duplicated data center. You might not even need the computing side of the cloud during normal operations; just use the storage side to keep the VM images in sync. Then, if disaster does strike, spinning up those sync'd images is as simple as flipping a switch.

Some of the key factors to consider include:

- How much of your operation can live fully in the cloud, and how much has to physically be on premise?
- Set up preprovisioning agreements with SIP trunking vendors to swing your incoming lines over to the new trunk. Since quite a few companies are moving to SIP trunking anyway, this could be as simple as making sure the right people have the authority to do the move.
- Set up key services either under a VM now or perhaps use something like the Paragon Software system to periodically spin off a virtual disk image as a "warm" image. Then it will be just a matter of laying in the incremental data restores over the latest "warm" image. If you use something like Global Data Vault, then it's a matter of sync'ing the image from their data store.
- Use something like Asterisk or TrixBox to duplicate as much of your dialplan on your PBX as is reasonable. Since it's all network-based, creating and testing your portable PBX isn't a huge resource hog.
- Since most cellular/3G/4G providers are located pretty high in buildings, using them for your WAN connectivity isn't that big a stretch, especially considering how many have generator capability now.
- Confirm that your backup locations have enough power and have enough reception for your cellular/3G/4G WAN connection.
- Put your bare-minimum system into a surplus road rack (aka Hardig or Anvil road case). Using something like an HP "Shortie" blade server, which provides both storage and computing capability, could go a long way toward bringing up essential services quickly.

- The School of Ocean and Earth Sciences and Technology (SOEST) at the University of Hawaii is an old hand at putting complete science labs and computing facilities into shipping containers. They're looking at using the portable NOC product from American Power Conversion that's pre-set up to your specifications. Power generation, UPS, cooling, control are all preconfigured in a rolling data center.

What we're really getting at is that virtualization and clouds pay dividends on many levels. What hasn't occurred to people is that having a portable computing facility can also pay huge dividends in terms of business continuity during disasters. It also means that moving your company for other reasons become a whole bunch cheaper too. The point we're making is that clouds free you of the data center anchor, giving your organization a level of portability never achieved in the past. If you're already in the cloud, then you only have to move the stuff that isn't already cloudy. We think this sounds like a good idea even if your apps are left in-house, just to remove hardware dependencies and provide for portability. Just in case.

Clouds Flight Path for Chapter 4

- *Development languages and environments keep changing to take advantage of new layers of abstraction.* We're moving toward finding programming tools that are appealing to a wider and wider audience. Each new programmatic abstraction layer means that business can home in on key topics faster and with less costly human resources.
- *Software development kits (SDKs) and applications programming interfaces (APIs) are really just the way we plug together various applications.* SDKs and APIs are the foundation stones for some amazing programs today. Imagine having a programming language that truly allows you to concentrate on the business task rather than the tedium of the language. Emerging systems are making it even easier to link rich internet applications to back-end cloud applications that are increasingly platform-independent, while giving Web-connected users capabilities previously found only on hugely powerful desktop workstations.
- *Thank you Admiral Hopper, who led the way to high-level languages that make clouds possible.* Admiral Hopper (who also gave us the term

bug) was truly a visionary technologist, whose COBOL was the first abstraction layer of the new rich internet application platforms. The future is extremely bright for amazingly feature-full applications.

- *Database abstraction methods and how a Hawaii company led the way.* Some folks truly got rich as the world started building abstraction layers, and this tiny Honolulu company was one of the leaders. Like other abstraction systems, the modern database management systems have evolved into some incredibly complex systems that remove a huge amount of care and feeding complexity for your precious data. With new database-light systems, even simple cloud applications will be able to take advantage of the speed and reliability of modern database systems.

- *Using storage clouds only for backup just scratches the surface.* At every turn, the cloud industry is finding new ways to utilize cloud storage. We took a look at a few and tried to imagine how cloud storage can continue to revolutionize business computing. It's already evident that Amazon is using its storage cloud as the glue at the center of its constellation of services. While Microsoft looks like it's playing catch-up, we wonder whether it may just leap-frog the competition.

- *Is Google jumping ahead toward true cloud computing by moving us farther away from the hardware?* We got pretty far out in our view of where cloud computing can go, and Google's view seems to match our view pretty well. Now the question is how far Google will take this, and whether the market actually wants it. We figure they must be on to something, with Microsoft's cloud offerings feeling very familiar and the amazing amount of buzz about cloud-enabled apps on the Android mobile phones emerging on the market.

Chapter 5

Business in the Cloud

Advances in computer technology and the Internet have changed the way America works, learns, and communicates. The Internet has become an integral part of America's economic, political, and social life.

— President Bill Clinton

In This Chapter

Technology is fine, but its deployment (or not) is a business decision that must be made using the same sort of hard-headed business criteria as are applied to other business issues. In this chapter we'll learn about some of the criteria that come into play, strategies that companies apply in deploying cloud-based applications, and what a cloud application can mean for your organization. We'll discuss:

- Can you even use a cloud?—We've talked a bit about regulatory issues, but what are the other issues, and is this really the next step?
- Do you have enough Internet feed into your organization to use clouds instead of local infrastructure?—Moving to cloud desktops might sound great, but you don't get something for nothing. We'll look at where the costs might potentially shift.

- Load balancing—What is it? How is it going to help us? How does it work with clouds?
- Global load balancing and auto provisioning—How can you apply global load balancing to use clouds for on-demand capacity?
- Computing on demand—Do you really have to upgrade your computing infrastructure for that special project, only to let it rot after that project is done? Why not use the cloud for special projects instead of building more asset liability?
- Clouds as the DMZ for partnerships—Why are clouds becoming the neutral territory for a growing number of businesses? Why did the authors decide against setting up a server to host our writing efforts?
- Federation—Are clouds going to be the key technology that finally makes federated computing a reality? Why does it make sense, and are we already starting to see the beginnings?

Business Concerns About IT

Let's begin with a quick review of the basic concerns of business about IT. It's all about return on investment (ROI) and the black hole that is a data center as a huge corporate investment. The care and feeding of a modern data center is a nontrivial affair with a decision-making process akin to dancing a polka through a minefield. While the business concern is about ROI, the biggest fights tend to be over control: who gets it and who wants it.

The data centers and switch closets of companies are filled with departmental servers that are there just because a couple of personalities argued about things such as remote access, operating system support (or lack thereof), who has root access, who can add/edit/delete users, and so on. It's often just easier to buy an additional server than to fight these battles up and down through the organization. For those who do decide to battle it out, it can feel like fight night at every budget meeting; meanwhile, those servers suck up power, add heat to the office, add noise to the office, and prevent facilities from being able to shut down the office on holidays.

On the flip side, new environments lead to new IT training and personnel costs, and with shrinking budgets, saying "No!" has become a fashionable knee-jerk reaction. So, while on-demand clouds or clouds in general might sound like a magic solution, business decision processes demand that we know just where the hidden costs lie.

That's the environment in which cloud computing is being considered and in which decisions are being made. Is the cloud decision just about numbers, or are there issues to be considered that are more difficult to quantify? What kinds of numbers are you going to need to consider making cloud decisions?

Can Your Business Cloud?

The first question is the most basic: Can you use a cloud? This is far from being a technology-only question. In some cases, regulatory issues mandate that your data stay within a particular country; with today's global load balancing, that can't always be put into a service agreement. "It's 10:00—Do you know where your data is?" isn't just a clever take on an old TV ad. The abstraction layers that were so exciting when we were talking about the technology can be incredibly complicating when it comes to policy. We know that the federal courts wanted to use some of the emerging cloud backup solutions, but proxied Internet access combined with out-of-country storage prevented at least one try at adoption.

Second, does the cloud service support your existing applications, or are you looking at migration costs on top of IT retooling costs? The phrase "total cost of ownership" has been greatly abused in the last decade, but when considering a substantial shift in technology customers, you must think about training costs, temporary productivity disruptions, and support costs in excess of normal run-rate expenses. You also have to remember to extend your search for app support all the way out to the edge and in some cases out to your business partners. Consider a company like Walmart, for example: Some of their applications directly affect communications paths with their supply chain. If they were forced to push a major process like supply chain into the cloud, would they also be forcing their suppliers to upgrade similarly? The answer is almost certainly "Yes," and while Walmart has the market muscle to ensure that suppliers follow along, most companies don't have that much clout. Understanding how far the ramifications of a shift to the cloud will spread is another key consideration for executives pondering the change.

A commonly overlooked application with organization-wide ramifications is the email and calendaring combo, especially as they connect to the enterprise directory infrastructure. When we reviewed Microsoft's online services, some of the key questions were about the costs and mechanisms required for the migration. We looked at whether it was better to migrate completely or to try to make a cloud application platform coexist with a large legacy active-directory infrastructure. Microsoft's online services had migration tools for active-directory infrastructure, but other cloud service providers may not.

In Chapter 4 we talked about the analogy of using the cloud like a rental car, and taking the technology for a test drive before buying something you'll have to live with for years. If you're serious about considering Microsoft Exchange for your business, take it for a test drive using Microsoft Office Online services for a representative segment of your user community. Live with it, learn it, and make sure you find all the warts. While the trial is going on, make sure someone keeps track of the hidden costs are. How much time is it taking to manage? Did someone have to go out and buy a whole bunch of books to learn how the pieces fit together? Can you realistically support this if you decide to move forward? Just think to all the pieces you already have to fund, and imagine the increase or decrease in support cost when/if the program is expanded.

It should also be reiterated that clouds are great because they're normally pretty easy to walk away from. Instead of holding the pink slip on a new data center, you can just walk away if the project turns out to be a bust.

Bandwidth and Business Limits

Next under the microscope is the question of external versus internal bandwidth. A decade ago some people thought we were about to enter an era in which bandwidth would be the cheapest possible commodity. In 2009, bandwidth costs were carefully watched and considered by every company. Moving application bandwidth from LAN links that aren't metered to WAN links that are is another of those costs that must be carefully considered when a move to the cloud is proposed. In addition to the dollars to move bits, there are the dollars represented by application performance to consider. Those critical enterprise applications that were so snappy when they had to travel only through internal gigabit pathways now have to make it through to a cloud, a pathway that includes the corporate firewall and the rest of the security infrastructure. Now, the list of factors to take into account includes pieces of the network infrastructure. Is that firewall even capable of handling the new aggregate throughput of shoving that application into the cloud? Is your external Internet feed even big enough for your internal users? The impact of network bandwidth and infrastructure is dramatic, but it is only one of the technology issues that need to be taken into account when working toward the decision to expand enterprise applications into the cloud.

Testing for Clouds

Determining whether you have the necessary bandwidth can run the gamut from simple to extremely complex, though as the complexity increases, so does the accuracy of the model. On the simple side, you can use a site such as Speedtest.net and choose a server target that's fairly close to your cloud provider. Speedtest.net will toss a bunch of files back and forth to give you a thumbnail of the throughput possible between your two sites. However, this simplistic view of the world uses fixed packet sizes over a short duration, and it measures the throughput at only a single point in time. You might consider using Iperf, where you can vary the packet size and duration of the throughput test. Although it has the ability to run under Linux or Windows, iPerf is still fairly simplistic, but at least it considers the fact that network traffic isn't all made up of single-sized packets. At the complex end of the spectrum, Ixia Communications is now the owner of the Chariot application throughput test tool. This piece of software consists of endpoints and a management console. The management console allows you to set up synthetic traffic patterns between the endpoints that can consist of varying amounts of different traffic types. For instance, you use a protocol analyzer and a network tap to look at the traffic exiting your firewall. You find a mix of HTML, SSL, IMAP, POP, SMTP, FTP, and some miscellaneous stuff. The Chariot console can set up synthetic data streams that simulate a variable number of users doing different types of network functions. Since Chariot typically has access to all the resources on those endpoints, a single modern computer can easily simulate several users' worth of data. This gives you the ability to run after-hour's simulation of your entire company. What kinds of synthetic traffic you can toss around includes a pretty big collection, with data streams such as

- YouTube video
- Skype VoIP traffic
- Real streaming video

- SIP trunks
- SIP conversations
- Web traffic
- SNMP
- And many others

The power of this system is the ability to put endpoints on just about any workstation or server technology on the market and even some switch blades from various network equipment manufacturers. The ability to do "what if" scenarios on your network during off-hours is an extremely powerful tool, easy enough that you could run a bunch of "what ifs": "If I moved my key applications to the cloud, would I have enough bandwidth for those specific applications?" "If there is enough bandwidth, is the link jitter and latency low enough to support voice-over-IP?"

Let's assume you've done a bunch of testing, and so far it seems the answer is a slow migration to the cloud. The first step is to get a handle on what's out there and exactly where it is.

Remote Access and the Long March to the Clouds

Not long ago, IT expansion meant more racks in the data center, more power to feed those racks, more air conditioning to cool them, expanding backbone connections to link them, and perhaps more IT staff for the care and feeding of those new servers. Those new racks meant capital expenses, physical assets, human resources, and recurring costs, all of which affect the bottom line. The question we've heard from CFOs around the world has always revolved around, "Is there a way to make that data center cost less?" The question has never been asked with more urgency than in the most recent two or three years, and the answers have never been more critical to the health of the organization. Cloud computing seems to offer an ideal way of reducing the capital costs and many of the recurring expenses, though we've seen that there are other costs that may limit the immediate impact of a migration into the cloud. While we're still thinking about the costs of cloud computing, we should consider a few additional items that can weigh on the pro or con side of the decision.

Just what, for example, is the life cycle of the project you're considering? Using the *New York Times* indexing project described in Chapter 4 as an example (http://open.blogs.nytimes.com/tag/aws), the *Times* was looking at several racks of blades, server licenses, Adobe Acrobat licenses, power, cooling, and personnel for a project that more than likely would have to be done only once. Then all those assets would either have to be sold, or re-tasked within the organization. This is where our CFO asks how much of our original investment can be recovered if we can return or sell these temporary assets. "Can't you just rent that gear?" is a CFO war cry heard all over the world. What cloud computing gives us is the ability to give it all back, for a small fraction of the long-term asset cost.

With all the issues we've provided to think about, it's possible that we've not yet considered the most important question: How, precisely, will you use the cloud? To begin answering this question, it's useful to think in terms of models.

One of the models we most often hear about is "local prototyping, remote production." This model had its roots in behavior that started in software development groups before cloud computing began. Programmers began installing VMWare or Virtual Server onto their workstations simply to provide prototyping for new systems. The reasons were fairly straightforward: Virtual machines were far less expensive than actual banks of new computers, and virtual operating system images that are hosting still-buggy applications in development can be blown away and regenerated much more quickly than similar images running on dedicated hardware.

So far we've talked only about savings on physical infrastructure. How about demand-based expansion? An application or set of information that is unavailable because the server can't keep up with demand is just as useless as an application that is bug-ridden. While excess demand can be considered a "high-class problem," it is a problem, and it can come from a variety of sources. Depending on your target market, your company might be SlashDot'ed or covered by CNN and get a massive surge in Web traffic. If you were to have enough foresight to try to plan for this, what would it cost you? We'll look next at a couple of ways to implement a strategy for this situation.

Traditional Server Load Balancing

The first server load balancing systems were simple: They just divided up the incoming Web requests among several physical servers. They did this based on simple algorithms that depended on basic round-robin scheduling or elementary demand-feedback routines. These load balancers had the advantage of also allowing for maintenance of a server by shifting its load to the other servers in the group. These Layer 4 (referring to the ISO seven-layer networking model) devices had a single public IP address for each service (FTP, HTTP, etc.) and were configured to split the incoming traffic up among two or more physical servers behind it. Coyote Point has a great demonstration on their website: http://support.coyotepoint.com/docs/dropin_nav.htm.

A typical load balancer configuration would go something like this:

1. The DNS name for the server cluster is set up to point to the outside or public address for the load balancer.
2. Inside or private addresses are assigned to various servers behind the load balancer.
3. The load balancer is then told which private addresses are serving what type of network service (i.e., Web, ftp, email) and whether a weight should be assigned to larger, faster servers in the collection.
4. Then a choice is made as to what kind of load balancing should be used: round-robin, Gaussian distribution, weighted average, etc.
5. If a machine needs servicing of some sort, the system administrator declares a machine to be out of service, and the load balancer shifts load to the remaining servers.

Key to this whole arrangement working is that each collection of servers has access to some sort of common storage system (i.e., NFS). Load balancing in many cases came in the back door as a method to extend the backup window for many critical services. By shifting the load off a primary server, it could be frozen in time and have a full backup done without worries about open files and such. In many cases backups were taking longer than the system administrator's window of opportunity, forcing the migration to some sort of load balancing.

The downside to this plan was that adding servers to respond to larger than anticipated loads was a long and expensive process, and the process was inherently reactive: In most cases, capacity couldn't be added until after the traffic surge had passed. More critically, the servers that were added were static, dedicated to a single purpose when deployed. Load balancing wasn't really dynamic in that FTP servers, for example, couldn't be reallocated to handle HTTP traffic without large amounts of human intervention. There's a way to balance in genuinely dynamic ways, but financial officers don't like it.

The workaround is to deploy a series of new servers, put all the necessary services for all applications on each server, but not route traffic to them until needed. This way a system administrator can quickly alter the load balancer's configuration to add additional Web servers to handle an unanticipated load spike. Once again, though, this requires encumbered resources sitting idle (and sucking up power and cooling) to handle a load spike that may never occur. This was all a guessing game played by IT groups all over the world, and a boon to hardware and software vendors worldwide. Now, this was not necessarily a bad thing, since backup facilities of some sort are part of everyone's business continuity plans. With virtualization and cloud computing, though, there may be a better way.

The Virtualization Load Response

Scyld Software (part of Penguin Computing) was the first company we know of to deliver products that saw computing clusters change from Beowulf scientific-style cluster computing to business clusters. In the Scyld system, a virtualization kernel was installed on each server in the cluster and applications were distributed across these. The distinctive feature of Scyld's software wasn't in the virtualization cluster, though, but in how this system could detect incoming application loads and apply business rules to the problem of how to handle unanticipated loads. The example the company gives was how they handled a massive spike in Web traffic. Their system would move the Apache Web server from a shared system (multiple applications all sharing a single physical server) to a dedicated server. If the setup was configured correctly, this happened automatically. An added benefit was that it was *not* bound to a single type or model or server, but rather could be run on a heterogeneous collection of boxes with weight assigned to them to vary the load.

A few years later, VMWare started offering a system called VMotion (www.vmware.com/products/vi/vc/vmotion.html), which took this idea quite a bit further. The VMotion concept was to have a collection of servers all running the VMWare infrastructure. Under normal circumstances, machine #1 could be running a collection of virtual servers that might consist of Apache Web servers and email services. Machine #2 might be running SugarCRM, and machine #3 might be running billing software. Let's imagine a case in which Company X has decided that if a huge surge in Web traffic occurs, the business won't be hurt if billing is delayed by a day. So their IT group has set up business rules that allow VMotion to shift the Apache Web server to a dedicated server if a huge load starts up. When the load disappears, the Web server will move back to a shared server and billing will be resumed. Those rules could be modified to also handle automatic migration of running servers to another physical server if a hardware failure should occur. This takes virtualization much of the way to the scenario that might exist when a company deploys a "private cloud." What's missing from this current scenario is how to detect when an application like Apache has crashed even if the virtual server is still up. Previously, IT professionals would write custom scripts for UniCenter or OpenView that would periodically probe to see if applications were running on the target machine and, if not, send a reset script to the system in question. Early efforts were more of a "Hail Mary" in that they would keep sending the reset over and over again if the application had crashed badly and restarting the system wasn't fixing it. More sophisticated scripts started appearing, and as the Microsoft Power Shell interface documentation became widely known, testing at the application level and then restarting more intelligently became commonplace.

Taking this knowledge base quite a bit further, Coyote Point has extended its application load balancer into the VMWare world to the extent that rules can be set up for spawning additional machines from prestored images. This generation of load balancers is able to probe higher in the ISO stack, and it has the ability to detect if a Layer 7 application like Apache has crashed and then do something about it. According to Sergey Katsev, Engineering Project Manager at Coyote Point Systems:

> Actually, we have a few customers who have a few applications "in the cloud" and still have a minimal datacenter "since they have control of it." Either way, app load balancing is needed since otherwise you don't know when your application has failed. . . . Amazon or whatever will guarantee that the "server" remains up, but they have no way of guaranteeing that your Apache Web server hasn't crashed.

With technology and deployment moving toward cloud capability, the next big question is where the servers and applications will live. This is the point at which the cloud begins to separate from simple virtualization, and decisions we've discussed earlier—decisions about bandwidth and networking infrastructure—are joined with business strategy concerns to determine whether it's time to move data and apps out of the local network. Now an IT professional has the choice to have apps live both in a local data center and in the cloud. It isn't a hard stretch to imagine that most of the time a key e-commerce app will live in a small but adequate data center in Corporation Y. Suppose, however, that a CNN reporter stumbles across their newest widget and highlights it every half-hour all over the world. Suddenly the Web load on this tiny little e-commerce app skyrockets, and if nothing is done the server in question will die a horrible death. However, preplanning has paid off, the meat-and-potatoes apps have already been set up in the clouds, and the load balancer is spinning up the cloud apps in a big hurry. Now, with the business surge spread across the entire North American continent (and the small but adequate data center), Corporation Y can reap the benefits of the CNN report.

Computing on Demand as a Business Strategy

Deploying applications or moving data to the cloud is rarely an all-or-nothing proposition. Instead, internal versus external computing is a balance whose formula is unique for every corporation. Using the criteria we've discussed in this chapter, you can build your own decision-making spreadsheet to aid in the process of deciding whether to try moving to the cloud. In later chapters we'll look at particular clouds and the impact they can have on your applications. In the rest of this chapter, we'll look at more general answers to questions about cloud strategies. Most of the answers will start with the assumption that you've already committed to move at least some of your data infrastructure to the cloud.

Regardless of which cloud you do choose, you should always keep in mind what mechanisms are in place to move data back to your internal data processing infrastructure if you decide not to continue the project, or if you decide that the initial balance of data or applications inside and outside the cloud should be changed.

An example may be useful here. While few would dispute that Salesforce.com is a great customer relationship management (CRM) system, the cost per seat is a key decision point in adoption for most organizations. One solution that we keep hearing about from different companies is about reducing the total seat costs by using Salesforce.com for the front-line salespeople, but something like SugarCRM for the call centers. Using two separate cloud applications isn't unusual, but it does lead to the question of where the data is stored and how it is moved from one application to another. One company had a middleware data mashup product from Apatar.com periodically moving data back and forth to make sure the call center knew about recent outside sales activity. This little company with roots in the old Soviet Republics also has offices in Boston, and is addressing the huge data conversation market. It's not hard to imagine a sales manager looking at the huge cost per seat for something like Salesforce, yet wanting to populate a hundred seats in a call center. This solution is tailor-made for this exact situation: The sales manager can download a free copy of Apatar and drop connectors onto the Apatar workspace. Each connector has a set of credentials for the data source, and has connector nubs on them for tools. Easiest are straight field conversions, where one program uses "firstname" and the other "fname"; harder are the items where one separates the first and last names and another uses only full-name, or where one program uses department codes and the other uses names. All this type of data manipulation is simple with this type of tool. Considering that we've heard of all kinds of companies paying some pretty big bucks for this type of data migration, it's no wonder that this tiny little company has gotten so much attention. Although it is certainly not the only tool of this type, this drag-and-drop data mashup tool is certainly worthy of attention.

While cloud computing has begun to take hold at the opposite ends of the computing spectrum, we're also seeing clouds gaining traction in the small-to-medium-size business (SMB) market. As the SMB world seeks to use Internet presence to compete with companies both larger and more agile, we've seen a shift in how they're starting to use cloudlike applications to leverage their Internet presence, allowing them to provide considerably more services to their customers than with traditional data processing methods.

As one example, we're seeing more and more Web designers taking responsibility for maintaining Internet servers. On the one hand, smaller organizations don't have the resources to dedicate workers to a single IT task. On the other hand, historically it has been these situations, where IT workers are required to perform multiple tasks, where systems administrators become less vigilant and attackers are able to exploit security weaknesses to turn those weakened servers into illegal download sites or zombies in a "botnet" army. This liability seems to be a new driving force for SMB organizations to look at clouds, to sidestep the potential liability of maintaining a server farm. However, this trend has some unintended consequences if we look further down the IT support chain.

Considering just how much Web design talent there is out in the world, it just makes sense to leverage this talent pool for special or new projects. Traditionally, you had to spin up a new server, customize it, add users, do penetration testing, fix the holes, load the application development environment, and then invite the contractors in to play. But all you're really after is some cool clean Web code for your smoking-hot new site. So why not spin up a site in the clouds, and get up and running on this new project in significantly less time? Since any cloud vendor worth anything has already done the patching, securing, and penetration testing, you can probably spin up a development site faster than you can steam a latté.

Clouds may sound like a do-all strategy, but that silver lining also is a stormy scenario for value-added resellers (VARs). Countless small and medium-sized companies look to VARs to provide the application development and IT support that they cannot supply from internal sources. What we question is whether the outsourcing trend is becoming a crutch. VARs aren't always going to look out for the best interests of the customer as they look to increase their profits. What we can't tell is whether this trend toward cookie-cutter solutions is also going to stifle the creativity that has made the Internet such a great resource. Or will this trend toward standardization make it even easier to migrate to generic clouds? The successful VARs that we've seen are the ones that have used hardware sales only as a service to their customers; and instead are using the outsourcing trend to provide high-profit services. We've especially seen this as giants such as HP, Dell, and IBM carve up the computing hardware market and somehow survive on tiny profit margins. The trend over the past decade has been toward services, and we just have to believe that those services are eventually going to live in the clouds.

A saving grace is that cloud vendors are working with many VARs to develop new profit models for this part of the industry, and the same vendors are looking to build direct partnerships with customers—direct partnerships that some say will reduce the need for SMB customers to rely on VARs for the bulk of their IT support. We maintain that with any paradigm shift in the IT industry, there will always be some pain as we see the adoption of the new technology. Some of the retooling examples we've seen are from mini-computers to PCs, from PCs to the Internet, from paper to intranets and the Internet, and from 800 telephone numbers to websites. Each technology shift has been a double-edged sword, with ramifications both seen and unseen. Said a different way, there will always be some fallout as the next disruptive technology appears, but the survivors will be those who plan for the change and manage it, rather than hiding from it.

It's difficult to forecast with any accuracy precisely how all the economic pieces of a major technology shift will work out. It's certain, though, that cloud computing is bringing about shifts in the way companies think about the allocation of costs in IT. Part of those shifts deal with recurring costs, and many of those recurring costs are built around partnerships with cloud vendors and with VARs. We're also predicting that as the comfort level sets in with clouds, the finance folks will start to get used to the concept of the rent-a-data center attitude that clouds can provide. If you look at the processes that went on during the *New York Times* indexing project, you can easily see how the temporary nature of cloud computing has really started to catch fire.

Let's now look a little more deeply at the cloud's impact on partnerships.

The Cloud Model for Partnerships

"There is no way I'm going to give Company X a log-in to my server!" We've all heard this before. It might be personalities, it might be regulations, or it might be just plain paranoia, but all the same, we often run into situations where it could save Company X a huge amount of money if Company Y's buyer could just log-in and check inventory for a fast-selling widget, yet Company X can't seem to loosen its corporate controls enough to let it happen. The problem in this case is where we put neutral territory that both companies can access and control without exposing their internal IT infrastructure. It's not an unreasonable position, really. Security surveys during the last couple of years have indicated that partners are a huge, legitimate security threat for most companies. If we assume that allowing access to certain "inside the firewall" information is a legitimate business need, how can we make it happen without unnecessarily endangering the inner workings of our corporate network?

The answer for some has been to use a cloud service as a common area for cooperative processing. Instead of spending the time and money building a neutral zone, why not use a service? After all, it wouldn't be hard to have several images to work from, with one running for Company Y and another running for Company Z. The common files, and common network access points, are outside either company's security perimeter, allowing the files to be shared without requiring that security protocols be breached. All data transfer can take place over secure VPN tunnels; policies and procedures can be put into place to govern precisely which files can be synchronized to cloud storage.

Let's look at a scenario where all the public-facing systems for Company X live in the cloud, but finance and human resources live in the company's local data center. However, finance certainly needs to get data off the public e-commerce site. Depending on what consultant you ask, the answer is most likely going to be some sort of proxy. The whole idea is to hide from the outside world the details of what the inside of the company looks like.

On a more personal scale, the authors used the Microsoft SkyDrive cloud to write this book. Instead of going through all the hassles of setting up a DMZ server in either of our facilities, we found it much easier to use a cloud service to store drafts of the book along with support material, images, and notes to ourselves. We could have easily built a system on a spare server, but that would have taken a machine away from our testing infrastructure and someone would have had to maintain it. This way, we can always get to our material, it's backed up by someone else, we aren't paying utility bills, and we didn't spend all the time to bring up a content management system. We've heard the same story from countless others who needed a common storage area for a project, but who couldn't or wouldn't open the firewall for the other party.

Going a bit further into Microsoft's cloud offerings, the folks in Redmond didn't leave SkyDrive to handle all the cloud file storage chores; a separate service called Live Mesh automates the process of synchronizing files between a computer (or a series of computers) and the cloud. Of course, Microsoft is far from the only provider of services like these. Dropbox, for example, is a popular file synchronization service that provides cross-platform automated updating. Media Fire is one of the many cloud services that allows you to share files with any number of people with whatever level of security suits you best. Of course if you're using a Mac, you've practically had Mobile.Me rammed down your throat.

What systems like these provide are a fertile ground for customized connections that provide data synchronization and a place for applications to more easily exchange information. Amazon's S3 storage system is a frequently used platform for development, and we've started to hear about developers writing wrappers for the system that will allow multiple parties to mount a common storage area with full read/write privileges. So we can easily imagine a special directory on both Company X and Company Y servers that are a common area. In this example, neither company is exposing its entire infrastructure, but both companies are able to access a shared directory. One provider of just such a solution for Linux servers is SubCloud.com (www.subcloud.com), where an application installed either in the cloud or locally extends the server's capabilities to share the S3 storage. A good analogy is how an income tax preparer uses a special set of forms to convey your income tax information to the Internal Revenue Service. Formerly, the common data transmission medium was the U.S. Postal Service. Now, those same forms are electronic, so the tax preparer sees an image that is very familiar—just like the old forms—but the IRS sees tagged information fields transmitted to a public proxy and eventually input into the IRS processing system. The point is that the data can enter a DMZ in one format and exit in another. It can also scrutinized at several levels, so that a certain level of trust can be established. Perhaps you could call your proxy "Checkpoint Charlie"?

At the workstation level, there is a cross-platform solution by Bucket Explorer (www.bucketexplorer.com) that utilizes a file explorer-like interface to provide team folders on the Amazon S3 system. That has a direct analog from both Microsoft and Apple. The point is that data can be input on a Mac, examined by a Linux machine, and then perhaps a Windows machine could be the SQL host that stores all the transactions.

The issue of interface—how data moves from local network to cloud application or from desktop to cloud server—is one of the issues that differentiates one cloud system from another. There are, if not an infinite number of ways to make these things happen, at least a large number of options. We've already seen the drag-and-drop interface of Skydrive and Media Fire, and the automated synchronization of Mesh, Mobile. Me, and DropBox. There are many others as well, including some with roots in earlier, nonvirtualized operating systems. Some developers have significantly stretched the original intent of the "named pipe" interfaces by having processes on different servers using a shared file system for interprocess communications. The concept is that a Python app running on Amazon EC2 might have a file mount to Amazon S3, but Company Y's Linux server also has that same Amazon S3 share-mounted on its accounting server. With a shared file area, the IT personnel can work cooperatively to implement a named pipe on the shared area so that immediate information on widget orders can be transferred from one company to another without exposing anyone's internal infrastructure. Peter A. Bromberg, while exploring the possibilities on the Egghead Café for .NET programmers, noted:

> The point we're trying to make goes back to the quote from Sir Isaac Newton about standing on the shoulders of giants. Just because the original intent of this was X doesn't mean it can't be extended to do Y. It should also be pointed out that named pipes aren't the only method for inter process communications, just one of the legacy methods commonly found.

(*Source:* www.eggheadcafe.com/articles/20060404.asp.)

Seeding the Clouds of Federation

Before we leave the topic of cloud applications that allow data to be shared among different systems, we should look at ways in which user information—user identity—can be shared in the same way. The concept is called *identity federation,* and it's one of the big ideas that cloud computing is bringing to reality a bit more quickly than might happen if clouds didn't exist. In simple terms, identity federation is a single authenticated user identity that is accepted as valid across a wide variety of systems. While the concept of having a particular type of user identification exist in two organizations might be easy to picture conceptually, the implementation has been fraught with heated arguments in the standards committees. Because the company that owns a customer's directory has a huge advantage in owning the rest of the organization's network infrastructure, vendors tend to want to feature their own solution to the exclusion of all others. With Sun Microsystems pushing LDAP, Novell pushing eDirectory, and Microsoft pushing Active Directory, the battle is a three-way slugfest among some of the biggest IT providers on the planet. Each bases identity management on a directory structure that vaguely resembles the work done in the X.500 standards committee but is tweaked to the individual company's benefit (www.infoworld.com/article/05/10/07/41FEidm_1.html?s=feature).

We'd like to point out that one of the huge roadblocks to federation has been the issue of government regulations. The medical industry's HIPAA rule set has certainly affected consumers by requiring a large number of new forms to sign acknowledging that their medical providers are compliant with HIPAA regulations and that they'll make every effort to protect your personal medical information. What hasn't been said is that HIPAA, Sarbanes-Oxley, and other federal legislation doesn't specify technology, only overall effects. The government doesn't say you must use AES256 encryption, but instead alludes to "secure communication pathways." This fact is creating a new era in the way medical providers share information and communicate with patients. A typical hospital doesn't own its laboratory, but rather provides space to a contractor to provide med tech services. When HIPAA first went into effect, many hospitals reverted to paper records to avoid having to answer privacy questions they really didn't know how to answer. However, as the scare faded and clearer thinking prevailed, medical providers realized that setting up a clearly defined procedure and risk management could provide just as much privacy as paper, perhaps even more. The Japanese have even gone as far as providing an even easier way for patients to identify themselves, so that they can start from a strong position of trust. Fujitsu Limited has produced a whole series of kiosks that scan the blood vessels in the palm, allowing for positive identification but without the resistance faced by other biometric identification systems. The Japanese figured out that if you start your information chain from a strong position of trust, much more can be done with less risk.

Let's clear the air a bit and say that each of the players in the debate about federation does seem to have the common goal of being able to interoperate. Each of the vendors agrees that creating a facility that would allow you to create special-purpose users on your system is a good thing *only* if it doesn't also expose your internal infrastructure to attack. That's it—we're all talking about literally how to implement that simple Venn diagram showing an overlap in authority between two organizations. The fight is really about how you determine trust so that you can more comfortably manage the risk for each transaction.

Suppose that Mary, an employee of Whapapalooza Widget Works, needs to place an order with Fergenschmeir Sprocket Works for 100 dozen size 20 sprockets. She and dozens of other defense contractors do this often enough that the folks at Fergenschmeir have been screaming for three more order-entry people. However, the enlightened IT staff at Whapapalooza and Fergenschmeir have discovered that their two internal IT infrastructures have an agreed-to standard for "federation." Each IT group has created a special user group that has privileges *only* in specific areas. Each has also assigned a group manager so that personnel changes in one company won't affect the other. *InfoWorld* magazine did a huge article on just this kind of thing way back in October 2005. The scenario mapped out a merger between two companies and followed the changes to a single employee. In this early comparative review, federation was only a buzzword, but the authors had long conversations with the vendors on just how federation would be implemented. Identity management, security event management, and federation all seem to be intertwined and no longer really exist as stand-alone subjects. All of these are being woven into the base operating system regardless of whether it was designed to be a monolithic system or virtualized. Considering the massive changes made to Windows Server 2008, the borders have certainly blurred.

However, the fight isn't over yet, and right now there just isn't a standard for federation in the world of identity management. However, there is a silver lining, and it's in the cloud. All Whapapalooza and Fergenschmeir really wanted to do was automate the ordering process so that neither company would have to encumber additional personnel to handle intercompany orders. A common area in which to place and acknowledge orders might be set up in any of the cloud services available. In Amazon it might be a virtual DMZ server, or maybe a shared storage area on Amazon S3 for named pipes, or a Python application in the Google App Engine. Like a Swiss Army knife, there are lots of ways to use the tools at hand.

Let's step back a few years and look at the early days of credit card validation. Although it was not the first, Verifone was founded on the idea of small simple devices that could read the magnetic stripe on the back of the credit card, call a credit bureau to validation the transaction, and then get back some acknowledgment by IC Verify for the transaction. This simple idea was applied to network applications in a simple DOS application that looked for files in a specific directory with a specific file extension. Upon finding those files, it would do something very similar to what Verifone did, but this time with a regular old computer modem. What made this different was how the system would keep the modem link up as long as it kept finding files in that directory. So, in many high-use cases these systems didn't drop the line all day. Credit card clearing houses now exist all over the world, but the concept is still the same. You've acknowledged a level of trust with the clearinghouse that in turn has a level of trust with the banks or credit card companies. Each in turn passes data along in a particular manner, but can't do anything beyond what is agreed on—thus dramatically limiting the potential for mischief. Key to this trust relationship is a third-party validation service called a Certificate Authority. In any typical browser today there exists a list of hosts that are considered trustworthy, and each of those servers takes part in a validation dance that utilizes dual-key encryption technology.

As a historical sidebar, modern encryption systems all spring from work originally done at MIT by mathematicians Ron Rivest, Adi Shamir, and Leonard Adleman (RSA Corporation was named for their initials), who were the first to create a commercially viable encryption system that utilized one encryption key to "lock" the transaction and a completely separate encryption key to "unlock" it. This dual-key encryption became the basis for almost all secure Internet communications today. More important for this discussion is how this same mechanism can be used to authenticate information. The "private key" is used to create a numerical representation of the message. To validate this message, the recipient retrieves the "public key" from a trusted Certificate Authority (all a Certificate Authority does is hold onto public keys for servers). The original work that led to this advance was done in Honolulu, Hawaii, by Wesley Peterson, PhD, in 1964. His paper on the mathematical representation of data for error correction became the basis for all modern data transmission error checking and all modern encryption. Today, Peterson is acknowledged as the father of the cyclical redundancy check used in every data transmission.

Is federation happening now? You bet! Just look at how Amazon's massive Internet sales site can place orders with hundreds of companies all over the world. The sophistication of the federated identity varies widely from organization to organization, but the goal is the same: Provide more services between companies but not at the added expense of human resources. After all, the biggest cost in just about any organization is warm bodies.

Clouds Flight Path for Chapter 5

- *Will government regulations prevent you from using the cloud?* We all know that government regulations play a huge part in how various organizations do business, and clouds have to learn to play along. We've looked at some of the issues you might stumble across as you think about moving into the cloud. Considering that we've had some friends retrieve their files and discover that they came from Italy, it really pays to do your homework and make sure you buy the right options. While the big boys are all offering regulatory options, you must ask for them, and they might very well need to be part of your service-level agreement.

- *To use clouds internally, you really need to examine the size of your Internet pipe.* It doesn't pay to move your internal computing facilities into the cloud if your Internet pipe is tiny. It's all about balance, and about looking at every piece in the puzzle. Remember that some applications are very timing-sensitive and don't lend themselves nicely to being shoved into a cloud. Here is where taking it all for a test drive really makes sense. Don't take the word of the salesperson; test it yourself and make sure it's worth risking your reputation on the move.

- *There are different types of load balancing, and a good load balancer can also provide auto provisioning.* We looked at some big Web surges and how various organizations handle them. Load balancing is a way of life as your audience grows. We mentioned some key factors you should consider, and we discussed why load balancing is making even more sense today, especially because it can actually help you strike a balance between in-house infrastructure and the cloud.

- *You can use a cloud as a DMZ between partners, just as good fences make good neighbors.* Setting up some neutral ground makes a whole lot of sense and limits risk for everyone involved. We're only human, and there is always potential for mistakes. It's said that good fences make good neighbors, and that's certainly the case with business partners using the cloud as neutral territory for exchanging information.

- *The seeds of federation are finally sprouting.* That no man's land might very well finally give federation a chance to bear fruit. Will this be the beginning of the business world coming to some sort of agreement on just how to handle foreign trust relationships, and will clouds become the Switzerland of the computing world?

Chapter 6

Cloud Providers

The science of today is the technology of tomorrow.

– Edward Teller

In This Chapter

The number of cloud computing providers changes by the day, and the number of applications offered through the cloud changes by the week. How do you go about keeping up with who's offering what, and how the definitions are connecting to the marketing terms? It helps to have a solid understanding of the concepts used by most cloud providers, and to back up that understanding with some clear examples. That's what this chapter is about. A list of providers comes later in the book, but in this chapter you'll learn the commercial concepts as they've been applied by some of the early market leaders, and why those concepts can be expanded to cover many of the other market players you'll encounter. You'll also get a better idea of just how you can take the marketing terms you'll hear and apply them to the software problems you have, to best match cloud solutions with your on-the-ground IT situation.

- Market positioning—We attempt to separate fact from fiction and politics from technology. Just remember that the more technologically sophisticated solution isn't always the one that wins out. Just look at Betamax versus VHS, or Ethernet versus Token Ring. Much will depend on how well cloud providers convince the executive suite that their solution will give the customer a better return on investment.

- Amazon Web Services—The 1000-lb gorilla, Amazon's suite of services has built a cloud for here and now, but their amazing collection of toolkits and support offerings may also mean they'll be able to leverage their initial lead into a commanding pole position as clouds evolve.

- SimpleDB—There's a *very* good reason why so many database projects start off in something like Microsoft Access: because it's simple. Business doesn't care about elegance; it cares about return on investment. Amazon's simpleDB is self-explanatory and is their answer to providing for database-enabled Web applications without the huge investment in an "elegant" database back end.

- Cloud Front—If simple is better, and not having to think about the care and feeding of a full server just so you can provide Web access to your data store, then Cloud Front is Amazon's answer. Leveraging the fact that almost all Web servers are virtual-capable, this service provides a fast and easy Web presence without the heavy lifting of maintaining the kitchen sink.

- Amazon Simple Queue Service—Sometimes you just need to separate out functions, but you have to push/pull data back and forth between those machines. Amazon's Simple Queue Service provides a secure and easy-to-implement method for passing information back and forth.

- Microsoft Azure—Microsoft is the Johnny-come-lately here, but Azure is currently more like Google than Amazon in that it's a cloud that's designed to run .NET applications. It's unclear where Microsoft is taking its cloud strategy, but what is clear is that they play a mean game of chess and that they're still positioning the pieces around the chessboard.

- Google—The search giant is reaching for the Web developers and isn't even offering virtualized machines in its cloud solution. However, Google's push for forcing a bit of standardization in their cloud also means that it should be easier for Google to make sweeping changes to meet market demands.

- Global Data Vault—Virtualized systems provide for snapshots that are really only a short-term "oops" facility and don't replace backups. What Global Data Vault has done is provide a way for changes to your VMWare farm to be reflected in their virtualized cloud while also providing an easy way to load balance your VMs globally.
- Appnexus and GoGrid—If your cloud solution is still changing or you don't fit into the solutions from the Big Boys of the cloud market, maybe something like Appnexus or GoGrid might be for you.

Marketing the Cloud

As with so many pieces of the IT market, there can be a gulf between how engineers define a particular technology and the way it's described by marketing departments. So far, we've been looking at cloud computing from the technologists' point of view, but now it's time to bring the marketing folks into the discussion. Toward the end of this book we'll provide a list of current cloud computing vendors, but before we get there we should talk about how we're going to define cloud vendors, and the type of services they're offering as of the writing of this book.

You should understand that this is where we have to make some judgment calls as to what we call a "cloud" at this stage in the game. Right now the industry's definition is more "foggy" than a full cloud soaring high above the earth. The market is at the very start of the cloud learning curve, and the cloud makers are still trying to figure out what the market really wants. What we're seeing so far is the big SaaS-type vendors just barely sticking their heads into the clouds, but we're saying that they're really just in a fog bank and have a long way to go.

The way they're going is complicated by the fact that cloud computing looks to be a very popular category of services. This means that the definition is going to be stretched by companies looking for a marketing "hook," even if their products have only the most tenuous connection to the engineers' definition of cloud computing.

As an enterprise-oriented IT publication, *InfoWorld* magazine makes an effort to keep track of emerging IT trends. Useful resources are www.infoworld.com/virtualization, which has quite a bit of overlap with the direction the cloud market is moving in, and www.infoworld.com/d/cloud-computing, which will help you keep track of the developing "Cloud City Market."

The "Cloud City Market"

While the market for cloud computing services is evolving rapidly, some elements are remaining quite consistent over time. An illustration of both halves of this statement come in something written by John Edwards in the August 27, 2008, issue of InfoWorld:

> Currently dominated by Amazon.com and several small startups, cloud computing is increasingly attracting the interest of industry giants, including Google, IBM, and now AT&T. "Everyone and their dog will be in cloud computing next year," predicts Rebecca Wettemann, vice president of research at Nucleus Research, a technology research firm.
>
> Yet James Staten, an infrastructure and operations analyst at Forrester Research, warns that prospective adopters need to tread carefully in a market that he describes as both immature and evolving. Staten notes that service offerings and service levels vary widely between cloud vendors. "Shop around," he advises. "We're already seeing big differences in cloud offerings."

The list of players has changed considerably since Edwards wrote this passage. At that level, there has been extensive evolution since the article was published. On the other hand, his contention that "service offerings and service levels vary widely between cloud vendors" is, if anything, more urgently correct now that it was when written.

If we are to believe that "Everyone and their dog will be in cloud computing next year," then it will be up to the consumer to determine what is important. What vision is important to your business? Will it be just an iterative step into hosted server virtualization or a much bigger step into OS-agnostic services, where agents can talk to brokers and shop your applications around? Or would you be more comfortable with something in between? Ultimately, then, the question isn't how Wikipedia defines cloud computing, or how the phrase is used by any marketing department, but how you and your company define the term. Having a firm definition in mind (and, especially, having a *single* definition that is used by everyone in your organization) can be incredibly important when it comes time to have discussions about the merits of a given plan for moving functionality to the cloud, or about the merits of a given vendor for building a partnership to enable cloud computing.

One of the reasons the single definition is so important is that, as of this writing, many of the cloud services are their own noninteroperable universes. We happen to think that the internationalization trends of the global Internet will eventually force the market to evolve in the direction of greater interoperability and become fertile ground in which the federation concepts we discussed in the last chapter can finally take hold. The agent-and-broker model may be a lofty goal sounding like just so much science fiction, but global roaming by hand-held mobile phones were science fiction not long ago.

Until the coming of the federated future, the cloud-based silos of today will do. Let's take a look at some of the current offerings and what they represent. The products discussed in this chapter aren't all of them by any means—think of them as being representative of what's out there and how it can work for you and your company.

Amazon

Fueled by the marketing engine that is Amazon, Amazon Web Services (AWS) has made splash after splash in the news with case studies showing massive savings on projects at the *New York Times* and NASDAQ. AWS seems to be the kitchen-sink approach to clouds: virtual machine hosting (EC2), storage (S3), database (SimpleDB), content delivery (Cloud Front), and Queue service (SQS) for handling asynchronous message traffic between servers. With Amazon the cloud provider to catch, vendors such as F5, Coyote Point, and Paragon Software (backup and migration tools) have all jumped on the bandwagon to support this 1000-lb gorilla. What Amazon really should be commended for is sticking its proverbial neck out a million miles in the first place. The investment of building a cloud infrastructure of this magnitude is probably on a par with the gross national product of quite a few countries. What we're willing to wager is that AWS is an outgrowth of Amazon's huge sales engine, which has fingers reaching out and linking a huge number of vendors in what can only be described as a country open market writ *very* large. We would be willing to wager that as Amazon developed their connections with more and more suppliers for their online sales inventory, they found themselves setting up proxies and federation servers to serve as intermediaries for the sales transactions. We could easily imagine someone (perhaps Senior Bezos) thinking that maybe this would make a good business model. Well, we tip our hat to the Big Boy on the Block and wish him well. Amazon Web Services has paved the way for a new industry, or at the very least has become the pace setter that everyone else needs to catch.

Amazon S3

Simple Storage Service is just that, an extremely simplified Web-based storage system that has made massive amounts of storage space available for just about any amount of time you choose to pay for. With service rates published in the range of $0.15 to $0.12 (at the time of writing), the reality is that you definitely want to use their "rate calculator" to figure out your first month's costs, since transfer charges can be the magic "gotcha." In blog after blog we've found mentioned that your first month is always going to be much more expensive than subsequent months, due to the larger first copy of your hard disk to the service.

It's important to remember with many of the services we'll discuss that the "setup" costs can be significantly higher than the ongoing fees for run-of-business computing. Sometimes, this will be reflected in explicit start-up changes. Other times, as with S3, the additional fees aren't explicit but are simply the result of the charges required to move data or establish program services in the cloud service provider's storage and intelligence.

The biggest gotcha that's forgotten by nearly everyone (except Internet service providers) is that bandwidth isn't free, and the Amazon S3 service isn't going to let you forget it. This is one of the first times I've seen a provider of any type of service actually charge back for transit fees right up front, and make no excuses or apologies for it. While everyone might think the Internet is free, someone has to pay those transit fees, and Amazon is there to make money. As Amazon itself states:

> Data transfer "in" and "out" refers to transfer into and out of an Amazon S3 location (i.e., US or EU). Data transferred within an Amazon S3 location via a COPY request is free of charge. Data transferred via a COPY request between locations is charged at regular rates. Data transferred between Amazon EC2 and Amazon S3 within the same region is free of charge (i.e., $0.00 per GB). Data transferred between Amazon EC2 and Amazon S3 across

regions (i.e., between US and EU), will be charged at Internet Data Transfer rates on both sides of the transfer.

Storage and bandwidth size includes all file overhead.

(*Source:* http://aws.amazon.com/s3/#pricing.)

Note that if your datasets are near the point where the initial data transfer charges could become a showstopper, Amazon now offers AWS import/export services by which you actually ship them large physical storage media that can be transferred over their internal high-speed network instead of over the Internet. This service is dramatically less expensive than an Internet transfer; although it does carry some handling and service charges, it won't break the bank.

Again, according to Amazon:

Pricing

As with all AWS services, you pay only for the resources that you use. Pricing includes fees for each storage device used and for the number of hours it takes to load your data (data-loading-hours). Estimate your AWS Import/Export charges using the AWS Import/Export Calculator.

Device Handling

- $80.00 per storage device handled.

Data Loading Time

- $2.49 per data-loading-hour. Partial data-loading-hours are billed as full hours.

Amazon S3 Charges

- Standard Amazon S3 Request and Storage pricing applies.
- Data transferred between AWS Import/Export and Amazon S3 is free of charge (i.e., $0.00 per GB).

(AWS Import/Export is sold by Amazon Web Services LLC.)

(*Source:* http://aws.amazon.com/importexport.)

As with any pricing, of course, you should always check the source to get the latest numbers, but, using the above prices as an example, 1 TB transferred up to Amazon S3 (AWS Calculator with no usage, just transfer) come out to be 2.5 times more expensive, with the gap increasing as the amount of data transferred increases. So, while this is an overly simplified example, it does illustrate that for large amounts of data, you might seriously want to consider shipping Amazon your disks for the first data load. We remember an old adage, "Never underestimate the bandwidth of an old station wagon full of tapes"; sometimes, shipping the data is cheaper and faster than transmitting it.

Don't get us wrong: This is still really inexpensive storage, especially if you factor in the cost of maintaining a server in your data center. This fact wasn't lost on the University of Hawaii Botany Department after their Windows Web Server got hacked out from under them. After comparing the price of a new server (the hacked machine was getting old), including the cost to migrate everything over, it was decided that it was a much easier pill to swallow to migrate once to Amazon S3 with the departments massive collection of high-resolution photographs of rare and endangered plant species. This was a case of a group accurately comparing the full costs associated with a change, considering two competing alternatives. Data transfer and application transition costs aren't unique to the cloud, and building them into the economic equations will make for a far more accurate understanding of how the various options truly compare.

Amazon EC2

Amazon's Elastic Compute Cloud is a multiflavored beast on which virtual server images can be ordered up in a dizzying array of combinations of operating systems, system resources, and, of course, integration with the Amazon S3 storage system. You can choose to order prebuilt machine images from Amazon or literally upload your own disk images and perform a system generation from scratch. The options are plentiful, and it's this range of options that makes EC2 useful for so many different organizations.

One interesting option is support for OpenMPI, the Open Source Message Passing Interface (http://en.wikipedia.org/wiki/Openmpi), which is typically used for the creation of Beowulf-style computing clusters. With this possibility, managers needing short-term or intermittent supercomputer-level performance can ask themselves an intriguing question: Instead of building a supercomputer cluster with all the potentially nasty little infrastructure issues associated with big clusters, why not rent one for the occasional cluster problem? With charge-backs on a per-instance compute hour, the *New York Times* found it cheaper to go with a massive number of cloud-based machine instances over a short amount of time than with a smaller number over a longer period. Critical, intensive, time-limited projects are perfect candidates for a service like EC2, as are situations in which system demand can spike suddenly, or in which horse-power demand fluctuates wildly.

The flip side of the EC2 coin is what Amazon calls Elastic Block Store, where snapshot images of servers are stored on the S3 service and can be started up as desired. However, while Amazon's service-level agreement commits to 99.95% uptime for each region (U.S., Europe, etc.), it only guarantees that the virtual machine—not any particular application—will be up. It doesn't guarantee that Apache won't crash, leaving you without a Web presence but still paying for compute hours on your server. Amazon's answer is called Hyperic Monitoring:

> **Hyperic HQ** for AWS automatically manages and monitors the software on your EC2 instances, giving you total visibility into the health and well-being of your computing resources. HQ starts with auto-discovery for more than 75 common technology com-ponents—including databases, application servers, middleware, web servers and more—then seamlessly monitors the availabil-ity and performance of those services. HQ for AWS–Developer Edition provides rich visualization capabilities, trend analysis and capacity planning, advanced alerts, built-in and extendable diagnostics, and remote control of system resources, so you can prevent, detect, and solve problems.
>
> (*Source:* http://developer.amazonwebservices.com/connect/entry. jspa?externalID=1923&categoryID=101.)

EC2 also provides geographic dispersion of your computing resources and the ability to change which virtual server your assigned Internet addresses actually point to. So, for instance, your IT group can have two or more identical servers running. Then suppose that application upgrades are applied and an unforeseen problem crashes your production machine. Instead of having to wait for Amazon's engineers to switch your IP address to your backup, your IT group can do it through their account portal.

Something else needs to be mentioned at this point, though we'll deal with it in more detail later: the issue of uptime guarantees and what they mean to you. Amazon says that it provides 99.95% uptime for EC2, and that sounds very good. For many purposes, it will be more than enough to provide incredible reliability. If you're running a global business that absolutely depends on the application sitting on that server, though, that guarantee still leaves a bit over three and a half hours a year that you can be offline.

Do a bit of simple math to figure out just how much reliability a string of 9's actually guarantees:

Availability	Downtime per Year	Downtime per Month*	Downtime per Week
90%	36.5 days	72 hours	16.8 hours
95%	18.25 days	36 hours	8.4 hours
98%	7.30 days	14.4 hours	3.36 hours
99%	3.65 days	7.20 hours	1.68 hours
99.50%	1.83 days	3.60 hours	50.4 minutes
99.80%	17.52 hours	86.23 minutes	20.16 minutes
99.9% ("three 9's")	8.76 hours	43.2 minutes	10.1 minutes
99.95%	4.38 hours	21.56 minutes	5.04 minutes
99.99% ("four 9's")	52.6 minutes	4.32 minutes	1.01 minutes
99.999% ("five 9's")	5.26 minutes	25.9 seconds	6.05 seconds
99.9999% ("six 9's")	31.5 seconds	2.59 seconds	0.605 seconds

*For simplicity, a 30-day month is used.

How sure are you that you want to demand service levels in your contract. Is it really worth it? Do you want to pay for it? Can your provider even attempt to deliver it, or are they just blowing smoke?

SimpleDB

(As of the writing of this book, the SimpleDB service was in BETA testing.) An alternative to installing a full-featured SQL server, this database alternative is designed to provide easier Web scaling for Web developers. Instead of dealing with the complexity of an SQL back-end server for clustered Web servers, developers can instead use Web-like commands:

- *CREATE* a new domain to house your unique set of structured data.

- *GET, PUT,* or *DELETE* items in your domain, along with the attribute-value pairs that you associate with each item. Amazon SimpleDB automatically indexes data as it is added to your domain so that it can be quickly retrieved; there is no need to predefine a schema or change a schema if new data is added later. Each item can have up to 256 attribute values. Each attribute value can range from 1 to 1024 bytes.
- Query your data set using *SELECT API* or *QUERY API* and this simple set of operators: =, !=, <, >, <=, >=, STARTS-WITH, AND, OR, NOT, INTERSECTION AND UNION. Use *QUERYWITH ATTRIBUTES* to retrieve the information associated with items returned as a response to a particular query. Your *SELECT, QUERY,* or *QUERYWITHATTRIBUTES* results can be sorted using the *SORT* operator. Query execution time is currently limited to 5 seconds, limiting the complexity of queries that can be run against large data sets.

Amazon SimpleDB is designed for real-time applications and is optimized for these uses. If you want to run quarterly wrap-up reports for your amazingly large retail operation that has 2 million SKUs and 3000 stores, then you're obviously way out of the range of SimpleDB's intended customer base.

Now take a step back and ask yourself some hard questions and make sure you're answering them honestly. Do you *really* need a full SQL server? Can you manage with something like SimpleDB? We can tell you from experience that managing a full-on database management system (DBMS) is why there are so many jobs for SQL experts. It's nontrivial and can be quite tedious. Not to mention that authentication in this day and age should be closely tied to some sort of directory authentication system (Active Directory or LDAP or similar). Many times we've sat around sucking down some cold suds and wondering out loud just why so many people like using database engines like MySQL. While we don't have a definitive answer, we suspect it's because that's the path of least resistance in many application systems. It's there, and because it's open source, quite a few developers don't feel bad at all tossing it fully integrated into their installer image. The same goes for SQL Express from Microsoft. The hard part comes when you have to scale up and suddenly finding yourself searching for a DBMS administrator. We're thinking that as the word gets out, SimpleDB might find success for the same reasons that MySQL and SQL Express have.

Cloud Front

Most people never really stop to think about how Amazon, Google, or other large and distributed services work. They long ago passed the point at which a monolithic server farm, no matter how large, could meet the needs of all their users and customers. Instead, they built widely distributed networks of servers and appliances that fulfill as many requests as possible as geographically close as possible to the individual making the request. Once in place, those distributed servers could be asked to work for cloud-service customers as well as the host vendors.

Simply put, Cloud Front provides access to Web content stored on the S3 service through these edge devices sitting close to the requestor. Cloud Front is marketed as a *content delivery network* (CDN) because that's its very basic job: By caching Web data closer to the end user, delivery is speeded up. This is the sort of service that can be vitally important to you if your business depends on maintaining a good user experience for your customers, or if you're concerned about trouble on the Internet in one part of the world having an effect on all your customers around the world.

Amazon Simple Queue Service

Also part of the constellation of Amazon cloud services, Simple Queue Service (SQS) is designed to provide a secure communications pathway between systems. SQS also integrates guaranteed message delivery into the mix, so this package is critical to companies that depend on systems to place and receive orders within specific time frames. If you think about the time-critical nature of financial trades or resource allocation during natural disasters, you're on the right track. Is your business sufficiently time-critical to require SQS? You and your IT team have to make that decision.

SQS provides a way for Web-based services to exchange information in a secure manner. It consists of three major components:

1. Authentication of the services involved is achieved through the use of additions to your standard AWS credentials. Through a registration

process, the developer creates an appropriate set of credentials so that the processes can achieve a secure handshake.

2. Message delivery is guaranteed and is valid up to 8 KB. What is noteworthy is that sequence is not guaranteed, and if such a thing is needed, then sequence numbers of some sort should be embedded into the message.

3. Message deletion from the system should be handled by the application programmer, but timers do exist for automatic deletion (4 days). If messages are not deleted after a certain time (typically 30 seconds), then their visibility is removed for a certain period of time and then made visible periodically until the ultimate timeout of 4 days.

We could easily equate this to a much more robust "named pipe" allowing message passing between globally separate applications.

Google

The Google App Engine is designed to divorce you from operating system-dependent issues and provide native Python and Java Virtual Machine support. What makes this even more significant is that you can leverage the amazing amount of free resources available to anyone, and you only get billed as your site starts to exceed the limits of the free accounts. The software development kit download is available for Mac, Windows, and Linux and allows for offline prototyping even without an App Engine account. According to Google:

> Google App Engine lets you run your web applications on Google's infrastructure. App Engine applications are easy to build, easy to maintain, and easy to scale as your traffic and data storage needs grow. With App Engine, there are no servers to maintain: You just upload your application, and it's ready to serve your users.
>
> You can serve your app from your own domain name (such as http://www.example.com/) using Google Apps. Or, you can serve your app using a free name on the appspot.com domain. You can share your application with the world, or limit access to members of your organization.
>
> Google App Engine supports apps written in several programming languages. With App Engine's Java runtime environ-

ment, you can build your app using standard Java technologies, including the JVM, Java servlets, and the Java programming language—or any other language using a JVM-based interpreter or compiler, such as JavaScript or Ruby. App Engine also features a dedicated Python runtime environment, which includes a fast Python interpreter and the Python standard library. The Java and Python runtime environments are built to ensure that your application runs quickly, securely, and without interference from other apps on the system.

With App Engine, you only pay for what you use. There are no set-up costs and no recurring fees. The resources your application uses, such as storage and bandwidth, are measured by the gigabyte, and billed at competitive rates. You control the maximum amounts of resources your app can consume, so it always stays within your budget.

App Engine costs nothing to get started. All applications can use up to 500 MB of storage and enough CPU and bandwidth to support an efficient app serving around 5 million page views a month, absolutely free. When you enable billing for your application, your free limits are raised, and you only pay for resources you use above the free levels.

(*Source:* http://code.google.com/appengine/docs/whatisgoogleapp engine.html.)

With a system finely tuned to provide support to the Web development environment, the App Engine system has tightly integrated database, Imaging API, Mail API, and MemCache to handle CDNs.

Google is thus providing a development environment that has a common set of tools, and resources that by their very nature force code to have a greater level of interchangeability than what you would find in a virtual machine-based system like Amazon's. The analogy is similar to the differences between the Apple Macintosh and the Windows PC. The Apple had a very narrow set of tools and resources limited to only those offered by Apple. This created an environment in which code developed for the Mac had a much higher chance of working as expected, since the controls put on it by Apple combined with the strict hardware standards made for very few variants in the operating environment. In contrast, the Windows PC hardware world is the Wild West, with tiny garage companies developing whatever widget comes to mind. This wide-open development environment has made for some amazingly original applications and hardware, but at the same time has created an environment in which incompatibilities are the norm rather than the exception.

Google has long believed in the "carrot" approach to attracting developers. A rich set of software development tools, and the ability to prototype in the free environment, has the potential for the eventual emergence of a huge collection of applications that with little or no modifications can interact with one another in a building-block approach for the creation of huge systems. We're not sure if Google took a page from Apple's playbook or the other way around, but it sure looks like Google is ramping up for its own version of the iPhone AppStore but with apps that can run either in the Google App Engine world or perhaps in the Android mobile environment. In 2009 Google launched XMPP support, which has the potential for loosely connecting client applications in the Android mobile world to the server-based applications in the Google App Engine cloud. What this really means is a continuing commitment by Google to extend the App Engine platform to meet emerging technology trends and, most important, to provide tools to implement cloud applications across the Google world, up to and including the Android mobile platform.

Microsoft

Microsoft's Azure is actually part of a multipronged cloud solution that is rapidly changing shape. So far, it has not been presented as a "cloud solution," but it certainly consists of a bunch of solutions that are very cloudy in nature. Only time will tell what the analysts decide on as packaging, but it's certain that Microsoft will be a player, if only because of its dominance in the workstation and server marketplace.

According to Microsoft:

> As part of Microsoft's continued commitment to interoperability, the Windows Azure platform has been built from the ground up with interoperability in mind. As an **open platform**, Windows Azure **offers choices** to developers. It allows them to use multiple languages (.NET, PHP, Ruby, Python or Java) and development tools (Visual Studio or Eclipse) to build applications which run on Windows Azure and/or consume any of the Windows

Azure platform offerings from any other cloud or on premise platform. With its **standards-based** and interoperable approach, the Windows Azure platform supports multiple Internet protocols including HTTP, XML, SOAP and REST—key pillars of **data portability**.

1. **Windows Azure** provides a scalable environment with compute, storage, hosting, and management capabilities. It links to on-premises applications with secure connectivity, messaging, and identity management.
2. **SQL Azure** is a **Relational Database for the Cloud**. Your Data: Anyplace, anytime. SQL Azure is a full relational database in the cloud.
3. **AppFabric provides Network Services for the Cloud.** AppFabric offers identity management and firewall friendly messaging to protect your assets by enabling secure connectivity and messaging between on-premises IT applications and cloud-based services.

(*Source:* www.microsoft.com/windowsazure/products.)

As with Amazon and Google, Microsoft's cloud solution isn't a single product, but rather a collection of products as a suite. While Microsoft's overall strategy is still unclear, various products will be appearing as they position their chess pieces around the cloud chessboard. Similar to the Amazon global content delivery system, Windows Azure is the Microsoft-flavored version.

Introducing the Windows Azure Content Delivery Network

As part of the Windows Azure CTP (Community Technology Preview), we are announcing the Windows Azure Content Delivery Network (CDN) to deliver Windows Azure Blob content. Windows Azure CDN offers developers a global solution for delivering high-bandwidth content.

Windows Azure CDN has 18 locations globally (United States, Europe, Asia, Australia and South America) and continues to expand. Windows Azure CDN caches your Windows Azure blobs at strategically placed locations to provide maximum bandwidth for delivering your content to users. You can enable CDN delivery for any storage account via the Windows Azure Developer Portal. The CDN provides edge delivery only to blobs that are in public blob containers, which are available for anonymous access.

The benefit of using a CDN is better performance and user experience for users who are farther from the source of the content stored in the Windows Azure Blob service. In addition, Windows Azure CDN provides worldwide high-bandwidth access to serve content for popular events.

(*Source:* http://blogs.msdn.com/windowsazure/archive/2009/11/ 05/introducing-the-windows-azure-content-delivery-network. aspx.)

From material on the Microsoft Azure website, it appears that Microsoft is presenting an environment not unlike the concept that Google would have us adopt: support for a specific set of programming languages, a DBMS, and connection technologies—all designed to reduce the amount of heavy lifting necessary to bring an application into the world. So far we've not seen any type of coherent cloud strategy from Microsoft, but we're certainly starting to see some very interesting pieces. As quoted above from the Microsoft Content Delivery Network, the ability to delivery globally load-balanced blobs (binary large objects) means that we won't have scenarios in which the Victoria's Secret lingerie show crashes the Internet service provider, because the massive load would be shared across the entire globe.

Another cloudlike offering from Microsoft is called S+S (or Software plus Services). These online services seem to be standing apart from the Azure group, and they feel like a separate business group. However, the summary of a speech by Ray Ozzie (Microsoft's chief software architect) would have us believe that these product silos are actually pieces of a very large puzzle, with Microsoft uniquely positioned to create what sounds like ubiquitous computing and is starting to sound like our "Jetsons" view of cloud computing:

Microsoft's investments in Software-plus-Services are framed by three core principles. Firstly, experiences should span beyond a single device. In our world of ever-increasing devices, choice in the right computing power in the right place at the right time is paramount. UX environments that span seamlessly from the browser, to the PC, to the mobile and console need to be brought together to provide flexible yet unified experiences.

Secondly, infrastructure and solutions should extend from the server to the cloud. Cloud services developed hand-in-hand with on-premises server counterparts will deliver much needed choice to enterprise customers—enabling flexibility in developing, scaling, operating and migrating systems that are distributed between the cloud and the enterprise data center.

And lastly, tightly coupled systems should give way to federations of cooperating systems and loosely coupled compositions. With the right transparency, standards and interoperability, these small pieces of code loosely joined help developers build new applications and services out of base components—enabling agile and cost-effective development.

(*Source:* www.microsoft.com/softwareplusservices/software-plus-services-full-story.aspx.)

The big difference is that this might be a much more appropriate environment for shops that have an investment in the Microsoft world of .NET and MS-SQL. We've also seen marketing pieces suggesting that Microsoft Azure or Software+Services might be appropriate for shops that don't need or want an IT infrastructure but still want to utilize environments such as SharePoint or the Microsoft Unified Communications (UC) world. One key concept is introduced at the very end of a cartoon overview on the Azure site, where Microsoft introduces a concept that looks suspiciously like federation and is suggesting that organizations use this new facility to provide seamless access to IT assets in a secure manner for partner organizations.

A key concept that many consumers forget is that Microsoft is a massive organization with very deep pockets and has the technology base to create products and strategies with the potential for touching the lives of billions of people around the world. So, while I'm certainly disappointed that we were unable to interview people in various Microsoft teams, they have given us a pretty interesting future view on their website:

Over the years, Windows has begun to dissolve the artificial barriers between devices, people and information—delivering new capabilities and unprecedented choice to a billion people and businesses around the world. Now, as the power of devices increases and the ubiquity of the Web unfolds, Microsoft's Software-plus-Services strategy is helping Windows leave even more walls behind.

Through the combination of Windows, Windows Live and Windows Mobile, Microsoft is delivering the platforms, tools, infrastructure and solutions to enable new kinds of applications and services that extend from the server, to the datacenter, to the cloud—and from the browser, to the PC, to the phone and beyond.

With this work, we hope to empower the world's software innovators and unleash a new wave of software and services that truly deliver on the promise of the digital lifestyle, with experiences that go wherever people's lives take them and simply work wherever, however and whenever they want it.

(*Source:* www.microsoft.com/softwareplusservices/software-plus-services-strategy.aspx.)

Client-Server and Other Asynchronous Methods

SIMPLE (SIP for Instant Messaging and Presence Leveraging Extensions) is an offshoot of the Voice-over-IP protocol called SIP, which for all intents and purposes looks very similar to HTML conversations. SIMPLE's most significant supporter is the Microsoft IM systems that are woven through-put the Microsoft Unified Communications offerings.

XMPP (Extensible Messaging and Presence Protocol) is an XML-based instant messaging protocol that is used in Google Talk and Jabber. The significance behind XMPP support is that developers can now divorce themselves from having to manage intermachine communications. This instant messaging support has been implemented as a way for your application to communicate with users or other applications. Instead of implementing a new protocol, as Amazon did with SQS, Google leveraged XMPP, an existing protocol (as opposed to SIMPLE, which is the IM protocol for Microsoft). It should also be pointed out that SIMPLE and XMPP are far from being the only protocols for instant messaging, but they are also connection-based message-passing technologies that are capable of being run over several different types of transports (TLA, SSL, etc.) for varying levels of security and delivery assurance.

What we find fascinating is just how many mobile applications provide XMPP client support already. It's not hard to imagine having lightweight apps on mobile phones that can talk directly to applications in the Google cloud (the capability is already in Google's Android). It's all handled by a protocol that looks very much like HTML married to XML, which can be easily encapsulated in a wide variety of transport systems, already has strong encryption and authentication, and already has a wide variety of supporters already writing apps for it.

Note that while XMPP and SIMPLE are competing protocols, it was proven at the 2006 Interop show in the iLabs that the Jabber gateways do indeed work, and the team was able to show some primitive interdomain communications in order to update presence information between XMPP and SIMPLE systems.

Allowing only one or two programming languages to work with the power of the cloud may sound like an incredible limitation. In truth, Python and Java do a large part of the heavy lifting of Web-based applications anyway, so this isn't really a dramatic limitation at all. Google has built much of its cloud-application presence on the idea of providing simple versions of services that are given additional features as the basics become reliable and well established. It wouldn't be at all surprising to see them take the same approach with their cloud offerings, bringing out enhanced features as customers respond to (and thoroughly test) existing features.

Other Clouds

Amazon and Google provide services based on vast arrays of widely distributed processors. Cloud don't have to be globally hosted to be useful, though. The next two offerings are almost identical—they're both large collections of servers, both with lots of remote management, both with the continuity assurance that comes from auxiliary power generation, load balancing, advanced network operations centers, etc. Appnexus has two data centers and will have three; GoGrid has a single data center located in San Francsico.

Both Appnexus and GoGrid provide services that are much closer to the hardware than the offerings from either Amazon or Google. On the one hand, that means there tends to be less programmatic hand-holding at the smaller companies than at the large, with programming and management interfaces that tend away from the incredibly simple. On the other hand, we could easily imagine either provider giving you the flexibility to handle services most likely not supported or allowed at either Amazon or Google, because of those larger systems' requirements for standardization across very large customer bases. Let's take a look at what the smaller clouds can provide for customers.

Appnexus

Appnexus (www.appnexus.com) is, at its simplest, a data center without the long-term investment. The Appnexus offering is a large collection of virtualized servers and storage, load balanced and delivered to the customer with a self-serve front end. Their offer sounds very much like what someone building a world-class data center might offer, but with a system that lets you purchase small bits at a time.

With a data center on each coast of the United States and one opening soon in Europe, Appnexus is in a position to provide content delivery services and global load balancing.

What is Appnexus not? It's not a system that focuses on any one programming language or set of capabilities. It's not a system with the market reach to strike alliances with ISPs around the world for automatic billing of services through the ISPs' monthly statements. It is a way to have on-demand overflow processes find a home in the cloud, or to quickly have the services of a cloud-based sandbox in which to test large-scale distributed applications.

GoGrid

GoGrid (www.gogrid.com), a Servepath company, has a full network operations center (NOC), a pair of 2-megawatt generators, multiple Internet feeds, security, and everything you'd need to run a world-class data center. The data center is wrapped in a Web-based customer self-service system that allows for provisioning of Windows or Linux servers to provide whatever type of virtual server infrastructure you want.

With a Web services front-end account, administrators can choose from a wide variety of prebuilt system images and deploy them with connections into user-assigned public and private VLANs. The GoGrid API is available for programming systems including Java, Python, PHP, and Ruby. The API provides a variety of provisioning options that can be utilized by applications monitoring systems or network monitors such as GroundWorks OpenSource, CA Unicenter, HP OpenView, or others.

Global Data Vault

Global Data Vault (www.globaldatavault.com) is a cloud provider that isn't trying to be a full cloud. Global Data Vault's claim to fame is business continuity by providing PC and server backups. The Interop NOC team uses them to (nearly) continuously backup the Interop show servers and then provide an easy way to get back up and running at the next show.

According to its website, Global Data Vault is

- The only enterprise-class remote backup solution offering a path to Failover.
- A technologically advanced online backup solution specifically for file servers including Exchange and SQL
- Includes message-level Exchange backup and restore

These cloud providers give you the ability to keep your servers in sync with their service and the ability to swap over to the copy within minutes if your main location should fail.

What we're waiting to hear more about are the offerings from the "big boys," such as IBM, HP, and Cisco. So far they're all being fairly tight-lipped about what they're planning on rolling out, but we're very sure they'll be leveraging the successes and mistakes of the folks who came before them.

Emerging Cloud Tools

While every Tom, Dick, and Harry was jumping into the cloud arena, we had an opportunity to get under nondisclosure with Terracotta Corporation (www.terracotta.org) fairly early in the game. What Terracotta provides is a stepping-stone to what we consider true cloud applications. The Terracotta system offers yet another abstraction layer providing inter-VM communications and creating durable shared-memory data sources even across virtual machines. Its Ehcache product provides high-performance caching that optimizes data source connections by bringing applications data into its scalable virtual infrastructure. With Terracotta Ehcache, changes in memory on one node are distributed in a very efficient manner across the network, enabling a coherent view of in-memory data that is transactional without the use of a relational database management system (RDBMS). Because of the database offload capabilities it can deliver in this fashion, Terracotta provides significantly higher scalability capabilities by eliminating the database bottlenecks found when every VM has to exit the virtual host to query the RDBMS.

According to Ari Zilka, Terracotta founder and chief technology officer:

> Scaling the data layer to meet the needs of a dynamic virtualized compute layer will be a critical capability for enterprises to realize the benefits they seek in clouds. Much of the time, the database by itself will not provide a complete answer to this problem, and that's where Terracotta can help. The Terracotta platform will enable users to easily scale applications in large virtualized environments and private clouds and to efficiently distribute the massive workloads characteristic of these environments. Our products, like Ehcache for caching, and Quartz for job scheduling, allow this powerful scalability platform to be readily accessible for all developers through robust industry-standard APIs.

Another player in the emerging cloud tools market is Layer 7 Technologies (www.layer7tech.com), whose approach to security and the world is migrating from service-oriented architectures to the world of clouds. According to Scott Morrison, CTO of Layer 7:

> Layer 7 is the leading supplier of security and governance technology for Service-Oriented Architectures (SOAs). Layer 7's flagship product is the SecureSpan Gateway, a Policy Enforcement Point (PEP) optimized for high-performance processing of application-layer communication streams. SecureSpan provides fully configurable security processing, offering security professionals fine-grained, policy-based management of services. This includes privacy, integrity, access control, validation, threat detection, audit, as well as key and identity management. It provides orchestration of transactions, virtualization of services, and

enforcement of Service Level Agreements (SLAs). SecureSpan also features acceleration of CPU-intensive XML-based operations, such as schema validation, query and transform.

SecureSpan Gateways offer a range of deployment options customized for different environments. Hardware-based appliances are available for deployment into enterprise DMZs, offering wire speed transaction processing, hardware-accelerated processing of XML and cryptographic operations, and secure hardware-containment of private key material. DMZ-based deployment provides cloud-based SaaS services such as GoogleApps and Salesforce.com with secure, managed access to internal resources such as identity stores, applications and databases.

Virtual SecureSpan Gateways are available customized for deployment directly into cloud providers such as Amazon's Elastic Compute Cloud (EC2). Virtual gateways protect cloud-resident applications by managing all access in or out of the instance. They also provide a secure channel for cloud-resident applications to communicate with existing on-premise applications and data, all under enterprise control.

Application Clouds

The clouds we've discussed so far are all about giving organizations the power to extend or enhance their own applications. For many users and organizations, however, the point of moving to the cloud is to find an application or set of applications. What kind of applications can be found in the cloud? The answer is that there are nearly as many kinds of apps in the cloud as there are on desktop clients—and gaps in the market are being filled weekly.

Let's take a quick look at three different types of application clouds. The first is personal productivity clouds, through which you can do things like create documents, build spreadsheets, and pull together presentations. The second is enterprise applications such as customer relationship management or expense report accounting. Finally we'll look at applications designed solely to enhance other cloud-based applications. They're not quite stand-alone apps, and they're not quite application frameworks, but they may be the most representative of where the cloud will ultimately take the notion of application delivery.

Personal Productivity Clouds

Most individual users, and many enterprise professionals, first came into contact with the cloud through a personal productivity application. The most famous of these is Google Docs, the online document development service tied to a user's Google account. Google decided not to try to dazzle users with a plethora of features, focusing instead on basic document creation and editing functions along with the ability to share documents among groups of individuals. As such, Google Docs quickly became a system used by many who wanted to write basic letters and reports, or keep up with school or essential business work while not worrying about a personal productivity application tied to a single computer.

One of the key abilities of Google Docs, and a feature that sets it apart from its competitors, is the ability to use information created and stored in a Google document as the basis for other Google functions. As an example, data stored in a Google spreadsheet can be used to create a presentation that's published on the Web using Google Maps for its geographic component. In the end, it's this ability to build and publish complex online documents that makes Google Docs so powerful, while its simple ubiquity (and its price—free) makes it so popular. Between them, it can be argued that they provided much of the impetus behind the "netbook" computer phenomenon, in which small, low-cost, ultraportable computers are designed to be portals into cloud applications, rather than platforms for applications themselves.

Trends Driving Us Toward Clouds

The rise of netbooks is one of the reasons many users are excited about the entry of Microsoft into the cloud application market. We've already seen that Microsoft entered the cloud through storage services such as Sky Drive and Live Mesh, but the company recently announced the availability of cloud versions of some of its Office personal productivity tools, including Word, Excel, and OneNote. For many users there is an expectation that the user experience for the cloud-based applications will be exactly the same as for the desktop-based versions, and that the functionality will be identical as well. Microsoft is still experimenting with functionality and will almost certainly develop new pricing models after the original, no-cost trial period has ended.

Zoho

Much greater functionality is the hallmark of Zoho, a cloud application platform that comes much closer to providing the features associated with traditional desktop personal productivity applications than does Google Docs. Zoho is an example of a cloud application platform that provides functionality very similar to that of traditional desktop-hosted applications. It also provides examples of two additional traits that application clouds are featuring on an increasing basis: an ability to work with functions from other cloud-based applications, and a mixture of free and fee-based functionalities.

Zoho's ability to work with features from other cloud-based applications is highlighted by its reliance on Google Gears for offline functionality. Google Gears was developed as a response to the rather reasonable question of how individuals could continue to work if the network connection to the cloud application was interrupted. Google itself uses Gears to enable offline work in applications such as Google Docs and Google Calendar. Zoho uses Gears for the same purpose, allowing users to continue to work on documents and projects even if Zoho's cloud is not available for a time.

The range of applications available through Zoho is different than what is available through Google. Zoho does have the standard array of personal productivity applications, but it also includes options such as a wiki, a planner, and an email service. Small business or enterprise applications include features such as invoicing, online meeting applications, customer relationship management application, and human resource functions. These business applications tend to be available on a limited basis at no charge, with a fee applying for those who wish to use the applications on a permanent or large-scale basis.

The business applications that are part of Zoho are the sole reason for the existence of many enterprise application cloud providers. Perhaps the most well known of these is Sales.com, a company that provides customer relationship management software to large and small businesses on a cloud platform. Other enterprise applications available from a cloud platform include human relations management packages, expense account reporting and management tools, and accounting software. In each case, the functionality is available to customers without a requirement for hardware purchases or ongoing infrastructure management. Though these promises are enough to convince many IT managers that the cloud is the best way to proceed, for others the deciding factor is the knowledge that the cloud application provider's staff will be responsible for updating software to incorporate changing tax codes or financial regulations.

SaaS Apps Turning into Clouds

A third category of business cloud applications is comprised of those designed to extend the functionality or improve the performance of existing cloud applications. Salesforce.com, because of its popularity among enterprise users, has become the gravitational center of a constellation of customizing applications that enhance its features for particular markets or geographies. In some cases these enhancements consist of features that allow the cloud application to integrate more closely with existing enterprise software to form a complete solution for a customer. Often, these cloud-to-enterprise glue applications are not described as "cloud applications," but as Software as a Service (SaaS) packages. The difference between a cloud application and SaaS can be subtle, with the most compelling distinction being the global scope of the cloud application versus the more centralized hosting platform of the SaaS offering. For the customer, though, this is frequently a distinction without a difference, as both product categories offer enterprise software functionality with the requirement to purchase and support hardware and other infrastructure at the customer premises.

The Edge of the Cloud

The vast majority of those working in IT have made the assumption that we're only going to see cloud computing in data centers. This might be called a center-weighted view of the world, but when we interviewed Dan Putterman, CEO of Cloud Engines, we heard a person passionate about changing this. Cloud Engines, founded in 2007, has brought to market an easy-to-use cloud storage system called the Pogoplug. This simple device is radically different from the popular Network Attached Storage (NAS) systems that are currently taking the SOHO/SMB market by storm.

The Pogoplug is a simple white block of plastic that plugs into the wall and has only two other connections on it: a single Ethernet connection that goes to your home router and a single USB 2.0 socket that can be connected either directly to a USB storage device (hard disk, thumb drive, etc.) or to a USB 2.0 hub with multiple storage devices on it. What makes this radically different from the standard-issue NAS is that you no longer have to know how to do port forwarding (aka poking a hole through your firewall) or depend on the uneven and often unreliable universal plug-and-play "auto configuration" system now found on many home network devices. The system instead creates an outbound encrypted connection to the Cloud Engines data center, where the entire user authentication and other heavy-lifting tasks are done. Authenticated users then ride back over that same connection, and since this is in answer to the initial outbound connection, the firewall treats it as if a Web server was just answering you back after you type a URL into your Web browser.

To say this a bit differently, when a Web browser opens up a website, this is considered an outbound connection. The Web server answers back in response to this outbound connection, and the typical firewall treats this as the second half of the conversation and allows it through. If, however, someone tries to open a Web connection (or anything else, for that matter) through your firewall uninvited, this is counted as a new inbound connection and is turned away by most firewalls unless a specific access rule was created to allow this. So it's all about who started the conversation. If the conversation starts from inside the firewall, then it's considered a trusted conversation and the firewall allows the answers to come back in. If the conversation started from outside, then it's turned away.

What Cloud Engines has done is create a platform for the home network that does *not* require an IT specialist to set up, but still provides remote access to your storage device from anywhere in the world. Pogoplug clients are available for the Web, 32-bit Windows, 64-bit Windows, Mac OSx, 32-bit Linux (beta), 64-bit Linux (beta), and the iPhone. The remote storage shows up on your client just like any other local storage device. Sharing various levels of access to those devices is as simple as clicking a button.

The significance of this product isn't just that you can now store and share your files from just about anywhere; it's that the Pogoplug is a development platform. Instead of leaving in a massive amount of legacy applications like a typical NAS, Cloud Engines has literally started with a clean sheet and designed a new network file system, network transport, application programming interface, and software development kit, and then created a community of developers who are passionate about extending the capabilities of this tiny device.

Energy Clouds

What makes this development even more significant is that we can easily foresee someone writing software to add ZigBee (a home wireless system capable of daisy chaining from one device to another throughout a home) capability to the Pogoplug so that it can harvest energy usage information from your home photovoltaic array, electric meter, and other ZigBee-enabled appliances around your home. *Make* magazine published an article in late 2008 that described adding a Digi brand XBee (zigbee variation) interface into the Kill-A-Watt power measurement device. In this case the simplistic program would periodically take power readings off the Kill-A-Watt and push it up to Twitter. Thus the "Twitter Watt" was born. We can imagine these types of devices then sharing the information with energy monitoring clouds such as Pachube (www.pachube. com), which is leveraging Google Earth to display live energy usage from around the globe. The intent of the Pogoplug platform is to leverage the foundation that Cloud Engines have created so that developers can extend the cloud that last mile into the home.

Who's Who in the Clouds?

This was by far the hardest chapter of this book to write, simply because so many cloud providers are still in stealth mode. We could not include some of the providers we know about because we've signed nondisclosure agreements (NDAs). Chapter 10 will include some references and resources on future products that we've been collecting and will also contain many more of our predictions on where we think this industry will be going. What we will do is update the book website as our NDAs expire or as we learn about new entrants into the market.

We're both of the opinion that the market has a very long way to go, but we also feel that as the market responds by voting with dollars/pesos/ yen/euros, etc., the development speed will become exponential in nature. It is also our opinion that cloud computing has the potential to make nearly as big an impact as the Web browser.

Clouds Flight Path for Chapter 6

- *Market positioning: Where are the cloud vendors positioning themselves, and how is the market shaking out?* Amazon is leading the pack, with virtualized servers (EC2) becoming their bread-and-butter service. However, Google's non-operating-system-specific offering feels much closer to fulfilling the dream of ubiquitous cloud computing. What's a bit frustrating is that clouds are the proverbial moving target, and it's going to take quite a bit of introspective thinking to decide among Amazon Web Services, Google Apps Engine, Microsoft Cloud Services, or some of the smaller providers. It's very clear that it's going to take actually trying out the various solutions, not just taking the salesperson's word.

- *Amazon Web Services.* With Simple Storage Services and Elastic Computing Cloud, Amazon's Web services are the current power house in cloud computing. Amazon's offerings are many and varied, and this market leader will be hard to catch. Amazon is certainly the "big dog" right now, but it's unclear whether a solution so closely tied to virtualization will be the long-term answer. Today, however, it's a pretty good way to extend your IT services without breaking the bank.

- *SimpleDB.* Based on SQL as a virtualized service, this simplified system is designed to make SQL "lite" available as a tightly integrated Web services offering. Sometimes you just need to store simple stuff and don't even want to consider setting up a database management system.

- *Amazon Simple Queue Service.* Secure and guaranteed message delivery between Web services that could very well be the key piece to federation becoming a reality. After all, who says you can only talk to your own servers? Why not pass those transaction notes across the hall to your business partners?

- *Google.* Getting closer to the idea behind true clouds, this Python- or Java-based system abstracts from the underlying hardware and may be the closest to our "ideal" of true cloud computing. Our ideal sounds like an app engine that you can toss anything into, and Google's support resources are certainly luring developers into the fold, especially considering just how tightly their cloud is tied to their mobile platform, Android.

- *Appnexus.* The data center-for-rent system where short-term resources can be found is the story of how an ISP can still compete in a market dominated by Google and Amazon.
- *GoGrid.* A smaller regional cloud service bureau offering virtualization in addition to virtualized Web and application servers.
- *The Cloudy Edge.* Some unconventional technology bringing the cloud edge into the home and small office. We looked at how using the cloud as the back end for mobile apps is a natural, and how the PogoPlug has extended cloud storage from the edge outward. If anything, these unconventional solutions really only punctuate just how much and how quickly the cloud frontier is changing.

Chapter 7

Cloud Issues

If we continue to develop our technology without wisdom or prudence, our servant may prove to be our executioner.

— General Omar N. Bradley

In This Chapter

If you're going to depend on the cloud for all or part of your business applications, you'll need to make sure that the functionality you depend on will be there when you need it. In this chapter, we'll look at some of the technology issues to be considered in determining just how dependable a cloud-delivered application can be, and some of the management and contractual issues that can be used to guarantee the necessary level of reliability. Key concepts are delivered through interviews with and observations by IT professionals who have been working "in the trenches" to make applications perform reliably for their own organizations.

When any rapidly developing technology hits the market, vendors set up "war camps" to battle for their view of the world. Shiny ad campaigns try to get you to overlook imperfections and draw your attention instead to shiny bells, whistles, geegaws, and widgets. The reality is that, as with any business action, there needs to be a thought process on just how this technology will affect the bottom line. We've already discussed several critical issues to be considered during planning for deployment of cloud applications, but we've yet to take up the issues of stability and reliability.

These issues are part of the larger topic of business continuity, and far too many managers have shown themselves unwilling to take up business continuity questions regarding any aspect of their organization. There are those who point out that cloud-delivered applications can contribute to robust business stability and reliability, and so they can, but the contribution doesn't come without serious planning and work to ensure performance.

The first steps of planning involve questions that touch on many of the basic points of both cloud computing and general business IT. They include:

- How much stability do you need? What is the largest gap in application or service availability you can afford to experience? We look at the issues you need to use when asking these questions. Are you willing to go to court to enforce a service-level agreement (SLA), or should you back off and just make it easier to walk away? Asking for "five 9's" of reliability may just not be a reasonable thing to ask for, especially for young applications.
- How much stability are you willing to pay for? In other words, are you willing to pay for all the stability you need? Should you even be considering a cloud if your app is still under development?
- Are your partners the weakest link? Where in the chain of application delivery does the weakest link lie? Did you buy a Ferrari and then put it on retread tires? You need to be even-handed throughout your entire chain, not just at the cloud provider.
- Has your provider been around a while, or are you adding additional risk by going with the new kid on the block? Where is your optimal balance point between bleeding-edge technology and institutional longevity and stability? Remember that those services may be less expensive for a reason; and you need to take an introspective look at your goals to see a balance.
- Have you thought about what might happen if the house of cards falls down? Business continuity planning includes worst-case scenario exercises: If the cloud application provider simply goes away, how will you deal with the loss? Who owns the data, and can you even get to your system image if the provider collapses? What does

the standard agreement provide for, and do you need to put in a few specific riders?

- Are SLAs worth the paper they're printed on? How serious are the enforcement mechanisms, and are those mechanisms meaningful to your business? We offer the opinion of a technology-oriented lawyer, but also the opinions of service providers and application developers. The results are a collection of differing opinions that all have great points to think about. As we like to say, mileage may vary, and what you put into an SLA needs to reflect your overall business plan.

- What are the issues for cloud security? Who owns the responsibility for security at each stage of the application's delivery? Are there gaps in security responsibility? How prepared is your cloud provider, and do you need to consider adding addendums on security to your service agreement?

Stability

As we've seen in earlier chapters, the decision to move from a self-hosted IT infrastructure to a cloud or cloudlike service is all about return on investment. No matter how good the deal is, if the service isn't stable, it's not worth a cent if my business is depending on it. So we're very happy to see folks like Amazon committing to 99.95% uptime instead of the bogus five 9's of reliability that marketing folks spew without thinking. Even three 9's of reliability is a pretty big deal, and with the two outages that Amazon had in 2008, we're not quite sure they even made the 99.95% they claim.

However, Amazon's bad luck in 2008 aside, anyone who wants to set up housekeeping in the clouds should plan on spending a lot of investment capital on designing stability into both the infrastructure and the fiscal house. What sort of questions should be asked as part of the process of including that stability in the design? Some of our favorite due-diligence questions are these:

- How many Internet feeds do you have? Do they come into your data centers through different cable paths? After all, the "backhoe fade" that results when the road crew cuts through the fiber bundle is going to take a whole lot of time to fix. Better that only one pathway at a time can be put into harm's way, with others left to maintain a connection to the Internet.

- What kind of backup power do you have? If you use generators, what kind of fuel powers them, and how much fuel do those generators have? Are the generators tested and serviced at least once a month?
- Where is your DNS hosted? Is DNS available only on-site or also upstream someplace at a key point in the Internet?
- Are the computers on your network in real address space or addressed through network address translation (NAT)?
- Where is the network demarcation point? Is it a switch in an on-site rack, or does the ISP provide data connections all the way up to your servers?
- Is there an out-of-band network for things such as service processors, console ports, etc.? If so, how is access to it provided?
- Does the service provider supply remote access technology such as secure console servers, IP KVMs, and service processor aggregation?
- What kind of security is in place? Is there some kind of protection against an intruder just walking in and flipping the power switch? We're hoping the card keys require some sort of challenge, such as a PIN or biometrics. Stolen keys or copied keycards are just too easy to get.
- Is the security force on-site or across town?
- Is there some sort of change-management system in place to avoid accidentally powering down production machines instead of a machine slated for maintenance?
- Are there both machine and network specialists in the network operations center 24/7/365? How are they staffed?
- If I use the provider's hardware, are spare parts stocks or spare systems kept on the premises?

This is, of course, not an exhaustive list of every question you will want to ask, because each organization will have a unique set of concerns that a potential partner should address. The key is to look at your concerns and ask very detailed questions about them. Never assume that a particular issue is so basic or trivial that it is always present as you need it to be. Always ask the "stupid questions"—the answers are no less critical than those in response to more strategic queries.

Partner Quality

There's a cliché bumper sticker that reads (in paraphrased form): "Stuff Happens." It's certainly true, and a complex cloud computing environment comes complete with scores of places where stuff can happen. No rational person can think that the stuff of everyday life can be prevented from happening, so the issue isn't whether a cloud computing provider can keep the evil stuff away, but rather what it's doing to minimize the bad stuff, and how it'll respond if it happens.

Not even a company as large as Amazon can control all the pieces of the cloud computing infrastructure from the server back to the clients. So much depends on partners that anyone getting ready to bet the company on a cloud should probably ask questions not only of the provider but also about the relationships the provider has with its partners. For smaller or newer cloud service providers, it would not be unreasonable to ask some of the same questions we've suggested as the heart of your internal due-diligence process. Larger, more established providers may deserve a modified set of questions, but when it comes to business-critical services there is no provider, and no function, that is either so large or so trivial that it should escape close scrutiny. At the very least, you want to make sure the provider will be able to cope reliably with the demands of your business's normal circumstances.

It's when you get outside the "normal circumstances" that the relationships your provider has with its upstream ISPs really make a difference. It doesn't take anything nearly as earth-shattering as the "Slammer" worm and the havoc it created to reveal just how well your provider's engineers work with their ISP partners. Much more limited challenges, such as a particularly effective advertising spot and its resulting traffic surge, can pose significant bandwidth challenges to your provider. The real question concerns how fast the provider can work with its upstream counterparts to characterize and set up access control lists (ACLs) to block attacks and limit bandwidth-filling traffic as far upstream as possible. The goal is to find where an attack or other traffic surge is coming from, and filter it out or limit its negative effects as far away from your server as possible.

Another time when relationships pay dividends is when inadvertent changes in the Internet routing for a domain suddenly take place. In its architecture, the Internet resembles a road atlas, in which cities are interconnected not only by superhighways but also by little country roads. Traffic flows back and forth, but sometimes a road is closed or congested for some reason and traffic has to take an alternative path. The problem is that some applications are very timing-sensitive and that detour to a country road isn't going to cut it: the application will start failing. It's under these circumstances that your cloud provider's engineers need to be on friendly terms with their partners to ask gently for help balancing changes to the routing tables in order to even out the pathways.

A similar dance happens when inadvertent changes somehow reroute all your traffic over a country road instead of the superhighway you've been paying for. How could something like this happen? It can easily occur when changes are made to any of the major protocols of the Internet. One such protocol is Border Gateway Protocol (BGP), the protocol that sits at the core of the methods used by routers to send data properly from one system to another across the Internet. One of the pieces of BGP is the peering table, a list of IP address domains and ranges that helps routers know the fastest way to send data between networks that are similar to one another or that are in close physical proximity. These tables change as new computers are introduced to the Internet or companies make changes to their networks.

In general, a network engineer must make the changes to keep the packets flowing in the most efficient manner possible. As an example of just what sort of trouble can result if the programming goes awry, someone made a mistake in the BGP peering tables in the city of Honolulu. When a particular FTP session was initiated between computers at a university and an engineering consulting firm in Honolulu, things got complicated. Instead of crossing from the .edu world to the .com in network segments located entirely within Honolulu, this particular FTP session was routed all the way to Chicago before it crossed over from the Internet to the commodity world. Thousands of miles of data transit and all that effort were required just to download a file from a business literally 1 mile away. It slowed the FTP session, but FTP is a resilient protocol and the transfer could take place. If the connection had involved more time-sensitive applications, such as VoIP or video replay, the difference in the distances involved would likely have had much different consequences.

Longevity

So you've been working through your due-diligence questions and everything is looking good for a cloud computing deployment with a particular cloud provider. There's yet another set of questions to be asked, and this one can be uncomfortable. This set of questions revolves around the quality of the cloud provider—not from a technology service point of view, but from the standpoint of the business plan. Simply put, how long can you depend on your supplier to stay in business?

This question is far more important than the question of how long your office paper supplier will be in business. If the paper supplier shuts down, it doesn't come to your office and take all your printed records away. A cloud failure, on the other hand, can be disastrous. The fear of a cloud failure isn't a simple mental exercise, either. Many professional photographers were affected when cloud storage vendor PictureBug suddenly closed its doors in October 2007. Those photographers who had not kept on-site backups of their photos were faced with the loss of critical data and very little recourse for recovery.

That leads to one of the most important questions to be asked: Can I get my server images and apps back if the provider closes its doors? What happens to my backup copies? Can I only do a complete image restore, or can I get individual files back? What recourse would your company have if the provider announces that it is going out of business? All these have to do with judging whether your provider is going to stick around and what you might want to consider putting into your contract.

Of course, the question of precisely how one figures out the future economic viability of your potential cloud provider is not necessarily easy to answer. Sometimes, annual reports on provider performance are available, but most times they're not, especially if the provider is a private company. You could fall back on looking at the essential foundation of the company as an indicator. In an industry as new as cloud computing, many of the "safest" companies fall into one of two camps: Either they're a cash-rich, large player like Amazon; or they're backed, managed, or directed by people with a great deal of experience in related industries. It is, to some extent, that cash backing and experience that makes it possible for the cloud provider to become a cost-effective provider of services to your company.

Many people tend to think of a cloud as an *über*-data center that has wrapped the typical data center trappings in layers of automation, security, and contractual agreements. Remember that you could probably build something very similar in function to what Amazon is providing to your company, *if* you were willing to spend the bucks. The hoary old adage, "There's no such thing as a free lunch," applies to cloud computing as much as to everything else. One of the trade-offs that you make when you outsource computing functions to the extent implied by cloud computing is to assume risk. So examine just how much risk you're willing to take on when looking for a cloud provider. The little guys are probably going to be much more willing to wheel and deal, but with their flexibility also comes the fact that they probably don't have a gazillion bucks in the bank to keep them running through a deep economic depression. Companies need to take this into account and negotiate contracts (with proper enforcement methods) accordingly.

It's the layers of abstraction and automation that are the largest intellectual property investment for most cloud providers, and it's that investment that will keep a provider afloat for the long term. What we're already starting to see is tiny ISPs scrambling to play catch-up as the world migrates to a hosted environment. When you look for a provider, you shouldn't be afraid to ask the hard questions right up front.

If the potential cloud provider has made the right investments in planning, then those answers should be readily available. If each question requires a call to the "back-room guy or girl," then perhaps you might want to consider if the pricing is worth the risk. We've seen way too many small ISPs started out a single super-talented geek, only to die a horrible bankruptcy when that single point of failure has an accident. How the provider staffs up should be a big part of your risk calculation.

No provider can afford to staff all three shifts with "router gods," and it is the automation created by those super-talented folks that allows a provider to leverage the expertise of the alpha geeks. The depth and quality of those scripts and templates are like an iceberg: The user gets to see only a small fraction of the total, while the bulk of the development effort goes into support products that allow the provider to use key features as "cookie-cutter" code. The ability to reuse code as a template for continued improvement is key to the cloud provider's key motivation: to stay profitable.

In the world of hosting, we tend to look for configuration templates as a way to guess at the provider's overall automation investment. For instance, in the case of a Plone (a popular content management system) provider, you can look at just how many "skins" and "plug ins" are already available. You should also to look at how easy it is to get a mysql/MS-SQL database created for your application's use. Investment levels tend to be tightly related to the quality and variety of configuration options. If every request becomes engineering time, then there's a high probability that this provider may not last over the long run. Templates mean development, testing, and documentation, and they also mean that the provider is trying to resell that investment as many times as possible. "100% custom solutions" is a very quick way to go broke in the world of cloud computing.

Scripts and templates combined with documentation represent the intellectual property value of the provider, and what you should see in any good one is a full set of operations guides with all kinds of different contingencies allowed for. This way the third shift is just as good as the others, and at no time are you more than a pager call away from someone to un-wedge you from a nasty situation.

Business Continuity

Regardless of the history of your provider, sometimes there are unforeseen instances that will drop even the best-prepared service provider off the air. The events of September 11, 2001, took out a huge swath of some of the biggest telecommunications centers in the United States; to a lesser extent, the 1994 Northridge, California, earthquake also silenced a large portion of the U.S. Internet. The lesson we've learned is that we can't always afford to put all our eggs into a single basket. This lesson is why Amazon, Microsoft, and others have put their data centers all over the world.

Microsoft has gone a step further in purposely choosing "greener" locations, where carbon-friendly power sources exist and air temperatures are low enough to give them as many "free cooling days" as possible. ("Free cooling" refers to days on which the outside air temperature is low enough that heat transfer can occur in building air conditioners without running the compressors and using additional electricity.) Being "green" goes a long way toward keeping a cloud provider's recurring costs in the realm of reality, as well as being politically correct.

Service-Level Agreements

With functionality, reliability, longevity, and business continuity considered and dealt with, it's now time to look at the sort of agreement that will bind the cloud provider to particular levels of service and functionality. After you've asked your questions and researched the stability of your provider, the service-level agreement is the contract that determines just what each side expects of each other. The SLA between the customer and the provider is thus the key document defining the relationship, and a properly drafted SLA can ensure that cloud computing carries as few risks, and as many benefits, as possible.

Since every SLA is a contract, we asked the IT professionals on the Interop Past-NOC mailing list what they expected in a service-level agreement. (The Interop trade show features a large, advanced-technology network that is built by volunteer engineers from just about every major network equipment manufacturer from the United States and a wide variety of other countries. Past-NOC is an restricted, invitation-only listserver for individuals who have served on the NOC team in the past.) Considering how often this group has been involved with shaping the global Internet, we thought it appropriate to ask them what they would expect a cloud service agreement to look like. Here are some of the answers we received.

Differing Opinions

Erik Cummings is past InteropNET head engineer and previously of Pathworks. Erik emphasized that he's already been through the process of moving to Amazon's cloud services and noted:

> Having recently designed a platform SaaS application—and having gone and said "cloud computing is AWESOME and we'll need to do it soon, but not now!"—the biggest concern in SLA terms I have is ALL ABOUT troubleshooting.
>
> For mature applications and systems where I understand and am familiar with the performance profile and bottlenecks, then SLA's and Cloud computing sounds good—in a fledgling, new, unknown application—well—I need to be able to tune and manage and report on too many parts of the system—cloud computing hides too many details for me to effectively build and develop a growing solution. . . .

Karl Auerbach describes himself this way: "By-the-way, I'm one of the inventors of IP/TV™ in the mid 1990's—I was part of a good (but small) team. Also my position in ICANN was unique because I was the North American elected board member." A long time member of the Interop team, Karl had these comments:

Of course it should be negotiable—and you can leave the door open for period review and adjustment (by mutual agreement, of course.) That's why it is important go get your own legal counsel involved from the outset—they know, or should know, how to create agreements with the desired degree of rigidity and flexibility.

When writing contracts it's often a good idea to try to think of everything that could possibly go wrong, and what to do about it, and what to do about it if the other side can't, or won't do what it needs to do. And then assume that you've covered only a part of all the bad things that can happen.

Remember, the other guy might look at the contract as the price he needs to pay to walk away and leaving you hanging—The legal process generally tries to turn contract failures into money payments, so if you absolutely need something done no matter what the cost, you need to build in contractual mechanisms that turn into money—for example, failures of the other guy to react should be measured in some sort of liquidated damages per unit of time of the failure. (Those liquidated damages need to have some ties to reality—terms like a billion $ per hour will probably not fly should push come to shove. The legal system tends to frown deeply on contract provisions that are clearly punitive and not reflective of some actually incurred harm.)

When specifying performance metrics, i.e. the service level, be as quantitative and object as you can—qualitative and subjective measures are an invitation to dispute. So set up real metrics that both sides can see and use—and it's useful to go through some tests to make sure that both sides see the same numbers. And make sure that those numbers are recorded as part of your and their routine practice and not only when things go awry.

And when I say quantitative I mean that you specify the data sources and formulas. For example, what does 99.999% uptime mean? That you can ping a box and that over a period of 7 days (measured by a GMT time base) that every ping you send (you need to specify the sending pattern) you get exactly one proper response, except for one? Or does that 99.999% mean something at a higher level than mere pings—for example, if you are offering database services do you mean that 99.999% of the SQL queries are properly handled within a time window of X milliseconds for each query?

Even a service outage of the first full year still meets a 99.999% threshold if the service company can claim that for the next 99,999 years that they will be perfect.

But don't use the contract only as an after-the-fact weapon should things go wrong. Rather build into the contract some specific procedures to be followed at the first signs of trouble—it's better to quickly solve a problem than to fight over the wreckage later. And it's always useful to occasionally exercise those procedures—like give a call to the other guy's NOC on occasion to make sure that the phone number still works. If you have a really big dependency, go visit every now and then so that you know some faces, and they know yours; that'll make it a lot easier to work through an ongoing problem without anyone flying off the handle and making things worse.

And always have a Plan B that you can use if the other guy simply vanishes and leaves you with no service, with the data on their boxes unavailable to you, and nobody to talk to, to get anything done.

And remember, in these days of tough financial times the other guy might be forced to do things that do not make you happy—so make sure that the ownership of data and code is clearly specified: you hardly want your data to be tied up inside some bankruptcy proceeding with some creditor of the service company claiming that they own your data.

And be sure of the physical jurisdictions involved. I was surprised with Amazon S3 when I retrieved some files and discovered that they were coming back to me from Italy!

There's other stuff as well—for example, if you are doing anything involving trade secrets you need to do the right thing to protect your interests. A large local university backed away from some Google based services because they realized that they could lose their patent rights because they were arguably disclosing unfiled ideas to a third party, Google. And if you have medical data or stuff that has privacy import, you gotta make the service company responsible in accord with whatever those particular laws say.

Writing a good SLA takes both tech smarts and legal smarts—it's not the kind of thing that can be written by techies and thrown over the wall to the legal group.

Jeff Young is a long-time member of the Interop NOC team, a senior analyst for the Burton Group who has had a large amount of experience with Internet service providers. His comments are a bit different:

> The normal SLA's service providers offer as part and parcel to regular service isn't worth it, no.
>
> If you want something better, it's a question of what you want to pay for it. If I go to one of the big guys with the intent to engineer a service that delivers five 9's, I might be able to get the provider to give me a real, negotiated SLA. But now I'm into him for engineering services and some type of engineered reliability (often redundancy).
>
> I've spoken to clients who have clauses for "damages" in their SLA's. They tell me that "damages" go beyond a refund for monthly service and are actually in proportion to the money they would lose during an outage. I've only ever personally been on the other side, the provider side, so my direct experience is limited. I tend to doubt that any provider could/would make such claims but the customer is always right.
>
> The more difficult question is, how can I prove a provider is at fault for an outage? Better to spend the time engineering a resilient service yourself.

Joel M. Snyder is a senior partner with consulting firm Opus One in Tucson, Arizona, and a member of the Network World Lab Alliance. Joel is also a long-time member of the Interop NOC team and has been heavily involved with the Interop Labs (iLabs) NAC demonstration team. His spin on SLAs is a bit different:

> SLAs are un-negotiable because the provider doesn't have the time, energy, or interest in negotiating them. If you think about it from a provider point of view (and I've been on both sides of

the fence, as a provider, and as a consumer of providers), they have a service that they engineer and monitor and that's about it. You can request all sorts of performance guarantees, but they won't be doing anything differently from your point of view than for any other customer (unless you actually buy a different service, like multi-home fiber/SHARP). In other words, if you say "I want 99.99 uptime" and the default they sell is 99.97, then it's not like they're going to do anything different for you—what would they do differently?

At the same time, measuring SLA compliance is difficult if not impossible. Are we talking uptime? Well, then what are all the components in the path? If the loop provider cuts the loop, does that break the SLA? As you get out of simplistic services such as point-to-point copper, the SLA gets very complicated to measure and define. When you're talking about application availability over the Internet, it's essentially impossible to come up with a meaningful definition (with emphasis on "meaningful").

And, let's suppose you negotiate an SLA and the provider doesn't meet it. So what? How does this help your business? It's your responsibility to engineer for a reliable service that meets your needs, and you can't simply dump that on someone else and assume that it will magically solve the problem.

Now, SLAs internal to a company, department-to-department, I have seen work pretty well. In that case, they actually lay out expectations and help both sides understand what is expected. This is clearly true in situations where the service being provided is not one that naturally is up 24x7; things like Email hosting are a good example, where we all know that some maintenance is required, but we need to agree ahead of time when and how much is allowed.

I'd close by noting that Opus One, my company, has paid, literally, millions of dollars to service providers; we have collected hundreds of dollars in SLA penalties. After 20+ years buying these services, I can't imagine how the SLA would have changed our experience with anyone. That time is better spent selecting the right service provider, doing due-diligence, and making sure that you and they understand what you need—rather than trying to stick it in a document which is only of interest to the legal department.

Agreeing on the Service of Clouds

The SLA negotiation process is where you absolutely *must* take a step back and look at just what constitutes an important service to you. We would like to suggest making a two-column list. First, list the features that you *must* have available in order to continue doing business. Second, list the features that make your life easier, but that you could do without for a little while. This second list is what you can "afford" to sacrifice in favor of business continuity.

It's good to remember what Erik Cummings had to say about the maturity of the application that you want to move into the clouds. Immature applications need quite a bit more attention than more stable code, and this remains true even after you've prototyped the application in your offices on a local server. It's also important to note that prototyping on local servers doesn't mean you won't need cloud-based testing facilities as you deploy.

The two columns of the list will be unique to each organization, but we'd like to suggest a first item for every organization. The absolutely most important item on your list needs to be common sense. Keep asking yourself whether the risk of feature X is worth taking. The risk factor definitely has a relationship to the cost of these services, and should also be part of the decision-making process on whether cloud computing (or any outsourcing, for that matter) should even be considered. Just because clouds are the "new thing" doesn't mean they're a perfect fit for your organization. A good analogy is when a spouse gets all excited about a huge sale at his favorite store: "Remember, honey, it's not a sale if you don't need it."

At the current level of cloud computing, few organizations will be able to move every part of their infrastructure to the cloud, so let's concentrate on virtualized servers since they're a common theme of many services. Neal Allen of Fluke Networks has literally written the book (The *Network Maintenance Troubleshooting Guide* [Addison-Wesley Professional, 2009]) on network troubleshooting, and he points out:

> Virtual servers in blade server chassis are a royal pain for monitoring and troubleshooting.
>
> Improvements in the VMware code permit the virtual switch to send NetFlow or IPFIX summaries for monitoring, which

helps. However if you actually need to look at some packets (IDS, billing, etc.) then you have to ensure that a tiered server speaks to servers in other blade server chassis. Otherwise you have a hard time causing the packets to appear somewhere convenient for monitoring. Yes, the built-in switch in the blade server chassis permits a span port, but this is often already in use for regular traffic. And it does not help at all if you are seeking inter-server traffic for two VMs on the same blade.

For example, in a simple three-tiered architecture you could put the App server on a different blade chassis, so communications between the other tiers pops out where you can get to it. It can get really tricky when there is direct communication between multiple tiers.

Client → Web server → App server → DB server

We are seeing more and more situations where the customer has loaded more than one tier on a single blade, and the rest of the application on adjacent blades. When something goes wrong they practically have to re-architect the installation in order to gain access to inter-server traffic.

So, while Neal Allen points out network troubleshooting issues, Joel Snyder of Opus1 and Network World brings up some issues that feel more like human engineering and behavioral issues:

I think it depends on the size of the network and how complicated things were before.

In our "data center," we have multiple racks and a pile of VLANs. Before virtualization, we would jack a device into a switch, and then go to the switch and tell it which VLAN that device was on. The switches are top-of-rack and connected up using fairly standard core-and-edge technology.

With VMware, we pump multiple ports into each VMware server (seven, one for management, two for SAN, two for vMotion, and two for data traffic) and just treat the VMware server as the "vlan switch" that the top-of-rack switch was in the past.

If we needed more bandwidth, then we'd simply bank up multiple ports, so bandwidth and funny stuff like proprietary network fabrics don't seem to apply at least in the mid-size case.

As Neal noted, when you need to look at the inter-server traffic, it's not as easy as it used to be ("Hey, can you drop a hub into that link so we can sniff traffic" or monitoring ports), but we really didn't/don't do a lot of that. So while the tools are different than they were, we didn't commonly use network-layer tools for application-layer issues.

In other words, from our point of view, it's really not all that different.

Now, there is a HUGE ENORMOUS problem with VMware and what we did, but that's a people problem. The issue is that the switching and host management are now mooshed (that's a technical term) together. In other words, in the old days, the network side of the house handled per-host traffic and the host simply was told "here's an IP; jack in."

Now, what's happening is that the VLAN assignment is a function of the VMware administrator, and not the network administrator. So all of the typical management functions that you might do at the network layer have suddenly disappeared and moved over from the "network guy" to the "VMware guy." That is a BIG deal and, to my mind, much more of a problem than any hypothetical "where is the bandwidth coming from" question.

In fact, my observation is that folks who haven't actually done this are all focused on the wrong issues. I read this long story from a guy who was all weirded out about protecting his VMware hosts, but what it came down to was that he had made stupid decisions about network separation and was going to pull his hair out forever trying to patch someone else's "appliance" operating system when he should have simply made proper architectural choices in the first place.

Most of the people complaining about VMware performance and/or security seem to be doing so from a position of stupidity rather than experience. I guess they're too busy blogging to actually know what they're doing.

Anyway, that's the real issue, as I see it: not the inaccessibility of network traffic (which is true, just not something we care about for application-layer design/debugging), but the shift in responsibility for the networking from trained networking guys to "someone we sent to the VMware class" (if that).

You can also read a lot more about my thoughts on the security issues in this white paper that I wrote in the Fall (and eventually got paid by Juniper to stick their name on, thanks Juniper!)

(*Source:* Joel Snyder, "Virtual Machines, Networking Security and the Data Center: Six Key Issues and Remediation Strategies," www.opus1.com/www/whitepapers/virtualization.pdf.)

Solving Problems

From the time we started writing this book, a great number of changes have occurred in cloud/virtualization technology. Among the biggest have been in the world of network analysis, with new products from Network Instruments and NetScout directly targeting the "hidden" network that is the virtual switch. Network Instruments takes the approach of a very lightweight software tap that takes advantage of the promiscuous mode configuration for the VMWare vSwitch to export the switch data out a physical network interface to an analysis tool. In simple terms, this means that the VMWare vSwitch is capable of entering a mode in which it will receive and accept every packet transported on the network, not just those packets addressed specifically to that network port. Most standard computer/operating system configurations aren't in promiscuous mode because of the dramatically increased processing load that sorting through all the "wrong" packets imposes on the system. For many network security and maintenance tasks, though, it's a critical capability. The philosophy is that an external analysis device is less likely to change the environment than one that coexists with an existing server, because it doesn't have to share the resources it needs to accomplish its job.

NetScout's approach is to put a lightweight network probe into the virtual switch to provide analysis in the virtual environment, only exporting what is necessary for the task. Regardless of whether you put the analysis in the virtual environment or not, the point is that analysis tools are becoming available for the virtual environment. We see this as only the tip of the iceberg, with what we're sure will be a flood of analysis products targeted at the virtualized environment and eventually the cloud. Already, external tools from Fluke Networks and internal switch tools from Cisco have come onto the market, and more are certainly on the way.

Why are the tools important? They're important because they offer additional ways to define performance and monitor the achievement of specific performance levels. Many SLAs define performance in only the most obvious terms, never looking at the factors within the network that contribute to overall performance levels. The availability of additional improved monitoring and analysis tools for virtual networks and cloud computing deployments gives customers options for defining levels of performance that will trigger corrective action before critical business applications are affected.

In the current state of network analysis, a large number of service-level agreements deal only with uptime, often defined as the performance of a specific network protocol, routing, DNS, etc. What all the experts we've interviewed seem to agree on is that access or capability for troubleshooting must not be neglected. Going back to Erik Cummings's statement on the maturity of your application, we propose that the newer your application(s), the more you need to concentrate on a troubleshooting clause in your SLA, to lock in certain minimal obligations of the cloud vendor to analyze and remediate within specific time windows, and to communicate specific details back to the customer's network engineering team.

It should also be noted that nothing in this world is free, and asking for anything beyond a provider's normal SLA is going to cost you money. This is where your needs-versus-wants list will come in handy. Is feature X really worth an extra xx% tacked onto the contract? Only you can decide.

What It Takes to Reach an Agreement

On some level, you already know the answer to the question of what, precisely, it takes to reach a service-level agreement. It's all going to boil down to money. If you have lots of it and are getting ready to roll out a do-all, end-all app that's going to change the world, then you'd better also make sure you have plenty of bucks for lawyers. If you're much smaller and the standard service contract sounds good to you, then maybe all you need to do is clarify who owns what and make sure you understand what your rights are if the provider comes crashing down around you. Can you grab your apps and run? Or are you going to be stuck in the bankruptcy litigation? If you need a refresher on why this is important, refer back to Karl Auerbach's comments.

Remember that our theory is that IT in this case makes up the bulk of your public-facing company persona. We assume that the loss of this persona will translate to lost business. However, you also need to be reasonable as to how much business you may really lose in an outage. If the outage is short, will your customers just come back a bit later? Will they go away to a competitor if they face even a five-minute delay in getting to your website? Think business planning; make sure that you really need to negotiate a more comprehensive agreement in the first place. Maybe it would be more cost-effective just to make sure there is a mechanism by which you can walk away cleanly if something goes badly wrong.

Quality of Service

Level of service and quality of service are intimately related, but they are not precisely the same thing, and they tend not to be measured in exactly the same way. Service level is the availability of a given service; quality of service is a measure of the user experience while the service is available. We're accustomed to thinking of quality of service in relation to VoIP and video applications, but quality can be an issue with just about any application that has a human user working at one end of the process. Defining service quality varies with each organization, but the process has some similarities in every company that needs to get the job done.

First comes the definition: What is the service? Remember the partner effect we discussed earlier in this chapter? If the metro area network provider that feeds the facility housing your application or data goes dark and they're forced to swap over to the backup provider (the provider that's still functional, but at a lower speed than the primary link), is this an outage? Quality of service isn't a light switch that you turn on or off; it means identifying the services that are important to you and the conditions you are realistically willing to operate under. You can't demand all the cloud provider's bandwidth and time—in that case, you might as well run your own data center.

Harking back to the comments by Erik Cummings, first you have to know the performance expectations of your application. A well-understood application can be profiled, and it's likely that some sort of metrics have been developed for measuring how well the app is performing. It's important, however, that you understand what any metrics you choose to use are really measuring. You need to make sure that the metric is measuring something that the provider can affect. There are several parts to this last statement, and it's worth taking a moment to understand all of them.

It's relatively easy to develop a tool to look at total transaction time. In the most basic case, an employee with a stopwatch can get this job done. The stopwatch-wielding employee cannot, however, tell you how the individual pieces of the application chain are contributing to overall performance. To be most useful, the metrics you choose and the analytical tools you employee should help you understand how each of the various servers, application components, and data transport pieces is contributing to the total application performance picture.

Once you understand how the overall application service level is achieved, you can begin to look at whether given components are under the control of your cloud provider. If your application slows down because you've cheaped-out by putting your database server onto a shared blade instead of a dedicated one, that decision was yours, not the provider's. Expecting a cloud provider to meet a particular service quality level in the applications and components they provide is quite reasonable. Expecting them to magically make up for your questionable deployment decisions is not. So do some introspective examinations of how the business is done with your application and then confirm that the quantitative expectations you're asking of the provider are reasonable.

Quality in the Cloud

Because cloud computing today is tightly tied to virtualization, you need to look very closely at how you deploy your server images and their associated communications paths. A key concept that is quickly forgotten when architecting your cloud is troubleshooting. We had some direct experience with this at Interop with the engineering team from Fluke Networks. In this case we gleefully adopted VMWare for all the show services and quickly found that we had made some bad decisions requiring some last-minute changes. Here are some key issues we ran into:

- Where and how can you insert a tap between key pieces of your server infrastructure?
- If you're using a virtual network between servers, does your virtualized NIC (Network Interface Card) even support promiscuous

mode to allow you to examine the data flows? (Note: At the time of writing, only VMware supports this; Windows 2008 Hypervisor is still playing catch-up on this ability.)

- Did you put key components onto different virtual machines all on the same physical blade? If so, you probably can't tap that at all beyond what you can get out via the Windows WMI interface.
- What else is using this data path? Are key transactions going to get lost in heavy traffic?
- Did you take into account the fact that things like VMotion and iSCSI access suck up tons of bandwidth? Did you plan for this?

One of the keys to the troubleshooting process is finding a way to look at the communications paths when key processes can't talk to each other. If, for instance, your Web application is talking to an SQL server, each on its own piece of hardware, and the two aren't handshaking correctly, can you even get a tap between them? Drilling down on this issue, you might ask yourself how you could determine whether your app is slow because of SQL server response or whether you have an out-of-control application that is wasting cycles.

Unfortunately, this isn't like the old days, when you could just slap a hub between the servers and look at the data stream. It should also be noted that application performance monitors need to be able to see the conversations between processes (rather than just between physical servers or large applications), and while the Windows Management Interface (WMI) provides a great deal of information, most systems also require that they get process timing information off the packet stream. Of course, this assumes that you both know how to use and need this level of troubleshooting. As Joel Snyder asked earlier, do you need network-level troubleshooting tools, or will aggregated statistics further up the ISO stack work?

The point we're trying to make is that great care needs to be taken when architecting your cloud. We're especially fond of the comments made by Erik Cummings about the maturity of your applications. Something brand new is going to need troubleshooting as you stumble across "gotchas" in the architecture. Keeping your options open for troubleshooting is an absolute requirement as you get ready to move your apps from the in-house sandbox to the cloud, and the requirement gains urgency with the relative newness of the application or applications involved.

Security in the Cloud

In the same way that moving applications and data to the cloud doesn't remove the requirement that you consider the performance of the application and protection of the data, a move to the cloud doesn't remove the obligation for you to properly configure and maintain security for your applications and data. Many companies have recognized that fact and responded by refusing to deploy any applications or data to the cloud. For those who decide that the cloud has benefits that are compelling, a significant set of questions must be asked and answered. "Our provider was supposed to take care of that" isn't an answer that a regulatory compliance auditor will accept, and it's not one that should be satisfactory to you either. How, then, do you make sure that a deployment into the cloud is not a descent into security trouble?

How Big Is Your Fence?

The first question is the most basic: Are you going to rely on the security suite that the cloud provides, or are you going to add more of your own? In the early days of the cloud this wasn't really a question that could be asked in a meaningful way, since the products weren't available to draw a unified security fence around an application that extended from a self-hosted application into the cloud and back to clients. Today, the situation is beginning to change, with the introduction of a variety of products that seek to address the problem in different ways. This exact situation might very well be why Astaro is now making its Security Gateway available as a VMWare virtual image (www.astaro.com/our_products/astaro_security_gateway/virtual_appliance). The concept of layering your security and putting a robust applications firewall between the real world and the virtualized network is a pretty big deal.

The ability to VPN (virtual private network) onto that virtual network also means that you've opened up a bunch of remote troubleshooting options, but that same pathway can potentially become a route for attackers. Great care should be taken when developing your firewall rules if you choose this option. We're probably sounding like a broken record by now: It's all about planning and trying to imagine what situations you might encounter.

A favorite imagination tool is to lay out the entire process on paper. While we're fond of flowcharts, the process could be as simple as creating a diagram of your business process. At each step we like using a writer's checklist: who, what, where, when, and how. The questions are not only *how* you do this process, but also *how* someone can do harm to me at this step. Or *what* I need to do here if the process fails. IT is really about automating processes; if you can't do them by hand, then how can you possibly think you can automate them?

Where Is Your Fence?

So far, we've talked about the advantages to be found in choosing a larger or more experienced cloud computing partner. Certain types of security implementations, though, may call for deployment of a mix of customer and cloud provider components that can fall outside the "standard" setup most providers expect. This is a situation in which some of the smaller cloud providers might have an advantage over their larger brethren in allowing for more freedom for customers to negotiate the extra devices that can be deployed into their data center.

In our conversations with Sergey Katsev of Coyote Point, he pointed out that the Amazon EC2 API set is very similar to the VMWare management interface. At the time we're writing this, Amazon's global load balancing is more about where the data appears, and it is uncertain just how the EC2 system will load-balance (or failover) your virtual servers in the event of trouble. This is why Coyote Point is expending resources on providing hooks into both VMWare and Amazon EC2, so that you can have more control over failovers and load balancing of your applications. Here's a scenario that we talked about as a potential near-future scenario:

> Interop currently has a rack of equipment in both the San Jose and Denver Qwest collocation facilities that handle load between shows. During this "off season" the Coyote Point load balancers will redirect service requests based on physical location. However, when the show is running, rules are changed so that the primary feed goes to the NOC in either the Mandalay Bay Convention Center (Las Vegas) or the Jacob Javits Convention Center (New York), depending on which NOC is in operation for a given show. In addition, each show location has a physical

backup NOC in a closet that handles the load if the NOC should become unavailable.

What can be foreseen is that regardless of whether a show is running or not, there exists a possibility of a huge spike that local servers might not be able to handle. Currently the load can be shifted to offsite locations, but should those sites become saturated, it really isn't that difficult to create a set of rules that would bring a virtual machine off the Amazon S3 storage facility into the EC2 cloud that was triggered by the Coyote Point load balancers.

It's our belief that planning for spikes like this is probably going to be the path of least resistance for most organizations to test the cloudy waters. With more and more organizations actually doing IT disaster planning, we imagine that it's only a matter of time before we finally see the market demand for clouds spike.

Regulatory Issues and Accountability

Security in the cloud isn't just a matter of firewalls and closing up ports on your server(s). It's also a matter of accountability, auditing, and plans of action. Government regulations are a big enough concern that Amazon's website has a dedicated section just about HIPAA health care privacy regulations.

One rude awakening for us came during a conversation with an IT group at a major university. Their corporate counsel decided that storing laboratory/experimental data in a cloud constituted publishing and could potentially invalidate their patents/copyrights to that data. While we personally think this was being a bit paranoid, it does show that clouds aren't well understood at this time. They won't be until some real standards (ad hoc or otherwise) start to appear, driving acceptance beyond the experimenters and early adopters.

The reality is that of all the server operating systems currently available, Windows is by far the most aggressive system for regulatory template availability. (While Linux and especially SuSE also have templates, the community-contributed templates aren't always well supported) Server roles in the Windows Server Setup wizard actually sets into place a large number of auditing rules, depending on what role you've chosen.

Just because a server is in the clouds, it doesn't mean you lose operating system capability. So, while EC2 is basically VMWare, the base operating system still has the ability to have auditing templates applied to it. Amazon has just gone a bit further to provide accountability in the virtualized management interface. A key point is that it isn't hard to break into a server if you have physical access to it; and the VMWare/EC2 virtual server management interface is sold as "just like being at the console" and thus needs to have auditing and security efforts just as aggressive as the effort you put into the OS.

Looking back to our comments on making sure you test everything before you toss it into the cloud, auditing is certainly a big component. Let's put this into perspective by talking about a few of the provisioning components in something like VMware.

Just as in the old mainframe days, each virtual machine is operating in a time slice on the physical machine. In order to keep all the virtual machines operating happily, a virtualization system such as VMware is constantly juggling the resources, including memory, overall CPU limits, and the number of cores allocated to each of the many virtual machiness operating on a given piece of hardware. Success in properly allocating all the resources means correctly understanding which applications have higher resource requirements and which are more frugal in their needs. Our experience in the defense arena is that auditing can actually outstrip huge applications such as SQL servers for eating up servers.

Look at it this way: one National Industrial Security Program Operating Manual (NISPOM) requirement is to record every time someone touches anything in the /Windows directory. So a simple log-in can generate nearly a hundred log entries just from this single rule. This amount of I/O combined with all the rest of the audit rules has in some cases cut available computing power by more than half. In addition, because the auditing dramatically slows down the machine, some timing-sensitive applications will start to fail out from under the management system. In reality, most of us really don't pay attention to logs because they're typically pretty small. However, when you're required to log every touch, the growth rate is much greater; and in the case of the NISPOM, you can't overwrite the logs. If you fill up the allocated space, you actually have to halt the machine.

The lesson here is to make sure that all the components, not just the applications, are set up in your sandbox. The other lesson is to find out early which regulatory requirements you'll have to work under and make allowances for auditing overhead in order to fulfill those regulations. Part of this lesson is that you need to start the SOP (standard operations procedures) manual as you do the planning, not in hindsight, since almost every single government regulation has components asking how the infrastructure was built. Lab notebooks have saved our bacon several times and never crash (but can burn).

One way to tell that Brian has been working on a server is if you find a composition notebook (aka a lab notebook) sitting near the server. He tends to use it just like a diary, with entries for time, date, and description, every time he touches the system. Do it in ink, and do it in a notebook that has sewn-in pages, and suddenly you have a notebook that will be acceptable in most courts. While it's perfectly acceptable to hope you never have to take any of your notes into court, it's not acceptable to be unprepared for court, or for a regulatory compliance audit. Prepare for the worst, and hope for the best—good advice in many situations, and particularly when it comes to cloud computing.

Security isn't about technology, nor do regulations such as HIPAA spell out what technology you have to use. Security is about policy and the application of appropriate technologies to achieve the goals in the regulation. Accountability isn't just on the server.

Clouds Flight Path for Chapter 7

- *How much stability do you need?* We talked about striking a balance when you ask for certain levels of stability and how you define your definition of acceptable risk in your service-level agreements. We think the big point is that you only get what you pay for, but do you really need to modify the standard agreement?
- *Are the partners the weakest link?* The provider might be loaded with talent, but if its subcontractors are prone to dropping the ball, they might not be worth the risk. Ask about partners and whether you should even consider this partner combination. You may also need to ask specifically about what's in between the provider and the cloud users, since no one is going to advertise that they use a fly-by-night upstream ISP.
- *Has your provider been around a while, or are you adding additional risk by going with the new kids on the block?* Just because the cloud

provider states it's been in business for decades, it could have been as an ISP and may not be experienced at providing the type of customer service you're demanding. Make sure the provider specifies what kind of business it's been in during those years. After all, premium prices don't always mean premium experience.

- *Have you thought about what might happen if the whole house of cards falls down?* You must think about business continuity and just what plans you have prepared should a disaster happen, regardless of whether the disaster is natural, financial, or criminal. You need to do some thinking about what you need to do in various circumstances. It might not be a bad idea to actually make the provider spell out under what conditions you can just walk away.

- *Are service-level agreements worth the paper they're printed on?* We got a wide variety of people from both sides of the argument to talk about the pro's and con's of SLAs. We think SLAs should be viewed as sharing the risk with the provider. But you need to be reasonable and make sure the compensation is worth the hassle. We polled the Interop NOC team and got the opinions of a lawyer, an icann board member, service providers, SaaS customers, and educators. Although they each had a different focus, they all agree that ignorance isn't bliss and that being realistic about what you ask for is highly recommended.

- *What are the issues for cloud security?* How big is your fence, and where should you put it? Security is about policy, and no amount of technology will change that. Just make sure you figure out what the balance needs to be for your situation. Can you use what's already being provided by the cloud provider, or is it time for you to spend the bucks to slide in yet another VM to run a firewall or proxy?

Chapter 8

Strategies for Clouds

Technology: No Place for Wimps!

— Scott Adams

In This Chapter

As we move from planning security to planning the overall cloud deployment, one thing doesn't change: It's still all about planning around benefit and risk, weighing the risk against the potential gains and planning to maximize the opportunities for benefit while minimizing the potential risks. If you can feel good about the balance, then maybe you're on the right track. If you're certain that you've carefully considered the possibilities and you still feel good about your plans, then that track is looking better and better. We're going to look at some of the cloud computing adoption strategies we've heard various organizations talk about, and we'll take a few educated guesses as to strategies that should work as the technology develops.

We've seen how many different aspects must be taken into consideration when it comes to cloud security planning. What sort of things do you need to keep in mind when it comes to planning for the deployment and operation of your cloud computing installation? Among the initial issues you'll need to think about are

- Remote access (who, what, where, when, and how). If you decided to take an intermediate step of drawing back departmental servers into an in-house data center, how can you persuade your users that they're not losing anything and that remote access really does work. How can the use of colo's get your users ready for virtualization and clouds?
- The views from collocation, virtualization, and the cloud. It's all about stepping stones and how to use carrots and sticks to get users to adopt new technology. We'll talk about using the energy stick/carrot and the paths some folks have already taken.
- Planning for peaks and valleys. Clouds might just be the answer to the old question of how to design for peaks and valleys in demand. How can clouds answer this, and what are some examples that worked?
- Energy issues. We've seen the energy card played in several organizations, and this card is strong enough that utilities all over the world are looking at this particular carrot.
- Experiments and wild hares. It's about *not* believing the salesperson and actually testing the waters. Take it for a test drive, perhaps even do a trial migration to a cloud, but make sure it actually fits.
- Testing the waters with virtualization starter kits. They're free, and a nearly perfect way to get your staff spun up on virtualization and eventually clouds. Here's where a bit of sweat investment up front can really pay dividends later.
- What does your timeline look like? Can you, or should you, wait?

Key Cloud Strategies: First Steps

When any organization is looking at adopting a new technology, success comes from proper planning, and clouds aren't an exception to this oft-ignored rule. The temptation is to do a physical-to-virtual migration just by "jumping into the deep end of the pool." Here the fallacy is that the virtualized server can't be that much different from a physical server. Well, yes and no: It can feel the same, but there are some differences that could potentially bite you. Here are a few that we've stumbled across:

- Licensing: How does your software vendor count CPUs? The VM might only have a single CPU assigned to it, but that blade might have something in the range of a half-dozen cores. Since virtualization is still new, the end-user license agreement (EULA) might not have a clause to accommodate the VM having only a single core assigned to it.

- Licensing 2: Does your software license even allow you to run it under a virtualized environment? If so, does the EULA allow you to run it on a single physical server or a single server instance? If it is by physical server, make sure the vendor hasn't updated its EULA, because many are catching on that they've left loopholes open that may allow users to run multiple copies of their software as long as all the virtual machines are all on a single piece of hardware.

- License dongles: Some pieces of software require a nice little USB dongle to be present in order for them to run. The unfortunate fact is that not all those license dongles can be replaced by a license server, and for those you'll need to get a USB network server such as the USB Anywhere networked USB hub by Digi (www.digi.com/products/usb/anywhereusb.jsp#overview).

- Licensing servers: You really need to be careful in adding up the virtual machines you'll have to run. In order to accommodate some licensing schemes, you might end up setting up yet another VM just to handle licensing. Even the Microsoft Windows Server 2008 Data Center edition might need one if you have certain types of bulk license agreements in place. (Windows 2008 Data Center edition seems to need an activation server for more than 25 machines)

- Not every OS will run under a virtualized environment, and not every release will either. We ran into a case where version 4.x of Debian Linux ran just fine under Microsoft Virtual Server 2005, but 5.x didn't. Since it isn't officially supported as a guest operating system, this customer ended up having to move to CentOS instead of Debian.

- Server throughput: This is a massive "gotcha," and the blog-o-sphere has been buzzing like mad about how VMs are sooo much slower because of those extra layers of abstraction. While not always the case, the truth is that you might find yourself doing a bunch more tuning on the virtual server than you did on the standalone. While not necessarily bad, it is a new line item in your project timeline. Xen keeps bragging that it's the fastest VM system around, but to date we've not seen any hard facts to support this. Considering the lack of real reviews in the trade press, we're not sure how long we're going to have to wait for quantitative VM speed comparisons.

So far, we've been talking about what clouds can and can't do (yet), and how to codify expectations in service-level agreements. We've also talked about the pressures that are exerted on cloud implementations by security and regulatory compliance issues. We haven't yet dealt with questions of planning horizons and how the current and most likely future versions of cloud infrastructure might work within realistic planning ranges. Cloud computing is no different than any other IT technology in many important ways that we've already discussed, and the need for proper planning is certainly a key arena in which there is no difference.

As with any strategic IT technology, clouds are tools that may or may not fit your needs. As with any new strategic technology, clouds should be thought of in both the long and short terms, and how the migration to the new technology will affect your long-term and short-term operational costs in relationship to the perceived return on investment. The real key is to ask the same question at every step along the way: "Does this really make sense for our organization?"

It's our opinion that a long-term strategic shift should definitely include regular revisits to the planning cycle as cloud computing changes from what is in essence a fancy ISP to a true cloud with a well-defined job submission and control system and several layers of abstraction removed from having to fuss around with operating systems. We're still convinced that over the next decade clouds will continuously morph as technology and standards evolve toward the "ideal" we pontificated about in the early chapters. (And we'll do lots more pontificating in the next chapter about how we think things should be.) The George Jetson science fiction ideal of being able to choose from a list of applications off the Web and then run it without regard to where it actual runs is still a glimmer in our eyes.

A common thread in cloud computing discussions is that the industry seems to want to achieve the science fiction goal someday, but, as with many other technologies, the hoped-for future will arrive only after a long series of iterative changes and compromises between competing ad hoc standards. What you really need to do on every technology refresh cycle is to keep asking yourself whether moving to a cloud even makes sense. The first couple of times the answer may very well be no. That doesn't mean you shouldn't keep asking yourself that question every once in a while. In the same way that many companies very legitimately decided against personal computers, PDAs, or smart phones the first time or two (or four), the question was asked, and eventually answered with a yes. The current state of cloud computing development might make clouds inappropriate for your company—today. The danger in any technology discussion is becoming set in an opinion that can't be changed, even when the facts change. Ask the questions honestly, with a willingness to hear and heed the answer (whatever it may be), and you can be well own your way to successful cloud computing deployment.

One of the many complications of planning for cloud computing is that it's quite possible to end up with a portion of your infrastructure in the cloud before you realize it. We hear a great deal about the importance of tackling problems head on, and how we can see products coming at us from ahead, but the truth is that cloud computing can come at you, well, sideways. What do we mean by that? Let's consider an example.

We're hearing lots of buzz about how identity federation, which we discussed earlier and is considered the holy grail of supply-chain operations, might actually force some companies into the cloud. The scenario we've been hearing goes something like this: Vendor X needs to streamline its ordering of the widget product line from Vendor Y. Remote locations from Vendor X are responsible for placing their own orders with Vendor Y, and then updating information in Vendor X central systems concerning inventory and order status. One of the critical things slowing down order entry is the process of authenticating the remote location's identity with both Vendor Y and Vendor X central. A single, unified authentication process would streamline the process and make widget order entry faster and somewhat less error-prone. What can be done?

Instantly, we think identity "federation," and for good reason; but what happens when you need some serious middleware to fit the square Vendor X peg into the proverbial round Vendor Y hole? Who hosts it, and most important, who pays for maintenance? Since clouds don't have hard assets to dicker over, perhaps that middleware might be appropriately put in a cloud? The interesting piece of the whole discussion is that, while Vendor X would logically make the decision to implement identity federation, Vendor Y must cooperate, and the required middleware becomes, at some level, part of each company's infrastructure. This is an almost ridiculously oversimplified example, but it does illustrate one use case in which we can see some very stodgy companies testing the cloudy waters.

Speaking of examples and use cases, user/customer adoption of virtualization and clouds has an amazing amount of inertia to overcome. The number-one complaint we've had to deal with has revolved around the perceived "loss of control." The perception, and the resistance to the perceived loss, has some very real dollars attached as a consequence. Just look at how the personal computer snuck in the back door in many corporations. Sometimes you find yourself in a situation where a technology has become an ad hoc standard in your company while you weren't looking. We think it's in everyone's best interest to at least take the tech out for a test drive and confirm or deny vendor claims. After all, every vendor on the planet is going to publish claims about its product in the very best of light. For the consumer market we have organizations such as Consumers Union, which publishes its test results in *Consumer Reports*. Sadly, the enterprise-networking world has been losing review-based publications in large numbers, and as a result, fewer and fewer of those vendor glossy brochures are being verified by an independent source.

On this subject, while numerous technology magazines tout that they publish "reviews," quite a few of those "review" articles were actually written by the vendor itself. This is called a "vendor-contributed article," and might as well be a glossy marketing brochure. Independent product reviews have become nearly extinct as magazine budgets shrink to the point at which reviews are either dropped or minimalized.

Moving on, at most universities, power consumption is a huge issue, but the insistence of departments having their own mini data centers running 24/7 has prevented them from shutting down office buildings on holidays, weekends, and evenings. If we could move those servers into more efficient clouds or even data centers, the university could potentially save millions of dollars in energy costs. To that end, many an InfoTech group is struggling to gain adoption of virtualization, but due to the inertia of departments and individual stubbornness, the university is being forced into an intermediate step of collocation first. It's a way of letting departments get used to the idea of not having the hardware within their walls, while not forcing them to give up the reassurance of a dedicated physical server that they could, if they wished, visit and touch. The overall lack of understanding and experience with virtualization, much less of the cloud, is the inertia we're talking about. This prime example of user and administrative ignorance shows just how big a part planning and education can play in your path to Cloud City. After several years of tinkering, early adopters are well aware of the huge advantages of virtualization and how clouds at this stage are simply an extension of that idea. But those are the early adopters, and those uncomfortable with the bleeding edge are going to take quite a while to wrap their minds around moving away from physical to virtual servers.

But intermediate steps can be good, right? Well, let's take a peek at what this intermediate step is going to cost the department in our example. Right now they have a server farm, but mostly for their own gear, and like most IT groups, they're experimenting with VMWare and/or Windows 2008 Hypervisor. In this case they're being forced into going the collocation facility route and are now looking at just how they can provide remote access for departmental servers, without giving the departmental sysadmins 24/7 physical access. Remember, the goal is to convince departments to move their servers out of their own buildings and into a collocation facility so that their buildings can be shut down on holidays, weekends, and evenings in order to save energy. The balance is to avoid needing high-end support talent on the second and third shifts, since the human resource cost could easily offset any savings from the server consolidation program.

Lots of remote control widgets exist, and even Best Buy carries some basic remote access tools; however, those "el cheapo" widgets are for a single machine with a single user. Many small shops use remote access programs such as Remote Desktop, GoToMyPC, VNC, or many others of the ilk. However, all of these products need an operating system to be running *and* a working network to connect with. What if someone changed the netmask on the server, and now it can't talk on the network; or what happens if the operating system is hung? Normally this would mean a trip to the colo, whipping out a credit card or purchase order to pay for the after-hours access (such things never seem to happen during the normal workday), just to hop on the console to change a stinking netmask mistake. Now, with something like an IP KVM (keyboard + video + mouse remote access, normally via an Active-X Web browser application), you can even get into the bios of the server, perhaps to turn off the physical serial ports to allow a virtual serial port to be Com1 instead of the onboard serial port. During the early development of the Fedora Linux distribution in the Advanced Network Computing Laboratory, Warren Togami utilized the IP KVM to remotely collaborate with RedHat engineers on some new iSCSI drivers for Fedora. Funny how Ring 0 drivers have a bad habit of hanging entire operating systems, and in the old days would have also dramatically slowed development on the driver.

Scaling remote access up to potentially hundreds of servers and sysadmins requires enterprise-grade tools. Even some of the multiport remote access widgets really only scale up to perhaps a dozen ports; what this kind of move requires is a system that can scale to hundreds of ports while not requiring massive amounts of management. Additionally, the system must be able to accommodate delegation of authority over various functions on a per-server or per-group-of-servers basis. It is extremely common to allow one group to have view-only capabilities and no power management, and another group to have it all. It's also pretty common that the remote access authentication is done by TACACS or RADIUS, but additional granularity be handled by the remote access system. Better yet, most modern systems actually hide servers from the potential connection list if the user isn't allowed to touch them.

Typically, the answer is to use an enterprise-grade IP KVM from someone such as Raritan or Avocent to fill the bill. In order to provide scalability to hundreds of systems, both solution vendors require some sort of aggregation server in order to scale up. Avocent's DSView software requires a dedicated Windows Server, while Raritan's Command Center is a dedicated purpose-built appliance. Both systems provide a single-point gateway and authentication that then fans out to hundreds of control devices that can span multiple sites. The same system can provide control to serial consoles, service processor aggregation (ipmi, iLO, DRAC, etc.), power control, and environmental monitoring. These modern systems even provide for mounting of the remote optical drive (e.g., from your laptop or desktop workstation) on the target server so that things such as server regens can still happen without setting foot in the data center. All these features are managed from a single interface and a single user pool. A fully loaded system for a data center in the range of a couple of dozen racks can easily put you back many tens of thousands of dollars if you want the kitchen sink.

Why did we fly off on this tangent? Easy: The exact same kind of control is currently available in both VMWare and Windows Server 2008 Hypervisor. What a virtualized environment looks like is a data center in a box. The typical virtualization console provides an easy way to find out just how many resources you've assigned to the VM (CPU load, ram load, disk usage, etc.), along with the ability to mount either physical drives or disk images (typically .iso images) and remote console capability.

The point we're trying to make here is that if you haven't already built a data center, perhaps you might want to skip the collocation step. We know that server consolidation into data centers do lead to rebates from several power companies, but really, for the bucks you would have to spend on remote access systems, you can buy one heck of a nice blade system and a lot of VMware or Windows Hypervisor licenses. Especially when you factor in the power costs: Blade servers typically use as much as one-tenth the power that the same number of standalone servers would use in a quarter of the space, and with one-tenth the heat output—even less in the rack space category, when you factor in not needing all the KVMs, service processor aggregators, serial console servers, and power management that are found in a typical enterprise-grade blade server. (Mileage, of course, will vary.)

Thinking About Peaks and Valleys

So maybe we've scared you off from building your own cloud, but you still like the concept. Perhaps it's more that we've made you sit back and take a good hard look at whether this "new thing" is a good match for your organization. Perhaps it is, perhaps it isn't, but how the heck do you find out? A great way to get your feet wet is to use a cloud service to smooth out the peaks and valleys that come with every IT job description. Find some project for which you would normally have to consider buying a server for (or at least re-tasking an old server). Then run two parallel projects: one version on the monolithic (stand-alone) server and the other on a virtualized server. Or, if you already have a project on a stand-alone server, consider migrating it to a virtualized environment using a tool such as Drive Backup Enterprise Server from Paragon Software, (www.paragon-software.com) which has the ability to do a physical-to-virtual (P2V) migration over the network or output to actual VMDK (Vmware Virtual disk) or VHD (Microsoft Virtual Hard Drive) files. This way you can take a running project server and sling it into VMWare (download VMWare ESX server for a free 90-day trial) and take it for a spin.

One of our favorite tricks is to copy images off these virtual machines and onto an NTFS formatted USB hard drive as masters. This way every new project can start from a template; all we have to do is swap out license codes. If you "copy" a VMWare template, the system will ask you if you want to redo the SIDs (system IDs) to avoid the system ID conflicts that are so typical when you create systems from copies.

Just like the service bureau in the mainframe days, services such as Amazon and Google can easily be viewed as a way to smooth out the cost peaks

for short-term projects by allowing you to "rent" large amounts of computing facilities without the long-term costs of acquiring and maintaining a
facility. The *New York Times* indexing project (we started talking about it
in Chapter 4) could have cost millions in equipment and human resource
costs for the one-time indexing of their story archives, but buying into
the Amazon cloud let their IT group walk away from the infrastructure
once the project was done. This is just the kind of short- versus long-term
capital investment that will put a smile onto any CFO's face.

We like how Galen Grumman and Eric Knorr of InfoWorld put it
in 2008:

What Cloud Computing Really Means

**The next big trend sounds nebulous, but it's not
so fuzzy when you view the value proposition
from the perspective of IT professionals**

By Eric Knorr, Galen Gruman

> Cloud computing comes into focus only when you think about
> what IT always needs: a way to increase capacity or add capabilities
> on the fly without investing in new infrastructure, training
> new personnel, or licensing new software. Cloud computing
> encompasses any subscription-based or pay-per-use service that,
> in real time over the Internet, extends IT's existing capabilities.

Conversely cloud services can also get you past valleys in that you
can "draw back" potentially expensive data center resources into cloud
resources that can be turned on and off at short notice. We've also heard
of clouds being used in corporate shutdown strategies, allowing for data
center assets to be sold off to recover portions of investment funds while
still providing services necessary to fulfill the terms of the shutdown.
This kind of thing is perfect for the last reminder on the Web, so that
customers can get information on where to go for cut-over services and
other such things as a company goes gracefully into shutdown mode.

The other "valley" that comes to mind is when an organization
can't fill IT positions or needs to provide services but doesn't have budget for a data center. Renting a cloud made a huge amount of sense for
the University of Hawai'i at Mānoa's Botany Department, which had a
huge amount of content but little or no budget for IT support. Moving

their huge collection of botanical images to the cloud is expected to dramatically increase access to this world-class plant image collection, while allowing the botanists to concentrate on botany instead of on keeping a server farm running.

To put this into perspective, treat it like a high-end temporary help agency. Hire the skills and the quantity that you need for a project, and then give them back when the surge or project is done. No fuss, no muss, and someone can get a whole bunch of credit card points out of the rental.

Another way to drag a cloud into your organization is to play the energy card. Enterprise-grade servers are designed to be loaded down and to a certain extent are purposely overdesigned for reliability. They're also designed with redundancy, with error-correcting RAM, parity disk drives, N+1 power supplies, and layer upon layer of remote access, to prevent getting painted into a corner. This all needs energy to cool and power it, light the data center, provide security, and suck up funding for things such as maintenance contracts. The overall fact is that a true server is purposely overdesigned to provide for constant operation. The concept is called a duty cycle and is best illustrated by the mundane paper shredder. A light-duty paper shredder can shred perhaps three sheets of normal copier paper at a time and is designed for perhaps 20 minutes of continuous operation. However, go too much beyond those 20 minutes and you might find yourself with the Salvador Dali version, as the overheated motor turns the plastic into goo. On the other hand, the military and intelligence agencies have super-duty shredders that can run for hours at a time. In fact, we've seen shredders into which you can toss the entire binder, and it turns the whole thing into a mass of powder. Servers have similar design criteria but based on how much load they can handle continuously. You might be able to turn an "el cheapo" workstation into a server; and if the load is light, you might get away with it. However, we've seen quite a few of these workstations die horrible deaths, taking critical business data along with them. Enterprise-grade servers typically have redundant everything and can run full-tilt 100% of the time and survive. The downside is that this level of redundancy costs money, energy, and heat.

Energy Issues

Let's look at some of the factors needed to figure out the real power draw for a server. The numbers we start with are

- Maximum amperage draw for each power supply at what voltage
- Stated wattage for each power supply
- Efficiency of each power supply (This is sometimes a graph, since most power supplies become more efficient as load increases. Typically, they're most efficient in the middle of their load range.
- Heat output numbers for the device, from the manufacturer
- Heat numbers from each disk drive, since those numbers are almost never included in the heat numbers for the server

So while this started out looking like a simple formula, it really isn't. You could just multiply the wattage of all the power supplies by time and get the maximum power draw, but that's not realistic because the power draw is in relation to the overall CPU and I/O load on the server. You also have to keep in mind that older power supplies can be as low as 60% efficient, with some of the new servers being up to 95% efficient. This is why we use automated systems from folks such as American Power Conversion (APC). Their *Data Center Efficiency Portal* allows you to build a model of your data center, plug in the make and model of each piece of equipment; and then run simulations for heat load and balance. On the "Pimp your Data Center Project," published by InfoWorld (http://www.infoworld.com/t/hardware/pimp-my-datacenter-307), we had both Rackwise Corporation and APC run heat load mapping programs to help us optimize the cooling-unit positions (computer room air conditioning, or CRAC) as well as the servers so that we could even out our heat load. We actually went quite a bit further and started asking the RackWise system just how much it thought all our gear weighed, especially when we got a huge surprise about our floor loading limits from the structural engineers. These types of systems are great because they also provide inventory control, change management, and light trouble ticketing in addition to heat and power simulation capability.

Another source for energy consumption numbers has slowly started appearing on manufacturer websites, as consumers demanded it. Since consumers are voting for green devices with their dollars, vendors have responded with whole marketing campaigns designed around green versions of their popular offerings. Dell, IBM, and HP all have been touting the greenness of their blade server offerings, and Netgear even has an entire line of green ether switches. We've even seen an ad campaign from Extreme Networks comparing their energy usage to the devices from the 1000-lb gorilla in the market.

A good reason for all these data center energy management systems is exemplified by the VMWare and PG&E (Pacific Gas & Electric) server consolidation project in northern California that we have mentioned before. One example project went from something like 40 racks of gear down to two; and literally chopped their energy bill by millions of dollars. The interesting side effect was that they also had to do some major changes to their now overkill cooling system and no longer had to budget for shoring up their sagging data center floor. We started out talking about energy, but the whole conversation is really about resources: whether it's floor loading capacity, power, cooling, space, or even power substation capacity. We also have to imagine that someone had to re-task all the human resources that used to maintain those 40 racks worth of gear.

> "Virtualization technology is helping our customers realize significant energy and cost savings, while addressing critical data center capacity issues," explained Helen Burt, senior vice president and chief customer officer for PG&E. "By providing financial support, we hope to increase industry adoption of this technology."
>
> PG&E customers in northern and central California who are interested in earning financial incentives for virtualization projects must apply for the rebate prior to pursuing a project. The incentives are based on the amount of energy savings achieved through data center consolidation. Qualifying customers can earn a maximum rebate amount of $4 million per project site.
>
> (*Source:* www.vmware.com/company/news/releases/pge.html.)

To play the energy/resources card, you need to collect some usage data. Just how much of that CPU are you really using for your human resources Web server? With most Web servers barely going double digits for CPU utilization, you've still got dual power supplies sucking down a full load of power, and then blowing out hot air into your data center. Combining all those "bits of servers" together into a virtualized array makes a whole lot of sense from an energy standpoint. Just stop and think about why utilities around the country are looking so hard at server consolidation as a method of saving billions of kilowatt-hours. We keep hearing stories about companies (and universities) doing server consolidation, and finding that the renovation pays for itself in energy savings over an amazingly short period of time. Combine that with massive rebate programs and suddenly you have one heck of a carrot to wave in front of your management. This is where the "test drive" system really comes into play. There is nothing more convincing than doing a trial P2V migration of existing systems and then running them parallel for a time. The shocked look of the CFO when he sees that you're now running something like a dozen servers in the space and resources of a single server is simply priceless.

While PG&E was certainly one of the first big utilities to push for virtualization, they're not the only one in the game today. Here's something from a website that seems to be doing a good job of consolidating this information:

> There are dozens of incentive programs from local utilities or state energy efficiency programs offering rebates to customers who can reduce their energy usage through improved efficiency or the use of renewable energy sources. While only a handful of these programs are customized for data centers, they offer potential savings for customers doing server consolidations or virtualization projects.
>
> The Database of State Incentives for Renewables & Efficiency (DSIRE) is a comprehensive source of information on state, local, utility, and federal incentives that promote renewable energy and energy efficiency. It maintains databases of incentives for both renewable energy and energy efficiency, broken down by state and individual utility, offering details on each program along with a link to the utility's web site. It's a great resource for identifying what's available in your area(s) with minimal research.
>
> (*Source:* www.datacenterknowledge.com/archives/2007/11/19/utility-incentive-programs-for-data-centers.)

Experiments and Wild Hares

In the Advanced Network Computing Laboratory, we're investing in a new blade server system along with an iSCSI storage area network in order to support what is in essence a "testing cloud" for the InfoWorld reviews editorial staff. However, as we keep pouring money into this constantly upgrading black hole, we've looked at striking a balance between maintaining an in-house cloud sandbox and buying time in a commercial cloud. We seriously doubt that Amazon (or another cloud provider, for that matter) will let us get away with the kinds of experiments we do in our lab. (Well, they might, but the charges would be staggering.) However, we're looking at a balance between the two worlds by moving our production server images off the expensive and time-intensive in-house VMWare cloud to a much less expensive EC2 image.

The story is similar in one organization after another. Try it out, run it in parallel to the original, and use those numbers to pitch it to the CFO. Whether you virtualize and then cloud or jump straight to clouds, there is normally a proof-of-concept phase to prove to the CFO that those numbers aren't just smoke and mirrors. Remember that we said that mileage might vary? Nowhere is that more true than in virtualization and clouds. How much you save is a variable that depends directly on how predictable your load is. If you can keep your virtualized servers loaded, they're more efficient. However, if you lean toward being able to handle peaks loads, then perhaps not so much.

Dipping Your Toes into Virtualization

We've said several times that clouds are not a one-size-fits-all technology. What we haven't seen has been any "starter kits" so people can eat the learning curve without waiting an entire budgetary cycle for funding. The hand-holding and starter kits we have seen for other technologies have only slowly started to appear in this field. Microsoft's Virtual Server product was an orphan for many years, with only a few Microsoft folks playing evangelist. VMware has also suffered, with some value-added resellers and consultants avoiding the initial product because of misconceptions about loss of revenue in server sales and consulting. Both camps had a slow start, and we'd like to attribute some of the kick-start for virtualization to the Linux User Groups around the world. Never has a group of users been more willing to tinker and to experiment—and experiment they did, first with primitive versions that forced operating system homogeneity and onward to some of the early hypervisors.

Recently, VMware has finally taken a page from the Linux world and is pushing users groups. The number-one question we've heard is how to get started without having to jump into the deep end of the pool, with blade servers and hugely expensive storage area networks.

By far the easiest way to test the waters is to run a hosted (workstation) virtualization system such as VMWare Fusion on the Mac, Microsoft's Virtual Server 2005 R2, or even VMWare Server, which can ride on top of Windows or Linux. These are all freely downloadable, and the best part is that the "test" VM's you create on these free systems can be scaled up to a full production version if the opportunity arises. Although they're free and run as an application on top of an existing operating system, they aren't crippled or stripped down. Those all-important conversion utilities to go between each of the VMWare hypervisor models are freely available if you're willing to register for a user account.

The University of Hawaii Department of Information and Computer Sciences used a recycled Xeon Compaq server running Windows Server 2003 and Virtual Server R2 to run four virtual servers for a database class. Each of the four project teams got a server all to themselves, complete with administrator rights and the ability to trash their server if they weren't careful. Other than the Windows Server licenses, it was all housed on recycled gear and the total cost was next to nothing, since they were just re-tasking a retired server. Notice that there was no storage area network in this case. They just used the internal IDE drives and sliced it up for the class. This project, more than any other at the time, demonstrated to various faculty members that virtualization was a key to getting students much-needed experience in building and administering database servers and actually eating the learning curve on how to build and maintain IT infrastructure. Virtualized servers also gave them a way to deal with the "oops" factor, with snapshots allowing the project teams to roll back their servers a couple of days if they managed to paint themselves into a corner.

Another demo project recycled an old Dell Power Edge server setup with the open-source "OpenFiler" system (www.openfiler.com). Configured as an iSCSI storage array, this free system can authenticate and mount requests against LDAP or Active Directory (the current version supports NIS) and are supported by both VMware and Windows Server 2008 Hypervisor. Since Openfiler is a standard iSCSI target (the iSCSI target provides services, the iSCSI initiator uses services), even Windows 2000 servers can mount it. Just to make life interesting, OpenFiler also provides NFS, SMB, NAS, Web, and FTP services all installed from a bootable CDROM. (*Note:* Don't accept the defaults for the Linux partitioning; leave *lots* of unallocated space so that OpenFiler has room to create partitions, volumes, and LUNs.) The only real catch with OpenFiler is that documentation isn't free; you'll need for fork over 40 euros for that. However, there are lots of "how to" documents available, and a basic setup really doesn't need the documentation. OpenFiler Corporation survives by selling consulting and services for their open-source product. The authors strongly suggest paying the 40 euros to download the PDF of the manual. The number of tips and tricks provided by the OpenFiler team make this investment well worth it.

We should also point out that although it is not recommended for a production environment, you could just as easily use that little Netgear NAS instead of OpenFiler or a commercial SAN. NFS is a very lightweight file-sharing technology and is supported nicely by VMware Server. It may be slower than a SAN (depending on the load), but it's a wonderful compromise for learning the intricacies of managing a virtualized environment. Another key advantage is that most of the new fast network attached storage appliances now support multithreaded NFS and actually work pretty well with VMWare through its native NFS support. We also need to point out that most of the higher-end NAS appliances provide iSCSI support (e.g., the Netgear Ready NAS 3200 can provide upwards of 24 TB very inexpensively). Note that we are absolutely not disparaging NFS as a storage system for virtualized environments. Network Appliance and others still sell a lot of NFS storage systems for VMWare installations, and they work just fine. As for any complex technology, moving from NFS to a storage area network is best done by working with subject-matter experts as you plan your upgrade. And, as always, your mileage may vary.

We would be horribly remiss if we didn't point out that one of the coolest bells and whistles of the commercial storage area networks is LUN (logical unit number) migration. Simply put, you can easily create a disk storage allocation for your project with more space and then use the SAN tools to slide the old one over to the new one. Network Appliances (NetApp) has taken this concept a whole lot further and now advertise "deduplication." The concept of deduplication depends on the fact that with an array of virtual servers, you're more than likely going to be running most of them with the same operating system version. So why store xxx copies of the same operating system? NetApp is so confident that this system works that if during the consulting process you determine you need 10 TB, they may come back and say you really need only 5 TB. If after a certain period in production it's determined that the 5 TB really isn't going to cut it, then NetApp will give you the remaining 5 TB for free.

> Of the available products, some only eliminate identical copies of files. NetApp deduplication works at the block level, so it can achieve a significant level of deduplication when multiple versions of a file exist. For example, imagine two copies of a 10MB file that differ by a single block. File-level deduplication would have no effect because the files are different, so you would still need 20MB of storage. Block-level deduplication would deduplicate all but the changed block, so you could store both files in 10MB plus one block.

> (*Source:*www.netapp.com/us/communities/tech-ontap/tot-dedupe-unstructure-0409.html.)

The cool part about diving into a storage area network is that, once you have shared network storage such as an iSCSI array, you can start playing with virtual server migration such as VMotion. An example is the way Interop normally has most of its services running on three or four shared VMWare blade servers. However, as load increases, the system brings additional blades out of standby and moves the heavily loaded virtual server out of the shared environment to a dedicated blade. What's significant is that those blades on standby are barely sucking up any power at all. All in all, this is a very green solution that still automatically scales up according to demand, all without human intervention and all according to the business rules that you define. All you really need to do is set up the business rules that define the power and performance profiles you're willing to live with.

Here's a bit of soap-boxing: We've been on several technology advisory boards, and every single one has been "examining" virtualization by arguing and cataloguing all the costs and issues involved with moving to this "new technology." Demo versions have been downloaded, and IT staff have been eating the learning curve as fast as possible. The flag we've been waving of late is that maybe some organizations might want to bypass building a virtualized server farm and go directly to a cloud. Keep the sandboxes to make sure you're completely familiar with your apps, but do you need to build that in-house cloud yourself? Should there be a balance?

Or do you jump into the deep end of the pool? In the case of our lab, it will be a balance of in-house sandbox and in-house cloud to develop and characterize any new applications. Then, once maintaining these apps becomes second nature, we can slide them into a cloud and free up resources for the next iteration. We even prototype our virtual machines on our Macintosh's under VMWare Fusion and then convert over to VMWare ESX server when we're ready. A similar process is also available for Amazon EC2.

Key to the conversion utility is the flexibility to migrate from legacy virtualization systems to the most current ones, and from physical "monolithic servers" to virtual servers. VMware's answer is a set of free conversion tools that provide ways of moving virtual server images from one platform to another:

> VMware vCenter Converter Standalone provides an easy-to-use solution to automate the process of creating VMware virtual machines from physical machines (running Windows and Linux), other virtual machine formats, and third-party image formats. Through an intuitive wizard-driven interface and a centralized management console, Converter Standalone can quickly and reliably convert multiple local and remote physical machines without any disruptions or downtime.

Benefits

- Convert physical machines running Windows and Linux operating systems to VMware virtual machines quickly, reliably, and without any disruption or downtime.
- Convert third-party formats such as Parallels Desktop, Symantec Backup Exec System Recovery, Norton Ghost, Acronis, StorageCraft, and Microsoft Virtual Server or Virtual PC to VMware virtual machines.
- Enable centralized management of remote conversions of multiple physical servers or virtual machines simultaneously.
- Populate new virtual machine environments from a large directory of virtual machine appliances.
- Ensure conversion reliability through quiesced snapshots of the guest operating system on the source machine before data migration.

- Enable non-disruptive conversions through hot cloning, with no source server downtime or reboot.

What's New

The VMware vCenter Converter Standalone release adds several new features including:

- Physical to virtual machine conversion support for Linux (RHEL, SUSE and Ubuntu) as source
- Physical to virtual machine conversion support for Windows Server 2008 as source
- Hot cloning improvements to clone any incremental changes to physical machine during the P2V conversion process
- Support for converting new third-party image formats including Parallels Desktop virtual machines, newer versions of Symantec, Acronis, and StorageCraft
- Workflow automation enhancements to include automatic source shutdown, automatic start-up of the destination virtual machine as well as shutting down one or more services at the source and starting up selected services at the destination
- Target disk selection and the ability to specify how the volumes are laid out in the new destination virtual machine
- Destination virtual machine configuration, including CPU, memory, and disk controller type

The following features are no longer supported:

- NT4 hot cloning
- ESX 2.5 destination

(*Source:*www.vmware.com/support/converter/doc/releasenotes_conv 40.html.)

Harking back to the comments of Erik Cummings and the rest of the Interop team, we suggest that, as for anything in life, moderation is the key. The answer isn't going to be black and white, but rather shades of gray where they make sense. Do you need an in-house cloud? On the other hand, can you risk moving everything into the cloud? You really won't know until you try a test drive. Since VMware and Microsoft both have test-drive versions available (if your provider does not, twist some arms), it makes sense to beg, borrow, or steal a few resources and take a test drive with *your* apps. Just because application X works great doesn't mean yours will.

Shades of gray certainly exist in clouds, and one of those shades might be storm cloud black—as in, "Don't do it!" Trying to force everything into a cloud is like trying to make a Ferrari tow a boat. Perhaps it can do it, but does it make sense, and just how much damage are you going to do to the Ferrari? There are some things that may simply not make sense right now; the reason might be security, copyrights, licensing, or lack of application stability. The key is to ask yourself if you really need to chase the hare down the rabbit hole at this time? Just because it can be virtualized doesn't mean it should be. A prime example is Apple's OSx Server: It is possible to shoehorn it onto VMWare, but it isn't legal, since the current Apple end-user license agreement forbids this. In fact, in 2008, Apple sued Pystar Corporation for copyright infringement, claiming that, by the Digital Millennium Copyright Act (DMCA), it has the right to lock its operating system to Mac hardware only. Psystar was eventually barred from copying any version of OS X, or helping others install it. So, while OSx might run on VMWare or other virtualization systems, it does not seem to be legal to do so at this time.

Planning for Success

You can't just buy into a cloud service provider and expect world-changing services to magically appear. Like so many other consultants, we always start off a new project by saying that our team has to learn the process well enough to do it by hand. Only then can we automate any complex process or procedure. The same goes for clouds: If you can't prototype it, how do you know it will work when you have less access and, for the most part, less intensive monitoring? Until we get to that magically homogeneous cloud programming and job control system, your people will have to make sure it works someplace where you won't go broke if a process tries to spawn an unlimited number of child processes or suddenly sucks up the entire disk farm. Like the advice given by Eric Cummings as he migrated his massive SaaS application from an in-house data center to Amazon, make sure you have your application well understood and well characterized so that troubleshooting doesn't eat you alive.

Trial Projects for the Cloud

There are lots of ways to get your feet wet in cloud computing. Some great short-term projects for the cloud include:

- Document indexing, such as our example of the *New York Times* giving its scanned story archive to Amazon EC2 for indexing
- Websites for special events, such as webcasting
- Short-duration websites, such as those for contests
- Mass format conversions, such as conversion of video content to another video format (e.g., AVI to MPEG4), creating thumbnails and adding digital watermarks.
- A "shutdown" website as a company starts the process of shutting its doors gracefully

There are also lots of great long-term projects for the cloud, including:

- A club or society Web server
- Well-understood SaaS applications
- Data repositories that are accessed worldwide
- Traveler backups
- customer relations management (CRM) applications accessed from multiple locations
- Federation sites as a "DMZ" between companies

Short-term or long-term, what really matters is that IT planning is being done at higher and higher levels in just about every organization we've encountered. The fact that MIS managers are becoming CIOs, and now we've starting to see IT vice presidents, illustrates how IT planning has become an integral part of corporate planning. Once you start talking about setting up some sort of trust relationship with an outside organization, it makes sense that the conversations start very early.

We stumbled on one great icebreaker trick when a new website was being prototyped for a university chancellor for an on-line sustainability magazine. During the presentation it was mentioned that not only did the magazine deal with green issues, it was also hosted on a virtualized environment along with a dozen or so other servers, with the aggregate using less energy that a single traditional Web server. The shocked look on the chancellor's face really drove home that education needs to flow both up and down in the organizational tree when it comes to the multifaceted advantages that clouds can provide.

Clouds Flight Path for Chapter 8

- *Remote access, the views from collocation, virtualization and the cloud.* Is collocation a good intermediate step, or do you jump into the clouds with both feet? What are some of the issues that will rear their ugly heads as you think about perhaps taking an intermediate step first. The InfoWorld gang pimped their data center, and we've seen how utilities are dangling millions of dollars in front of corporations to do data center consolidation and virtualization. The potential savings in operational costs are massive and may very well pay for the next technology upgrade.
- *Planning for peaks and valleys.* We're of the opinion that cloud computing is just tailor-made for the peaks and valleys of modern IT. Just ask the folks at the *New York Times.* The fact that you can just walk away from the hardware after you're done is a *big* win. The industry has long talked about how to handle workload peaks, and for the first time there seems to be a reasonable solution. Will those solutions grow and become the foundation for true clouds?
- *Energy issues.* Who pays the power bill, and just how green is your data center? There are huge potentials for saving energy, but weigh those savings against the investment costs. If you live in the land of ultraexpensive electricity, maybe you should consider using one of the new generation of green collocation services instead of trying to keep everything in-house.
- *Experiments and wild hares.* There are some very cheap ways to get into virtualization and the clouds. We think a bit of sweat factor in

the beginning will pay off huge dividends as you proceed along the path to clouds.

- *Testing the waters with virtualization.* Why not start with virtualization at the workstation? Prototyping on the free virtualization systems is a great way to start off, especially considering that upsizing is "easy-peezy."
- *What does your timeline look like?* Do you wait, or dive in? Sometimes the best idea in your planning is to wait a bit. But there are certainly some very good reasons for both short- and long-term projects to go into the clouds. We like the strategy of taking tech for a test drive on small projects as a great way to expose the warts of any new technology.

Chapter 9

Cloud Security

We've arranged a civilization in which most crucial elements profoundly depend upon science and technology.

– Dr. Carl Sagan

In This Chapter

In this chapter we'll look at the key features of security functions that are available through the cloud and how those features are delivered. We'll also present information on the key considerations for deciding which of the cloud-based security technologies can be considered for your organization's use now, and which can be looked at in the future. Finally, we'll look at the future of cloud-based security, including both technology- and management-related issues that could have a huge impact on what will be available through the cloud as the industry moves forward. In this chapter we'll discuss:

- Cloud security options. Where should the fence go, and what kinds of options are there out there?
- Cloud authentication. Do you have to migrate off-premise, or are there options for a hybrid approach?

- Cloud security limitations. Just how far can you take it, and is it worth the effort?
- Cloud security futures. Where is this all going, and what can we expect in the future?

What Can You Do with Cloud Security?

Security for information systems breaks down into two broad categories: protecting the assets (the hardware, software, and network infrastructure that makes up the IT system) and protecting the data. Twenty-five years ago the assets were considered the most valuable part of the system, and great effort went into making sure that no unauthorized use of those assets took place (and that no one could erase or damage the software in ways that made it unusable).

Today, of course, the situation is different, and most organizations recognize that data is the critical piece of the IT puzzle and requires the most significant protection. Physical and software assets may well be protected, but their protection is almost incidental, seen as a necessary piece of protecting the data that lives on the platform.

As cloud computing becomes a more important model for enterprise IT, the cloud will necessarily be a more critical part of the overall security infrastructure. We've looked at some of the implications of trying to protect the data that lives on and flows through the cloud, but the cloud can also be an important part of securing an enterprise IT architecture.

What sort of things can the cloud do in a security sense? First, it's important to understand what any security, whether cloud or on-premise based, can do to protect data. Despite all the different products that are available for security, the number of security functions can be broken down into just a few tasks. Security can make sure that only authorized users can access the resources. This activity is generally called user authentication. The rest of security is basically a series of steps to take over if this security layer fails.

Security can be a filter, making sure that only authorized data flows into or out of the network, whether authorized users are involved or not. Security can make sure that the data isn't usable if it is transferred in an unauthorized way, usually through data encryption. Finally, security can keep track of everything that's happening on the network and its constituent computers so lessons can be learned, miscreants prosecuted, and (with any luck at all) patterns of behavior detected before any criminal activity has taken place, so the illicit activity can be stopped before damage has occurred.

While firewall vendors will now be up in arms, remember that filters also include the new generation of deep packet and pattern inspection systems appearing on the market today. A little-known factoid is that for the most part the world's largest temporary network (Interop) actually runs with very few rules in place. Since vendors are trying to show off emerging technology, adding a lot of restrictive rules would be counterproductive. Instead, the InteropNET concentrates on looking for malware via signatures and patterns. As the NOC engineers identify malware, either through automated systems or human intervention, only then are filters put into place. Another new tactic is to hook an attack script by using the TCP congestion facilities so that engineers can keep the script online long enough to trace it back to a source. The Interop engineers actually had one script kiddy hooked for close to 72 hours. (The TCP congestion facility allows you to tell a connection to back off due to congestion; we just tell it back off to the maximum allowed by the protocol... hehehe.)

During the planning and execution of a series of firewall tests for InfoWorld magazine, the authors started to see a change in just how firewall vendors implemented security features. The challenge with the "all-in-one" firewall appliances has always been the amount of processing power available in these small devices. An aborted attempt was made by CheckPoint somewhere after the turn of the century to push things like email antivirus and antispam out into a cloudlike service. Instead of forcing CPU- and RAM-poor appliances to do deep inspection, the email was instead sent to a service for inspection. Cisco has just recently joined the club, and we expect to see a big marketing push around this "new" feature. Just looking at what a unified threat manager (UTM, aka all-in-one appliance) has to deal with, we're surprised that this feature hasn't appeared sooner. In our first series of firewalls tested for InfoWorld, it was SonicWall that came loaded for bear with a 16-core Cavium processor in thebox, and even then, turning on all the UTM functions severely spiked the overall CPU utilization on the appliance. So perhaps the heavy lifting of email antispam and antvirus really should be put in the cloud. Regardless of whether UTM vendors adopt this tactic, it has become very clear that spam has become such a huge problem that outsourcing has become a way of life for many corporations. When it's as easy as changing an MX Record in the domain name service records for your company, email-based cloud services are pretty easy to implement. Then it's just a matter of making sure you have enough hardware in the cloud to handle the heavy lifting of checking huge amounts of email for malware.

If your web presence is also in the cloud, then all of a sudden some interesting alternatives become available. Let's look at firewalls and realize that firewall appliances have been packing some serious CPU capabilities inside those boxes. With the SonicWall NSA series packing a 16-core Caveum, one starts to wonder where this arms race will end. Maybe folks like those at Astaro have caught a glimpse of the future with their virtual machine version of their firewall. Now the amount of resources assigned to that firewall is variable based on load. We can easily envision a load balancer setup to spawn additional firewall VMs as load hits predetermined levels, similarly to how it shifts application VMs around.

Keeping in mind that firewalls can represent a bottleneck to your Web presence, we can easily see this kind of scenario playing out: Corporation X has moved its CRM system into the clouds and has traditionally allowed its customers to update their own records. However, they managed to get an exclusive on an amazing new series of e-books that just hit both the New York and Los Angeles bestseller lists. All of a sudden, Web traffic has spiked to levels that would crash normal Web systems, but in this case we see this scenario play out:

- The load balancer detects the ramping up of Web traffic and compares it to the business rules that have already been set up.
- It first moves the CRM applications and the e-commerce applications from a shared virtual machine to dedicated blades in the cloud server farm.
- It then spawns additional copies of CRM and e-commerce to share the workload across multiple physical cloud servers.
- Finally, it spawns additional copies of the virtual firewall system to let the flood of customer traffic into the site.
- In the meantime, perhaps additional IDS (intrusion detection system) virtual machines are peeking at the virtual network connecting all the e-commerce and CRM machines to the back-end corporate database.

- As public interest wanes, the load balancer follows another set of business rules and slowly collapses the business cloud back onto a shared cloud server, thusly reducing overall cost of running the site.

Given the list of security activities, which fall easily into the cloud? You might be surprised to find out where clouds can readily support solid IT security.

It should also be noted that just because you dropped a facility/service into the clouds, this doesn't mean you can't monitor it. Just about every application monitoring system we've ever played with really cares only whether it can see the apps and yank in performance data. Virtual taps and probes mean that you can see the conversation between your application servers and the database servers. Virtual machines are still going to have SNMP (Simple Network Monitoring Protocol) and WMI (Windows Management Instrumentation) interfaces with which to pull system performance data. Just keep in mind that you can still set up VPN interfaces that will allow your people to peek into even the protected virtual networks; just design it in.

Our suggestion here: Draw pictures and draw circles around your virtual machines to show the Venn diagrams of trust. Our favorite saying is, "If you can't do it manually, then you can't automate it."

Cloud Authentication

Most enterprises will, with good justification, keep their user authentication in on-premise solutions. User information, with the attached permissions and roles, are quite sensitive, and a solid directory hosted at the center of the network infrastructure is a good, sensible way to start. The cloud, however, can be a realistic solution in a few specific situations.

The first such situation is when the organization has a widely distributed network architecture but wants a central authentication and directory structure. This is an ideal opportunity for a private cloud, in which the directory lives in a logically centralized and physically distributed architecture. Many companies are already in this arrangement, though very few want to call it cloud-based. They instead will turn to older language of primary and secondary servers with synchronization and mirroring, which ultimately creates a very cloudy-looking situation for the organization. One must keep firmly in mind just how directory systems can be architected, and the easiest way to picture this is through Venn diagrams. Just because the Los Angeles branch is a major sales hub, this doesn't mean it needs to contain the authentication records for the London office. Through intelligent carving, a corporation can reduce authentication database updates while increasing the potential authentication speed.

Let's look at authentication another way. If a hotel chain kept room keys for the entire hotel chain at every hotel in the chain, you would have an amazingly complex management problem. It makes sense to keep the keys for each individual hotel on the premise, but perhaps a few key managers might keep a set of special keys for other hotels in the chain as a backup security measure. How responsibilities overlap and intersect is only in those areas of responsibility that are common to multiple branches/locations. We've heard of several systems where the mobile sales force has their authentication in the cloud, but the corporate headquarters is the master. We've also heard of a design where a read-only copy of the master identity database is held in the cloud as a backup. In this case, though, the cloud version is read-only and the master authority is still at headquarters.

Other architectures that lend themselves to cloud-based authentication and distributed directory schemes are only beginning to be fully developed but will likely become far more common as we enter the second decade of the century. Identity federation, in which a single set of log-in credentials serves to identify and authorize a user across multiple systems and organizations, is certainly coming. With enterprise network boundaries blurring to the point of erasure and business partnerships (with interrelated applications and data stores) becoming the rule rather than the exception, identity federation will become a far more common practice (especially once standards are put into place for its implementation and practice). The cloud is an ideal way to authenticate users across multiple systems, and it will be used more frequently for this purpose as time goes on. Again, using the Venn diagram model, federation doesn't have any overlap in the circles, but rather a tiny circle that contacts both of the larger circles, and only in that way are the two organizations connected. Communications and authentication are passed through the tiny circle, and it is there that an opportunity arises for bolstering that trust through deep packet inspection and perhaps proxies to make sure that only acceptable business rules and transactions are taking place.

There's one more authentication-related topic that needs to be covered, if only briefly, before we move on. It's one thing to make sure that only authorized users can access systems, applications, and data. It's another to ensure that the end-point systems used to gain access are in compliance with enterprise security and configuration standards. This insurance is known as Network Access Control (NAC), and it is a candidate for cloud implementation as mobile users become the majority of corporate users.

NAC is implemented in one of two ways. In the first, a small application is loaded onto the individual workstations. This application monitors the configuration and status of the workstation and reports on those conditions to the NAC server when the user of the workstation attempts to join the network. In most cases this application will also play a role in receiving software updates to make sure that the workstation has the most current version of all enterprise-supplied software loaded (and, frequently, will prevent the installation of nonapproved software).

The second NAC implementation involves a set of queries from the authentication and NAC servers when a network join is attempted. The query must be answered and completed before the device comes inside the trusted part of the network if the scheme is to work, and the cloud is a perfect place from which to have the conversation because it can (rather remarkably) be both outside and inside the network at the same time. That quality—to be able to deal with security issues from a trusted venue without actually being inside the corporate firewall—will also be of value as we consider other security implementations involving cloud computing.

It should be noted that this is quite a bit different from workstation authentication as found in many authentication systems. In the case of Microsoft Windows, the workstation authentication only provides gatekeeper functions for network resources that are under its control. In the case of something like NAC (Microsoft calls its version NAP), the workstation+user combination must authenticate to a back-end database such as active directory, Radius, LDAP, etc., before *any* network access can take place. So, in the case of active directory workstation authentication, a person could cancel out of the authentication process and still get access to the network; whereas with NAC/NAP, no access is provided at all until authentication takes place.

The real goal of authentication, regardless of whether it's in the clouds or in an enterprise data center, is single sign-on (SSO). Users absolutely hate having to remember multiple log-in names and multiple passwords.

Make strong passwords a requirement, and suddenly you have stickies on monitors for everyone to see. Single sign-on, though, means that some sort of mechanism has to exist that contains a keychain of log-in credentials and a way to protect them. Workstation-based versions have existed for some time now, but how do you extend that securely for a traveler who may or may not be using the same machine twice in a row? At the 2005 InfoWorld shootout on identity management systems, Citrix showed just how it handles an enterprise-class key ring and demonstrated just how that key ring was utilized to log our demonstration users into Windows Active Directory, Sugar CRM, a white pages app, and an IBM mainframe using CICS. With Citrix making noise about cloudy ambitions, maybe we'll start seeing single sign-on migrate into the clouds.

Cloud Filtering

It's a simple premise, really: Some traffic (we'll call it "the good stuff") should be allowed to flow in and out of an enterprise computer network. Other traffic ("the bad stuff") should either be kept out or kept in, depending on the nature of its badness. There are a variety of appliances and software packages that perform this filtering, ranging from firewalls and IDS to Web filters and data leakage prevention systems.

There are differences in the filtering that happens along a couple of axes. One is the network layer at which the filtering takes place. Firewalls tend to operate at the lower level of all the options (generally looking for particular protocols or network ports to block or allow), while Web filters that look at data stream contents operate at the highest possible layer of logical filtering. In between, there are devices such as the IDS, IPS (intrusion prevention system), and UTM, which tend to look for patterns in the network formats, destinations, and network traffic contents.

The next difference is in the direction of the filtering. Firewalls are designed to keep bad traffic out of the network. Data leakage prevention systems keep unauthorized traffic from leaving the network. IDS systems typically look at traffic in both directions, applying algorithms to the traffic streams to determine whether the conversations taking place indicate that a break-in or infection has occurred.

It's not uncommon for organizations to contract with outside providers for both incoming and outgoing email service, so the idea of having a third party intercept or modify a portion of the organization's data stream is already acceptable in a business context. The real question is whether the magnitude of the data stream in and out of the organization is large enough to make it difficult for a provider to "keep up" with the demand in either direction.

There have already been significant cloud-based deployments in email filtering, and cloud-based Web-based filtering or application blocking (keeping employees from using, say, instant messaging applications) is growing rapidly. The functions that will take longer are the very basic firewall and IDS applications, because of the very real concerns about maintaining data flow. Interestingly enough, while the concern is real, it's likely that a properly designed system with sufficiently provisioned WAN links could actually protect segments of a corporate network against many of the more common traffic-based attacks by intercepting and filtering the offending packets before they have a chance to be launched against the core of the network.

It's in the world of intrusion detection systems (IDS) and intrusion prevention systems (IPS) that some pretty significant changes have been made. First off, these two systems are almost identical in that they must identify "bad stuff" on the fly and are typically set up to look at data flying by using some sort of network tap. The difference is what they do after the "bad stuff" has been identified. Think of an IDS as like a burglar alarm; all it does is make a noise. Think of the IPS as like a personal security force that can spring into action and detain or eject the malware. What makes this significant in terms of clouds is that this all takes computing power, and there is a marketing battle heating up in the two camps.

- If I'm trying to protect the overall performance of the system, why should I be putting a huge additional load on this system I'm trying to protect? It's much better that I put a very light load in the form of a probe or virtual tap that redirects the appropriate network traffic outside of the virtual environment to a system dedicated to examining the data. This methodology basically is one of light footsteps.
- The heavier-footstep version is one that points out that it isn't very expensive to spin up yet another virtual machine in the cloud, and considering that, why not examine the data closer to the source? In this case, let's put a heavier probe actually into the cloud so that we can "react faster" and stamp out our problems closer to the source.

Both camps have great points, and it will be the enterprise buyers voting with their dollars that will determine the winner.

Why Is Cloud Security Good?

Much of the question of why cloud security is good is answered by the basic architecture of the cloud. If suspicious traffic can be intercepted and stopped before it ever reaches the enterprise network, then many issues can be avoided, from the obvious but unsavory questions of liability for pornography or illicit files that remain on a corporate server after being screened out of email to issues of vulnerability exploits that might function even though the message never gets to the client's desktop. It's also important to remember that mobile devices are vulnerable to malware, but to date very few antimalware systems are available for the mobile market, and even those that are force the users to sacrifice quite a bit of performance. As users seek a lighter and lighter client, it makes sense to make sure that data is clean by the time these mobile devices get it.

Cloud security also has the advantage of stopping traffic at the provider's network, preventing large volumes of "bad" data from reaching the enterprise network. This attribute is utilized by email SPAM filter services that help corporate networks avoid logging and storing large quantities of unsolicited email. Cloud security can function in the same way for other security purposes, allowing the corporate network and its administrators to concentrate on targeting more sophisticated issues while the large-scale dross is skimmed off in the cloud. Just remember that it's easier to catch the malware as it transits your infrastructure than to root it out after it has buried itself inside your system.

Keeping in mind the changeable nature of clouds, this also means that there isn't any reason why security systems can't also be swapped in and out as necessary. What could potentially show up in the near future is a new breed of deep inspection system that is a combination of IDS and IPS. We could easily see a lightweight IDS looking at the entire data stream at the cloud ingress, between the app servers and the database servers, and watching all the authentication streams. It might even start looking at the netflow/jflow/sflow streams coming in from the cloud networking infrastructure (remember, switching also happens in the clouds), since many attacks begin with some sort of traffic spike. This cloud IDS could then spin up additional resources as it finds suspected malware. The idea is to provide a way to use as few resources as possible, but not leave the gates unlocked and unguarded. This on-call guard capability is still just in our imagination, but the architecture isn't too far from reality.

Finally, cloud-based security can eliminate one of the principal concerns about security systems: that they present a "single point of failure," at which a serious problem could disrupt the operation of the entire network. The cloud architecture is inherently distributed, eliminating single points of restriction and failure around lone data pipelines and processing elements. There isn't even a requirement that the cloud-based processing be passed back to the customer organization through a single Internet link, further reducing the possibility of disruption due to single-device or single-link failure on the part of the cloud provider. Another key point is that the cloud architecture is inherently changeable, and the ability to swap needed abilities in or out is something we expect to see in the near future. Just like Neo in *The Matrix,* we should be able to download karate on demand.

What Are the Limits of Cloud Security?

With the wonders of cloud security that have been described, could there possibly be limits or restrictions on what it can do? There certainly could be, and likely will be for some time to come. Part of the limit will be speed- or bandwidth-related, part will be related to the willingness of management to trust various aspects of the network infrastructure to the cloud, and part will be due to regulators' reluctance to trust what they have difficulty putting their hands on.

Speed and infrastructure concerns will likely slow the acceptance of cloud-based firewall and IDS or IPS technology. The fact is that large enterprise networks are pushing the limits of on-premise firewall technology, so a turn to a new cloud-based architecture is unlikely to be warmly received until there have been several very large demonstration projects that are viewed as unmitigated successes.

Trust has been an issue with security as a service, and the nature of cloud computing doesn't, in itself, have the qualities required to eliminate the concerns. This trust question is an issue that is larger than cloud computing itself, going to the heart of whether companies should focus on their "core competency" or handle all elements of the business infrastructure themselves. This is an essential philosophical question that can't truly be addressed by cloud computing alone. While there are some functions that companies are accustomed to leaving in others' hands—how many enterprises function as their own banks?—where the line is drawn between essential internal functions and tasks that can be performed under contract by others is a question that each organization must answer for itself before tackling questions of cloud security, or cloud computing in its most basic form, for that matter.

Another interesting monkey wrench in the process is the depth of the identity management database. Interestingly enough, developers have been eating the learning curve on these complex special-purpose databases and have been extending the data store in novel ways. A good example is how a major university in Honolulu has been pushing a very large LDAP authentication system, but has continued to draw flak due to departmental needs for additional granularity in identifying groups of users. We've also heard of corporations that have added in user-defined fields for data not anticipated by Microsoft or others in commercial identity management systems. It is our opinion that these user-defined fields are going to be a sticking point in just how far corporations are willing to migrate into the clouds, and how quickly. More important, some of these user-defined fields were created to meet the demands of regulatory pressure.

Regulators tend to be conservative sorts. As a society, we've learned that there can be significant consequences if they're not. The notion that there will be elements of the essential security infrastructure that might be outside the direct control of the IT staff makes regulators nervous. The same abstraction layers that can be so appealing to technologists can be seen as obfuscation layers by regulators seeking transparency in the processes and systems they view.

The good part of regulations is that they're all written down, subject to interpretation, and eventually reality takes over. The federal Health Insurance Portability and Accountability Act, HIPAA, is a very good example of pure terror eventually turning into standard operating procedure. We're pretty sure that as rules solidify into reality, cloud providers will all be following Amazon's example with regulatory-compliant virtual templates. In the very near future you should be able to answer a questionnaire about your business and the cloud provider will suggest a template, or will suggest that you contact their global services group for a custom template.

It is likely that cloud providers will be able to come up with architectures that ultimately allow regulators to be more comfortable with the presence of cloud-based elements in a security infrastructure, but the conversation to make that happen will not happen quickly, and will almost certainly be re-created across every regulatory regime that must consider cloud security. The process will be slow and deliberate, but that isn't necessarily bad. If cloud computing platforms are sufficiently developed to be able to satisfy regulators, that fact will speak very well to the platforms' ability to meet the genuine needs of a variety of different organizations.

What Is the Future of Cloud Security?

Improving bandwidth is almost certain to lead to greater acceptance of all security-as-a-service offerings, and cloud architectures will be a growing part of those offerings. Growing "fuzziness" of the network boundary will make cloud security a far more desirable security architecture as IT staff realize that they simply can't grow a fence big enough to stretch around all the mobile devices and telecommuting employees they must deal with. In many ways, it's a perfect storm—needs that can't readily be met in other ways will meet the supporting infrastructure to make them possible. The real question is how long it will take management to catch up with the reality.

A side benefit of all this thinking about how to implement security in the clouds should be increased cooperation among the data owners. Think about it this way: New and amazing things can be done if additional layers of correlation can be achieved. Our favorite example was at an InfoWorld security event manager shootout in 2004, where one vendor had the system correlate card-swipe physical entry data with network security log files. Separately, a card swipe to enter the facility by employee X was fine, and separately a VPN log-in from outside the country by the same employee was also fine. However, a correlation between the two suddenly would get any security specialist's attention. Sometimes, pushing people together with a requirement for change isn't always a bad thing. Make it easier to share data securely, and perhaps it might actually happen.

Ultimately, cloud-based security offers the promise of a single security infrastructure that can properly protect a wide variety of different platform types and operating systems no matter where they're operating from. This "end game" would make the enterprise far more secure while making the task of the security administrator much easier, since there would be a single relationship and management console to provide views into wide-ranging security features.

Clouds Flight Path for Chapter 9

- *Cloud security options.* Where should the fence go, and what kinds of options are out there? Unified threat management appliances are going in two directions, bigger faster CPUs or pushing functions such as antispam and antivirus into the cloud. Will virtual versions of firewalls like those from Astaro become normal? Firewall appliances are almost all now based on Intel chips and embedded Linux, so the potential is already there to start seeing cloud versions in the future. We think it's mighty convenient to have the security closer to the apps, and perhaps we'll start seeing dynamically allocated security functions based on load and perhaps a multitiered approach to security.

- *Cloud authentication.* Do you have to migrate off-premise, or are there options for a hybrid solution? Consider the success of services such as SalesForce and Microsoft Office OnLine, and how they both provide for both import and synchronous authentication methods. We just want to point out that there is a history for single sign-on, and the market really seems to want it. Will a greater amount of trust in the cloud also provide the fertile ground for federation to finally sprout?

- *Cloud security limitations.* Just how far can you take it, and is it worth the effort? Some effort certainly has to be taken to architect your system so that fences have a chance of working. We want to point out that you can't implement what you can understand. Making sure everyone involved understands their role means that trust relationships might actually have a chance at being implemented.

- *Cloud security futures.* Where is this all going, and what can we expect in the future? We are certainly seeing changes happening, and as clouds mature and options really start opening up, we're sure to see some really creative solutions popping up. Just the fact that taps and probes have already been virtualized gives us a clue that troubleshooting tool vendors are jumping onto the bandwagon, and we're sure that others will follow soon. When all is said and done, it's all going to be about how we vote with our dollars/euros/pesos/etc. If the market demands solutions, solutions will appear.

Chapter 10

The Future of the Cloud

The true sign of intelligence is not knowledge but imagination.
— Albert Einstein

In This Chapter

Trying to predict the future of clouds is like trying to nail Jello to a tree—what doesn't wiggle, slips and slides. What we can do is take a historical perspective and extrapolate forward, sprinkle lightly with educated guesses and perhaps add a dash of wild guess to keep things interesting. We're already starting to see the cloud warriors setting up the chess pieces, and we can only hope that the best solution will win. We must note that, in the time it's taken to write this book, some topics have moved from their original position in this chapter into earlier chapters on current cloud deployment. It's possible that others will change in the near future, but we'll forge ahead boldly, nonetheless. Some of our predictions will cover:

- Specialized clouds. Just because clouds want to be platforms and nonspecific doesn't mean that we won't find exceptions to the rule. Specialization is a natural occurrence, but will these become the norm or the exception?

- Media clouds. An example of how things change and grow. See how one industry has been changing to meet market demands.
- Clouds as the fertile ground for the growth of federation. Why we keep harping on federation, and why we think we might finally see federation happening in the cloud.
- Clouds as a DMZ or security proxy. How clouds can provide neutral territory that can be used in all kinds of ways.
- Office productivity clouds. Why do you have to buy a full copy of a productivity suite if you're only going to use it for a couple days? What's starting to appear, and how do we think it will be used?
- Compute clouds in a mixed environment. We're already starting to see the deemphasis of specific platforms and how clouds are starting to become the universal translator of the computer world. Wouldn't it be nice if we didn't have to care about the hardware on the back end?
- Mobile clouds. The universal constant is that mobile platforms just don't have enough horsepower to run the really cool applications, and it's looking like clouds are going to provide the back-end processing power to make them happen.
- Cloud-aware applications. Android-based phones are just the beginning of systems designed especially to leverage the back-end cloud. It's all about programming tools and how the cloud providers support developers.

Putting Our Crystal Ball into Perspective

It's very apparent that the world of cloud computing is still forming, and that the market is at a cusp—one that may be the first of many to come. We're hearing conversations about clouds everywhere, but as yet very few companies have actually jumped into cloud deployment to any significant extent. The common statement has been "We're experimenting" or "It's still being prototyped." We have seen some encouraging signs that clouds are becoming more mainstream, as pundits are starting to scream about "securing the clouds" to the tune of a "Chicken Little" song. The good news (if you're a cloud proponent) is that these are issues that tend to become important only when technologies are beginning to be deployed in production environments. The bad news is that the mere fact that the questions can be legitimately asked will keep some organizations on the sidelines for some time to come.

It's important, at the beginning of this chapter, to note one of the critical things we haven't heard much about. What we haven't heard is anything about some sort of meaningful cloud standard, ad hoc or otherwise. It's inevitable that standards will be developed, if for no other reason than it makes entirely too much sense not to have them. Now, there are, in fact, standards at different interfaces and levels used within the various cloud computing environments. From SOAP to Java to CGI, a variety of different standards are used to make cloud computing possible. What hasn't happened, yet, is the proposal of any sort of "one standard to rule them all" when it comes to the cloud. There's no telling what will push the industry into more cloud standardization, although the issues orbiting around identity federation are a reasonable guess, but the safe money will be on some degree of greater standardization sooner, rather than later.

Many organizations report that they're considering clouds as a way to extend their jump into virtualization, and virtualization is a trend that has moved far beyond the mere experimentation phase at most organizations. Since the Amazon EC2 cloud server is based on VMWare, it has certainly made sense to leverage that compatibility as IT administrators find themselves outgrowing their VMware server farms faster than expected. This is especially prevalent when they find themselves with a surge project that was unanticipated in the annual budget.

The *New York Times* indexing project (see Chapter 4) is a typical example of this type of deployment, and we're already seeing clouds become the answer for quite a few unanticipated expansion projects. One of the things we'll look at in more detail later in this chapter is the question of which specific types of clouds will be better suited to this sort of overflow capacity computing than others, and how those differences are likely to influence the future development of clouds for both public and private applications.

One of the unfortunate side effects of almost any wave of technology adoption is that marketing teams adopt the name of the technology as a means of selling products that may or may not have anything to do with the actual products that make up the trend. The industry has seen too many vendors adopting "cloud" as a buzzword and applying it to just about any kind of back-end processing that takes the load off the actual desktop. It's useful to keep asking whether product X is a true cloud application or just a client server implementation of a business service. Some will be cloud applications, while some will be classic client-server apps dressed up with a fancy new cloud label. We hope this book has helped give you the information to tell the difference. Whether that difference matters to your organization in any particular situation is entirely up to you.

Beyond handling surge projects, clouds will start off in most cases as specialized applications in order to attract various vertical markets. As profitability becomes a reality, the offerings will slowly creep sideways and become more general purpose in nature. How fast these sites become horizontal is also going to have a lot to do with how fast real standards appear in the market. Let's take a look at one of the special-purpose cloud applications that developed into a much more general-purpose platform for cloud apps.

Cloud Development Tools in Perspective

When you're talking about the future of cloud computing, you can get some real clues based on things that are happening right now. Let's look at one of those, BOINC, and how it might impact the cloud in the near future, and if things develop along certain lines, a little farther out on the timeline.

One of the first shared-resource computing applications that many people were aware of was SETI@home. The Search for Extraterrestrial Intelligence gathers data from a number of sources, the main one being the large radio telescope at Aracibo in Puerto Rico. SETI realized years ago that gathering data wasn't its primary problem—analyzing the data was. They knew that they would never be able to buy enough processing power to analyze data in a reasonable amount of time, so they decided to get people to give them processing time, instead.

The SETI@home software worked by taking advantage of the fact that relatively few home computers use even a substantial fraction of their overall computing potential. By downloading data to volunteer computers in discrete chunks, allowing the analysis to be done with otherwise-idle compute cycles, and then uploading the results whenever the work was complete, SETI created its own compute cloud long before the term was in use more broadly in the industry.

There are a couple of things to understand about the SETI@home project. First, the SETI data was gathered and constructed in such a way as to facilitate its division into regular packages that can be parceled out to a large number of computers. Next, the SETI project isn't time-sensitive—if a particular set of data takes hours or days to complete, it doesn't jeopardize the project or throw the application into disarray. Finally, the data SETI works on isn't confidential or sensitive, so there's no issue with volunteers seeing the processing take place or having information on their personal computers.

Eventually, other scientists realized that their data met the same basic criteria as SETI's. Several wrote their own distributed applications before someone had the idea of an open abstraction layer and application that would simplify the process of deploying a widely distributed app. The birth of BOINC was a major step toward a cloud for processing scientific data.

The Berkeley Open Infrastructure for Network Computing (BOINC) makes it relatively easy for scientists to give their data the SETI cloud treatment. This is a free processing cloud application, with the processing nodes provided by individuals who feel it's worthwhile to allow someone else to "use" their computer during odd seconds and minutes of processor inactivity. The applications making use of the BOINC framework include projects such as protein folding and a search for gravity waves in our galaxy.

BOINC allows scientists and project managers to easily develop applications that make use of the widely distributed cloud that makes up the BOINC processor grid. It also allows individuals who want to contribute to solving the processor-intensive problems to easily volunteer their computer cycles for this purpose. In serving as a broker for services, it allows application users and compute infrastructures to find one another with a method that is easy to use and economical for both parties.

That's now—let's look at the future.

The renewable energy market has begun working on the notion of traditional energy consumers (homeowners and businesses) who install no-impact or low-impact energy production technology (such as photovoltaic panels) to power the building when necessary, take energy from the grid when required, and sell energy back to the grid when possible. Imagine this model at work in a processing cloud. Business applications that require significant processing power could be parceled out to legions of users who allow their computers to become part of a cloud.

It would be relatively straightforward for a cloud application broker to anonymize data that flows to the crowd, or for the application designer to make sure that the data is broken into pieces that have no meaning to anyone who might look in on the data or the processing. The greater difficulty is designing a micro-payment system capable of keeping track of processing units and arranging for compensation in a cost-effective manner.

The question, of course, is who might have an incentive to come up with such a system, but there are several possible answers to this. The first is utility companies that are already adept at large-scale customer billing, and that frequently have communications infrastructures in place which would be able to handle the data transactions required for the cloud to work. The next might seem less obvious, but is an example of the sort of industry that could solve two of its major problems as a cloud broker provider.

Many traditional publishers are working on the notion of getting readers or viewers to pay for content, a notion that's generally opposed by the readers. One of the issues facing the publishers is the development of a micro-payment system that could charge mere cents (or even fractions of a cent) for access to certain material. What if the publishers acted as cloud app brokers, exchanging access to reader's CPUs for access to published material?

The reader could "pay" for content with CPU cycles the publisher could sell to those who need the processing. A new revenue stream for publishers might help lessen reader resistance to paid-content models by offering them a noncash way to pay for their reading. It's a win–win situation that requires nothing that has not been developed, to at least an early stage, already.

Now, let's take the micro-payment cloud application solution to another level. The publishing industry is one that has been in financial trouble as their existing business model shifted beneath them, but it's far from the only sector that finds itself in that situation. What if we expand the concept to other "industries in need"?

Truck transportation is critical for the North American economy, though it's subject to many different challenges on cost, revenue, and infrastructure fronts. Many trucks already have computers on board to handle scheduling and bookkeeping operations. It would be relatively easy to download raw data to the computers at truck stops, freight depots, or warehouses, have the computers process the data while on the road, then upload the results at a future stop.

Transportation companies are accustomed to dealing with sensitive physical cargo and developing strong relationships with customers. Based on these factors, transportation companies could easily handle applications that customers would be unwilling to turn over to an anonymous, much more public cloud infrastructure.

While there are absolutely limits on the type of cloud that could be supported by this sort of highly mobile, intermittent-access cloud infrastructure, there are also tremendous possibilities. Frequently accessed data storage is not an appropriate application, but large-scale project processing is. The fact that there are applications that aren't appropriate to the infrastructure may seem a limitation (and it is), but it's also a strength of the cloud concept.

If there were only one type of cloud, then it might well be true that there were significant limitations on the types of applications that could reasonably be deployed into the cloud. The wide variety of clouds that can exist means that there are equally wide varieties of applications that can be moved to some sort of cloud. Let's look at some additional cloud types that bear watching in the future.

Clouds of Different Types

Since we're polishing that crystal ball, let's step out a little closer to the cliff's edge and say that once the first stake goes into the clouds, the number and variety of cloud cities will be like the colors of the rainbow. Just like the myriad of service bureaus in the 1960s and 1970s, we're pretty sure that a whole lot of cloud cities will spin off from corporations, as, for instance, hospitals have been spinning off shared IT and billing departments for ages.

These specialized clouds that serve only a few organizations will be only the beginning. The true future is going to be in the commoditization of the cloud and how it becomes a generalized facility. What we see will be a combination of specialized and generalized clouds, just as in the rest of the world's markets.

This worldview has long been envisaged by science fiction writers such as Robert Heinlein, Isaac Asimov, and Arthur C. Clarke, who described world networks leveraging experience through a nearly unlimited selection of applications. It's already starting to happen with clouds such as

Google Docs and Microsoft Office Live Workspace, where groupware apps run in the cloud either complementing or replacing the desktop.

When a bunch of InfoWorld editors started working on a list of what we considered the best open-source applications available at the time, it was considerably easier for all of us to work on the same spreadsheet in Google Docs. Since the spreadsheet application actually ran in the Google cloud, there were no issues with compatibility, nor did we have problems with versioning, since we were all working in the same doc.

We could as easily have been working on spaceflight launch parameters, or the itinerary for a school field trip. The point is that we are now able to find some very complex applications running in the cloud instead of needing a full thick application on a desktop. Perhaps the world is subliminally telling the industry that this is the model it wants, since the concept of "good enough" has swept the world with things like netbooks and iPods. The netbook is good enough for light applications and Web browsing, and the iPod is good enough to listen to music on the train or watch tiny video screens to catch up on missed television programs. Do we need the full versions, or will the cloud become the "instant gratification" system for the Information Age?

Media Clouds

Exemplified by mediacloud.com, this vertical market cloud concentrates on the concept of leveraging the huge amount of remote reporting capability that the worldwide Internet provides. According to Media Cloud:

> Media Cloud is a system that lets you see the flow of the media. The Internet is fundamentally altering the way that news is produced and distributed, but there are few comprehensive approaches to understanding the nature of these changes. Media Cloud automatically builds an archive of news stories and blog posts from the web, applies language processing, and gives you ways to analyze and visualize the data. The system is still in early development, but we invite you to explore our current data and suggest research ideas.

(*Source:* www.mediacloud.com.)

We would be remiss if we wrote only about the production side of media. To a certain extent we could also say that copyright.com could be defined as the beginnings of a copyright registration cloud that then utilizes a payment cloud run by Amazon. Copyright.com's Ozmo service provides a clearinghouse service for both registration of copyrighted materials and the licensing of copyrighted materials.

Perhaps the litmus test for clouds is whether the application is both standalone and extensible. This is certainly true for copyright.com, since it is very clearly providing a front end for a whole lot of other organizations behind the scenes, but is also serving as a place for other organizations to leverage. Maybe a cloud should be colloquially defined as a middleman that is capable of standing alone?

Another media-related application is "What The Font," which combines the utility of the iPhone camera with back-end processing of complex images for on-the-fly identification of fonts submitted via the Web or iPhone cameras. So, while this system will only find a close match and then suggest a font that they sell, it is nonetheless a great example of just how complex the back-end processing can become.

Security Clouds

We're only just starting to glimpse what we might call a security cloud, with offerings from folks such as Symantec and SonicWall. These vendors both have a myriad of security devices, all feeding information regarding the status of the Internet at that location. With all this information being collected in a central location, these vendors are now better able to feed information to other security-related organizations on the attack vectors being used in Internet attacks that periodically sweep through the world Internet.

What these types of clouds provide is a way to potentially hack off attacks where they enter the country, or at least higher up in the Internet router hierarchy. Their overall goal is to provide a quicker way to characterize attacks and then provide a way to share this information so that the authorities have a better chance of catching the perpetrators in the act, and most important, pull the teeth on the attack by updating client security devices as quickly as possible.

We really first saw this appear when we did a review on security event managers for InfoWorld and got briefed by Symantec on their worldwide

Security Operations Center. Since then the security community has taken great strides in coordinating its efforts through shared databases and finally a common descriptor language and catalogue. Previously it was common to have different antivirus systems characterizing the same virus under different names or numbers, only to have it renamed something else. The use of the Common Vulnerability and Exposure Catalogue is quickly making attack protection a worldwide effort.

What we can also imagine are cloud service bureaus that concentrate not only on characterizing attacks quickly, but also being contracted to provide security auditing of Internet feeds before the attacks get to a company, and shutting down attacks before they have a chance to ramp up and do real damage.

At the consumer level, we first saw this type of back-end security processing from CheckPoint Corporation, where email scanning was handled at the CheckPoint data center, which allowed advanced security features to be offered on relatively inexpensive firewalls meant for home use. While this particular product didn't seem to catch on, this exact feature has reappeared in some small business products from Cisco Corporation.

App-Specific Clouds

We can certainly think of a couple of "one-trick ponies," and while those sites do only one thing, that level of specialization doesn't mean they shouldn't be considered a cloud. We think it really comes down to an application or site that allows its boundaries to blur so that it can have some sort of overlap with its peers.

When we pontificated about federation and how that will be the fertile ground on which clouds will sprout; we can also imagine that there will be sites sprouting that really have little or no public interface. These sites are the "one-trick ponies" we're talking about. Considering the amount of skill and time it takes to do color correction in video, for instance, we can easily imagine a site that does nothing but video color correction. It would have interfaces fed by retailers such as Walmart, Sears, and many others that only provide the aggregation and billing services at the front end.

Perhaps a better analogy might be the companies that make rear-view mirrors for the big automakers. They rarely do any sales direct to the consumer, but they sell huge numbers of rear-view mirrors because the automakers buy enough to outfit all the cars coming off their assembly lines. The litmus test seems to work: It's still a stand-alone organization, but designed to be extensible as other organizations utilize it through Internet connections.

Office Desktop and Groupware Clouds

The first example we ran across actually goes back to the old "bulletin board" days. CompuServe had all kinds of applications available, with some collections closely resembling the groupware applications we know today. We certainly remember a group scheduling application on CompuServe that Brian used with several other government employees to figure out who was in which city and when. It was all character-based and accessed via dial-up modems, but it could be viewed as one of the predecessors to modern clouds.

However, in more modern times, Google University and Google Docs has got to be one of the more modern incarnations of desktops in the clouds. With full spreadsheets, presentation tools, and word processing; Google's offerings not only give shared workspaces, but also don't require that any apps be installed on the desktop except a Web browser that support Java.

What we've found most surprising about Google Docs is just how aggressively Google has duplicated the capabilities of thick desktop apps such as Microsoft Office. Features such as forms support, footnote-to-endnote conversion, language translations, an equation editor, tables, solver (small spreadsheets), and the ability to import a large number of different formats is making this offering a very tempting alternative to Microsoft Office.

One odd function we found is called Tournament, by which NCAA statistics can be easily imported into a document. While this may sound frivolous, we have to imagine that this function will eventually turn into a full SOAP/JSON import function for yanking data directly off other websites.

One trend to watch is the "follow the crowd" syndrome, where managers are thinking that desktop virtualization will be just as successful as server virtualization. While the potential is there, it has to be tempered with caution about trying a "one size fits all" attitude. The success of Windows Terminal server can in part be attributed to the unevenness of Internet service providers worldwide. Remote users got really tired of apps taking some very *long* minutes to start up, as opposed to seconds when they were at the home office. Running the apps on your desktop physically at the home office and then sending only the keyboard+video+mouse information over the wide-area link have made some applications bearable. What the desktop cloud folks want you to think about is to instead have desktop images that can be loaded on demand into your in-house cloud instead of sucking up physical desktop machines. Microsoft raised the bar recently with Windows 7 and its built-in abilities for this sort of thing, and then sweetened the deal with their DirectAccess feature to take a huge amount of pain out of implementing IPsec VPN connections for secure remote access by road warriors. So while the Microsoft marketing hype may say that this is remote access without VPNs, that's not quite true; it's more like taking the massive amount of hassles out of VPNs by leveraging a tightly integrated client-server model between the Windows 7 client and the Server 2008 system. As Microsoft describes it:

Enhance mobility and manageability with DirectAccess

- **Working outside the office is easier than ever.** DirectAccess in Windows 7 and Windows Server 2008 R2 enhances the productivity of mobile workers by connecting them seamlessly and more securely to their corporate network any time they have Internet access—without the need to VPN. When your IT department enables DirectAccess, the corporate network's file shares, intranet websites, and line-of-business applications remain accessible wherever you have an Internet connection.
- **Manage remote machines more effectively.** Flexibility gives IT the opportunity to service remote machines on a regular basis and ensure that mobile users stay up to date with company policies. With DirectAccess, IT administrators can manage mobile computers by updating Group Policy settings and distributing software updates any time the mobile computer has Internet connectivity, even if the user is not logged on.
- **Enhance security and access control.** To keep data safer as it travels public networks, DirectAccess uses IPv6-over-IPsec to encrypt communications transmitted across the Internet. DirectAccess is designed to reduce unnecessary

traffic on the corporate network by sending only traffic destined for the corporate network through the DirectAccess server (running Windows Server 2008 R2), or the administrator can choose to send all traffic through the corporate network. In addition to authenticating the computer, DirectAccess can also authenticate the user and supports multifactor authentication, such as a smart card. IT administrators can configure which intranet resources specific users can access using DirectAccess.

(*Source:* www.microsoft.com/windows/enterprise/products/ windows-7/features.aspx#directaccess.)

In addition, VMWare is adding fuel to the fire with the PC-over-IP (PCoIP) protocol, which trumps the legacy remote desktop protocol (RDP) with a new protocol that quickly builds a low-resolution image and then, as bandwidth and time allow, layers in additional resolution. This is the type of architecture used over and over again by several vendors in order to provide quick application response time with potentially slow wide-area network connections. A great example is ARCGIS by ESRI, which provides planners with the ability to represent graphically large amounts of infrastructure and use that graphical interface to work with data layers and create complex "what if" scenarios with physical infrastructure. Typical is asking the system to display utilities in relationship to a proposed development and then get information on capacity and current usage. Such graphics and data querying heavy operations have been found to be nearly impossible over slow WAN links, so instead ESRI has been leveraging terminal servers so that data flows over local high-speed connections and only the "results" are sent over the WAN connections:

PCoIP is a server-centric protocol, meaning that we are doing the majority of the graphics rendering and processing on powerful servers. Compressed bitmaps or frames are transmitted to the remote client. This division of labor has some ideal properties for static content. First it's making use of the powerful processing capabilities of multi-core servers such as Intel's Nehalem to render the graphics. More importantly, by transmitting compressed bitmaps or frames, we can adjust the protocol in real time to account for the available bandwidth and latency of the communications channel. On a WAN connection with typically less bandwidth and higher latency, a less crisp image is produced quickly, typically with 0.2-0.5 bits/pixel producing a grainy, but still recognizable image. Kind of like an analog TV. . . . This rapidly sharpens with increasing clarity and detail visibility with each succeeding frame until the image is perceptually lossless. This is a high quality image at a total of approximately 1-3 bits/pixel. Think of it as now Digital HD to stick with our TV analogy. On a higher performance LAN, the images become sharp instantly and will build to complete lossless at 5-15 bits per pixel. Think of it as Blu-Ray!

(*Source:* http://blogs.vmware.com/view-point/2009/10/why-pcoip-is-the-best-protocol-for-virtual-desktops.html.)

Computing Clouds

We've not spent much time on computing-specific clouds (also called Beowulf clusters), since for the most part those are science-specific and already quite well defined. However, even those are seeing convergence of sorts.

The supercomputer centers around the world have all seen the writing on the wall and have been spending quite a bit of effort to provide easier ways to accept and account for large-scale supercomputing applications. With large-scale projects using more and more computing resources, the need to split projects across multiple supercomputer centers has driven researchers to seek better ways to manage these massive applications.

We mention this here because Amazon isn't just going for business applications, but has also set up the EC2 system to support MPI (Message Passing Interface, which is how supercomputer apps talk to each other in a cooperative fashion). Here are some examples we got from the Amazon public relations folks:

Eli Lilly and Company <http://www.lilly.com/> is a leading global pharmaceutical company that researches and develops innovative medicines that help people live longer and healthier. Among known brands such as Cialis and Prozac, the company is also responsible for many major pharmaceutical breakthroughs:

Gemzar, for treatment of pancreatic cancer; Humalog therapy for diabetes; and Secobarbital, a treatment for epilepsy. To support its research, Eli Lilly is using on-demand servers and storage from Amazon Web Services to help manage costs as well as providing high performance computing to the company's researchers. Not only that, but AWS also provides a resource for research collaboration so Eli Lilly and Company can focus on continuing to pioneer pharmaceutical breakthroughs.

Pathwork Diagnostics <http://www.pathworkdx.com/>, a molecular diagnostics company, turned to Amazon Web Services to get access to the kind of massive scale computing required to perform its research. The company develops high-value diagnostic tests to aid oncologists in the diagnosis of hard-to-identify cancer tumors; it chooses optimal models for its tests by analyzing large libraries containing gene expression profiles of clinically annotated tumor specimens. Pathwork scientists investigated several different cloud providers before selecting Amazon Web Services, based on its proven computing environment, ease of use and reliability.

The Indianapolis Motor Speedway hosts three industry-leading motor sport events: The Indianapolis 500, Allstate 400 at the Brickyard, and the Red Bull Indianapolis MotoGP race. To meet the demands of their growing fan base, the Indianapolis Motor Speedway built an online platform to stream their live events. As an entertainment company, IMS's first priority was providing relevant, accessible content to their visitors. But, with over 3.1 million online visitors, IMS's Online Services team had a challenge ahead of them.

Amazon EC2 serves indycar.com and indy500.com through web hosting, live video streaming, and live timing and scoring applications. IMS mirrors thier websites in Amazon EC2 and scales up as needed during events. Amazon EC2 enables IMS to use only the servers they need and save costs by monitoring servers remotely. In one month (during Indy500), they were able to save over 50% in costs.

NASDAQ used Amazon Web Services to launch NASDAQ Market Replay—an innovative new tool for replaying and analyzing mountains of stock market data. The Market Replay application enables users to view the best bids and offers at any point in time, replay the market in simulated real-time, and zoom to view events at the millisecond level. Investors can validate best-execution and regulatory compliance. Brokers and traders can review events at the time when their trades occurred to determine whether there was a problem or a missed opportunity. Brokers can send clients a NASDAQ-validated replay of the moment a trade occurred to validate their performance.

The application utilizes Amazon for housing of historical market data. Amazon S3 removes the need for a traditional middle-tier server, as the data is accessed in from the Amazon "cloud." Amazon Web Services helped launch the service without investing in data storage hardware and reduced the cost and risk of bringing a new product to market.

(*Source:* Kay Kinton, Amazon Public Relations, August 21, 2009.)

Mobile Clouds

The smartphone surge exemplified by the Apple iPhone can also be viewed as people saying they want access to their data anywhere they go. What mobile clouds promise is to extend that access regardless of how much compute power it requires. Picture yourself standing in front of a vacant lot where your friend's house used to stand and then asking the phone to find where you friend lives now. Potentially, that means cross-referencing phone book archives, possibly tax map records, and perhaps Facebook. Then the mapping program would to guide you to your friend's new home.

Extending this idea further, perhaps there's a mobile version of some digital image forensics program that can take the shaky video you just shot of the bank robbers driving away into the night. It submits the image to the back-end digital forensics cloud, where the image is de-skewed, enhanced, combined with surrounding frames to create additional resolution, and then perhaps centered on the license plate and lastly run a DMV lookup. Perhaps a little George Jetson, but desktop versions already exist, with a strong wish from the law enforcement world to push this into a mobile platform. A little more down to earth is the iPhone app from Nuance, which has a mobile cloud application called Dragon Dictation, which sends voice clips to a back-end cloud service and returns results over the 3G or WiFi connection. A demonstration seen while attending Digital Experience at the 2010 Consumer Electronic Show was performed in an incredible noisy ballroom but still yielded reasonable results. We expect to see more and more of the heavy lifting being done in the back-end cloud.

Certainly a tough task even for existing desktop computers, but a phone? It's really going to be about leveraging back-end compute power to deliver the results to the mobile platform. Like the old client-server model, the client (the phone) is simply a user interface; all the heavy lifting would be done by the back-end cloud applications.

We've noticed recently that both Microsoft and Google seem to be positioning their pieces on the mobile world chessboard. Our clues are the quiet release of Microsoft SQL mobile, MyPhone.live, live desktop for Windows Mobile, and, in the Google court, Android. What this kind of creeping technology release means to us is that the big announcements are yet to come.

What both big players are doing is creating a mobile environment that is extremely friendly to back-end services—services that when complete should rival full desktops in capability, and at the same time leverage the desktop and extend its reach. Just look at how the Google Android system already has a whole bunch of connections into the Google Docs desktop. Or how the Microsoft Live environment has become quite adept at exchanging and synchronizing with both the desktop and the back-end Microsoft Cloud. It will be back-end applications that enable mobile apps like augmented reality to handle complex tasks that enable labeling businesses or friends within view of the camera phone, all from a compass, GPS location, and accelerometers on the mobile device. Just think of all the processing this task takes up:

1. Look up the general location and altitude from GPS and multiple cell tower signal strengths to determine the location within a couple of meters.
2. Use the compass to determine the direction the user is facing and the accelerometer to determine the angle of view.
3. Then use 3-D geographic information systems (GIS) models of the urban area and execute ray-tracing algorithms to determine what's in the field of view.

4. Do a 3-D rendering of what's in view and generate a perspective overlay so that closer signs are bigger and distant signs are smaller but all are in perspective.

And everything has to be done fast enough to keep up with the user panning around in the field of view. Some of the other magic happening is that the whole system has also rendered a local model of the surrounding area in order to allow this panning around, without needing to suck up amazing amounts of bandwidth on the mobile device.

Another big front-end and back-end mobile application might well be unified communications (UC). The big players aren't labeling it UC yet, but that's essentially what it is, and we may begin to see it called that as more of the suite is exposed. Since enterprises have been extremely hesitant to adopt UC in house, UC may be a significant portion of the glue that will connect both Microsoft and Google mobile devices to their respective clouds.

It's the heavy lifting on the back end that will make mobile clouds more than just a novelty and into an enterprise tool. Regardless of the way the scenario unfolds, what's important is that being able to do all the computing in the cloud means that the line between the office and field will no longer matter. We're just wondering how long it will be until we see SAP clients for the iPhone.

We also think these special-purpose clouds will be fertile ground for federation to finally throw down roots. We've been hearing about federation for a very long time, but the trust relationships necessary to make it all work just don't seem to be forming. We think the DMZ or "no man's land" approach that clouds can provide might be the very ticket necessary to finally bring about adoption.

For that matter, we're predicting that the "no man's land" concept may be one of the first true cloud cities to stake a claim. Hey, maybe it will be in Switzerland and have a red cross as a logo? It has occurred to us that those trying to pull off a "no man's land" cloud really ought to take a page from those Swiss bankers in how to stay neutral.

If there were only one type of cloud, then it might be true that there are significant limitations on the types of applications that can reasonably be deployed into the cloud. The wide varieties of clouds that can exist means that there are equally wide varieties of applications that can be moved to some sort of cloud. Let's look at some additional cloud types that bear watching in the future.

It's one of the sad facts of modern life that business continuity and disaster recovery are critical aspects of an IT administrator's life. Natural disasters, infrastructure failures, and man-made catastrophes are all part of the universe of dangers that must be taken into account when making plans for how to keep a business running regardless of the circumstances. Many traditional plans have centered on the fact that critical pieces of data or processing infrastructure are in one place—a particular server farm or data storage center—but let's think for a bit about how planning might change if certain aspects of the business are in the cloud.

Cloud storage (with built-in redundancy) means that no disaster short of the end of civilization as we know it could take down an organization's data set. There are, of course, requirements that the data be managed so that redundancies are maintained and the data traversing the Internet is de-duplicated and cached at critical locations, but those are technical details that have existing solutions. No, the real issues that make this a "future" topic are cloud management and the internal political will to make such a project happen.

Computer and network vendors are being pushed by their customers to make private cloud systems more available and more capable than ever before. One of the major players that intends to become a cloud monster is Microsoft, with its Azure cloud environment. Azure was announced in late 2008 and was finally released as a service offering at the Microsoft Professional Developers Conference in November 2009. Released in a platform-as-a-service (PaaS) architecture, Azure became available on a pay-per-unit basis, with the units depending on whether the customer purchased application capability on a virtual server or storage in the Azure storage cloud.

While Azure was released as a public cloud offering, at the Interop conference in November 2009 (the same month Azure was released to the public), customers and potential customers began pressing Microsoft to release a version of Azure that could be deployed as a private cloud. In an interview with journalist Jeffrey Schwartz, Yousef Khalidi, a distinguished engineer for cloud infrastructure at Microsoft, said he was aware of the desire of larger enterprise customers for private clouds.

> In the visualstudiomagazine.com article "Interop New York: Customers Press Vendors for Private Clouds," on November 20, 2009, Schwartz quoted Khalidi as saying, "We believe there is a place in the spectrum for private clouds that offer many of

the benefits of the cloud including a scale-out architecture." Khalidi said, "Unlike public clouds, private clouds can be kept under lock and key. We have the benefit of capacity on demand, global reach and all of the benefits of a large shared multi-tenant infrastructure."

Private clouds under the complete control of the customer organization solve a number of security and regulatory concerns that are inherent in public clouds. The same abstraction of service and data from physical infrastructure that delivers the promise of virtual machines and clouds makes it impossible to apply many conventional control and security methods to data and applications in the cloud. Private clouds combine the architectural advantages of the cloud with the regulatory compliance capabilities of traditional architectures. The trade-off, of course, is that the customer is once again responsible for all the purchase, deployment, and maintenance costs of the cloud when the cloud is private.

IBM is another traditional computing infrastructure company that has made significant steps in both public and private cloud deployment. While the company was one of the early vendors to offer public cloud capabilities to its customers, in November 2009 it announced the deployment of what was at the time one of the world's largest private cloud environments. Blue Insight, a cloud application environment built to support IBM business analytics, provides its users with over a petabyte (roughly a thousand terabytes) of stored information that can be used to inform marketing and sales decisions. At the same time, IBM announced the IBM Smart Analytics Clouds as a platform on which customers can build their own business analytics applications using the same infrastructure IBM has deployed internally.

Changing the Definition of Virtualization

The concept of virtualization has been a moving target ever since we first heard of the concept from IBM in the old 360/370 mainframe days. It was big news when those systems could run multiple jobs instead of a single punch-card deck at a time. The ability to ask multiple questions all at the same time without the need for costly custom coding was the real reason why computer usage exploded. What we're seeing now is a repeat with virtualization.

Making Your Application Cloud Aware

Microsoft's Document Connection tool seems to intertwine Microsoft's unified communications investment with its Office suite of applications. These types of cloud connectors provide an extension to the desktop or handheld in order to provide services never envisioned by the original designers.

A massive example is how AutoCAD and others are leveraging their near-monopoly of the architectural world by extending AutoCAD into the world of clouds and calling it Building Information Modeling (BIM). So, as you click around your 3-D building model in AutoCAD, you can pull up additional data tables that might have originated in PeopleSoft, SAP, or any of a myriad of data sources. The systems also seem to have hooks so that you can use other applications that do things like heat modeling, so you can ask the BIM what a new set of e-glass windows might do for the offices. Each piece is pretty clearly a stand-alone item, but the BIM is many ways is a cloud that serves as a common group or DMZ between them, making a whole new category of facility management tool.

However, the amount of custom coding needed to "glue" these pieces together is still quite staggering, and so far all these functions have to be preplanned and designed by the team. We've also seen that only a very select few applications in the world of facilities management are compatible with the BIM systems currently available, and the amount of custom programming necessary to integrate foreign systems is enormous. What needs to happen is yet another layer of abstraction, so that the connection is not so painful to implement.

What Should a Cloud Descriptor Language Contain?

We've said a lot about how we see clouds becoming less and less specific and more and more about applications rather than platforms. Eventually, we should be able to submit a job to any financial cloud that does market analysis or some other compute- and/or data-intensive application. We can also see how someday "agents" may shop the job around to different clouds, getting estimates based on the amount of resources you request as described in a header file in a Cloud Descriptor Language (CDL). We can foresee the CDL being similar in function to what the old mainframe Job

Description Language did, but possibly in something a bit more modern, such as XML.

We see CDL as an offshoot of the work done by the supercomputing centers around the world for job schedulers. This current system contains resource requests such as:

- Number of CPU cores and type of cores
- Amount of working RAM per node
- Amount of working storage for the job and per node
- Libraries and toolkits to run the job
- Estimated time or time limits for the job
- Data sources either setup locally or off the Internet

We see CDL taking advantage of some of the lesser-known features of XML, such as schema exchange. Simply put, any conversation that involves XML exchange would also preface the communication with a descriptor of the data that it wants to exchange. In theory, little things like a field called "fname" instead of "firstname" could be handled more easily. It would be this type of information that middleware or data mashup tools could take advantage of to in order to "translate" one arrangement of data to another and allowing you to accommodate variations between the systems conversing.

What Are the Back Office Issues, and How Do You Pay for a Cloud?

While cloud computing certainly sounds like our future, what must happen first is profit. If you can't make money on clouds, then clouds just won't happen. The Amazon, Google, IBM, and other cloud offerings have all had a customized billing and accounting system designed for them. In late 2009 VMWare released a virtualization accounting system that will bring cloud billing into the realm of reality for the regional cloud service providers or even cost sharing for intraorganizational clouds.

In the mid- to late-1990s, one of us (Brian Chee) chose to publically support a very unpopular system called the Clipper Chip, not so much for the actual implementation technology, but rather for the promise such a device provided. Though it was flawed enough that the entire program died within six years, the concept of ubiquitous strong encryption was a good one, and a concept the world would have to wait a little more than two decades to see again.

The premise was that if everyone had in their computing platform a system that provided extremely fast and always available encryption, then perhaps we might finally start to see small transaction trust relationships—in this case, a system that would make a 5-cent transaction worthwhile as a fee to read a newspaper "right off the press." While the entire concept was poorly implemented, with the world roaring that it didn't want the NSA able to "back-door" their conversations, computing power finally caught up with the concept and SSL/TLS strong encryption is now ubiquitous.

The advantage of such a facility is that we now have in place a system of authentication that is trusted enough so we can have programs using credentials for acquiring access to resources and being able to pay for that use. As clouds become more and more available and the application "store" becomes available, then perhaps we will finally see enough usage volume to drive the pricing down to the point where we might see the nickel reading of a newspaper.

The back-office accounting systems for clouds are going to be very programmer/corporation-centric at first, in that they will have charging systems strictly for overall virtual application and/or machine usage. However, as time and the market develop, we're pretty sure that the usage granularity will reach the point where the nickels can finally start adding up.

One other back-office issue harks back to when we discussed how you protect your cloud, regulatory issues, and just how you can leverage the cloud architecture to protect critical and sensitive resources. We asked Scott Morrison, CTO of Layer 7 Technologies, for his spin on these types of issues, and here is his answer:

> The fundamental tension in the cloud is about surrendering control. We are attracted to the cloud because of its promise to increase agility and drive down costs; but we are simultaneously cautious because of the potential risk to applications and data. Our ambivalence comes honestly: the traditional best practices for security and visibility leverage physical control and rely on localized access to work. In the cloud, these fall under provider control, leaving us with little basis for trust.
>
> This problem is exacerbated today because the control boundary—the line between what we manage versus what the

provider manages—is blurred. In the future, enterprise IT must reassert control of security and governance in the cloud. To do this successfully, security architects will need to take a different approach and apply new technologies. Control and visibility must be applied at the application layer. Policy enforcement needs to become integral to the cloud provider environment; today this is separate and only available from third parties. Naturally, policy administration must be under control of enterprise IT, and this needs to become standardized across different providers so that customers are not locked into a particular platform by virtue of its having a proprietary policy enforcement engine.

The Cloud Is the Computer

We've talked about the cyclical tendencies that we see in the computing industry, and clouds certainly are feeling very much like the old mainframe days. The concept of a thin client has exploded in the market, with inexpensive and small thin clients that look for all intents and purposes just like the terminals we used on the mini and mainframe computers of the last decade. We still remember the French Minitel system, with its tiny clamshell terminals and how such portability gave the French a dramatic boost in computing and communications capability for the masses. Today's tiny netbooks are filling the old niche, and given how many of these now have built-in 3G modems, you can access the cloud from just about anywhere. The point we're trying to make is that we're coming full circle as applications execute in the cloud, and the next generation of "dumb terminals" just look prettier. Less and less computing is being done at the desktop/handheld, and pretty soon we'll be very similar operationally to what we had on the mainframes.

We're hoping to see clouds gain market share and, as a result, that market pressures will force ad-hoc standards. We're predicting that the software marketplace will be a rich and wonderful place where large numbers of solutions to every potential computing need can be found, and then run in the cloud of your choice. More than likely an offshoot of what we're seeing with the Apple AppStore, this open market would have the potential for developers to reach billions of users and as a consequence provide the potential for companies to thrive as the market model starts to move to software rental instead of outright purchase. The end-user license agreements from quite a few vendors are no longer providing for outright sale, but rather limited-time licensing. It's not a big stretch that we might start seeing more and more one-time usage licenses appearing, similar to the ones we discovered at Paragon Software.

What we're willing to predict is that this kind of cycle has brought with it some extremely good side effects in usability, security, affordability, and interoperability. Market pressures have forced various vendors to play more nicely with each other, and developers are seeing an unparalleled set of abstraction-layer development tools so that we can concentrate on the business rather than the tools. We're willing to say that there will be some really exciting times, as computing can now become ubiquitous.

Clouds Flight Path for Chapter 10

- *How it might start with specialized clouds.* The flight path is all about steps climbing the stairs toward true clouds. Seti@home and Sales-Force were just the start, as the layers are built one on the other. Once we get good at one layer, someone thinks of how to make it better and a new layer is born.
- *Media clouds.* A great example of how a copyright clearing house became something altogether different on its journey to becoming a cloud. This is also an example of just how diverse the cloud world is, and how diversity is going to expose more and more users to cloud potential.
- *Clouds as the fertile ground for the growth of federation.* Federation has been rearing its head every time a new authentication or security management system appears. The lack of traction seems to have been related to trust, and clouds may be the neutral territory that federation will need to succeed.
- *Clouds as a DMZ or a security proxy.* It just makes sense: You set up proxies and software firewalls on dedicated machines, why not use a dedicated virtual machine as neutral territory? The cloud is a perfect place, where snapshots are easier to manage, and if someone should get lucky, you can roll back to a clean image. Clouds also make sense for a place where partners can exchange information, sort of like Checkpoint Charlie between partners.

- *Office productivity clouds.* Sometimes you just don't want to suck up all those system resources and expense for a function that might only be used for a short time. Or maybe you want a full set of functions but on a really small netbook, thin client, or remote clients. Services such as Microsoft Office Online and Adobe Online are possible only because of huge leaps in last-mile bandwidth.
- *Computing clouds.* Just because clouds like those offered by Amazon are primarily targeted at business doesn't mean that you can't ask them for a couple of dozen machines to be set up as an on-demand Beowulf cluster.
- *Mobile clouds.* Face it, we would all love to have a mobile platform that could keep pace with the biggest desktop computer, but we're not there yet. What is within sight are applications that let the clouds do the heavy lifting. Scientists have been dreaming about augmented reality for decades, but it's looking like the consumer world was the first to bring it to fruition.
- *Cloud-aware applications.* It's not just the mobile world that wants more computing power than is currently available in the platform, and clouds are a good solution. We just keep thinking how much this is sounding just like what we used to have in the mainframe days.

Glossary

For further information on the terms on this glossary, we suggest you consult Wikipedia (www.wikipedia.org), which has useful information about many of these topics. Useful search criteria follow the entries in this Glossary.

Chapter 1

Beowulf Cluster   A collection of typically inexpensive microcomputers linked together by a message-passing buss (typically a high-speed Ethernet network), which allows the cluster or collection of machines to work on large scientific problems. Each problem is typically broken down into smaller subtasks controlled by a single master program, which is responsible for spawning child tasks onto computers in the cluster and then collecting the results as each child process finishes its task. (http://en.wikipedia.org/wiki/Beowulf_%28computing%29)

Abstraction Layers   A means of deconstructing a task or function into separate pieces to allow for a modular approach to programming. Each layer typically presents a programmatic interface previously agreed to as some sort of standard, so that other programmers can utilize this interface without needing to modify their code for any subsequent underlying layers. Like a child's building-block toy, the sockets at the bottom of the building block match the stubs on the tops of the blocks, regardless of whether the underlying block has some sort of special purpose. (http://en.wikipedia.org/wiki/Abstraction_layer)

Software as a Service (SaaS)   A description of a general movement in the information technology industry away from applications in which the bulk of the application code is executed at the workstation. SaaS is described generically as "thin apps," in which client machines typically need only a Web browser with perhaps some sort of plug-in to provide additional functionality. SaaS has been equated with a general trend toward Web-based applications, moving the onus for computing away from the client and more toward the back-end server. (http://en.wikipedia.org/wiki/Software_as_a_Service)

Web 2.0   Typically acknowledged as the "next phase" after Software as a Service, the use of more intelligent browsers and more plug-ins and/or programmatic abstraction systems (e.g. Adobe AIR, .NET) to provide a much richer client environment and features normally associated with "thick applications," which require installers and typically take up large amounts of resources at the workstation. (http://en.wikipedia.org/wiki/Web_2.0)

Virtualization   The system through which operating systems can be hosted within a shell system (e.g., Vmware, Xen, Windows Hypervisor), allowing the guest operating system to access either virtualized resources (disk, network, input/output, etc.) or other guest machines while maintaining control over each guest through the shell management system. The virtual machine host environment also provides known and consistent abstracted hardware connections that create a common interface and eliminate some potential hardware conflicts and incompatibilities. (http://en.wikipedia.org/wiki/Virtualization)

Russian *Matryoshka* Nesting Dolls   A toy usually associated with Russia and the Slavic areas of the world. Each doll is hollow and is designed to fit one within another. The concept is a common analogy for how the layers in the ISO seven-layer model works. Each layer fits into the one below, and each layer is slightly larger than the one before it. (http://en.wikipedia.org/wiki/Matryoshka)

ISO Seven-Layer Networking Model (OSI Model)   An abstraction model that eliminates the need for programmers to write different versions of code to accommodate any possible hardware combination. Instead, network interface card vendors write drivers for their product and present programmatic interfaces that complly with a standard for a class of operating system. Upper layers do similar things, but separate major tasks involved with network communications to allow greater variety of functions above themselves. For example, Intel writes a driver for the E100 card to be compliant with the Windows XP operating system. This driver in turn talks to the Ethernet layer, which talks to the IP layer, which then talks to UDP/TCP/ICMP/etc., layers all the way up to the application layer. This modularity allows for new programs to be "slid in," so that new functions can be created without rewriting the entire ISO model. Thus, for example, Layer 3 (IP) can just as easily be IPv4 as IPv6. (http://en.wikipedia.org/wiki/OSI_model)

NEMS (Network Equipment Manufacturer); NEPS (Network Equipment Providers) Acronyms for a collection of electronics manufacturers involved in the production of networking equipment. The terms are typically used to describe companies involved in the production of network infrastructure components such as routers, switches, firewalls, etc. (http://en.wikipedia.org/wiki/Network_Equipment_Provider)

ODBC (Open DataBase Connectivity Model) An abstraction layer that provides for programmatic access to various types of databases over some sort of network connection. Well understood and supported by a large number of applications, the ODBC model is used in the context of this book to represent how new models are built on what came previously and to show that database connectivity is changing rapidly to accommodate new programming systems. (http://en.wikipedia.org/wiki/Odbc)

OpenGL (Open Graphics Library) An abstraction layer for video display technologies such as graphics cards that removes the direct tie to the hardware in graphical programs. This abstraction layer competes with the Windows Direct (DirectX) system, with both systems providing a way for developers to concentrate on the software rather than hardware details. (http://en.wikipedia.org/wiki/Opengl)

HASP (Houston Automatic Spooling Priority) A system typically used on IBM mainframes to handle the prioritization and scheduling of job execution. Popular with academic institutions, HASP allowed for variations in job cost and access to resources. In many academic institutions, student jobs could run only after hours, while administrative jobs had priority during the work day. It could also handle multitiered pricing for CPU time and resource usage. (http://en.wikipedia.org/wiki/Houston_Automated_Spooling_Program)

JCL (Job Control Language) A scripting language, introduced by IBM, to handle requests for resources and provide a way to set up necessary modules to support the requirements of each job. It was possible to execute system programs for operations such as disk-to-tape copy, tape-to-tape copy, tape-to-punch dumps, etc., all without writing a single line of code in a language such as COBOL or RPG. (http://en.wikipedia.org/wiki/Job_Control_Language)

Grid Computing A loose collection of personal computers connected to the Internet that donate their idle CPU time to work tiny pieces of very large computing problems. Typically implemented with a toolkit such as BOINC, these volunteer machines check out small portions of the problem and work on them during idles times when their screen saver kicks on. Significantly, these grid clusters may have little or no association with each other, and in many cases their work is duplicated so that the system won't lose a critical piece of the puzzle. Results are then reported back over the Internet to a master controller node. (http://en.wikipedia.org/wiki/Grid_computing)

HPC Clusters (High-Performance Computing Clusters)   A tightly grouped collection of personal computers that typically have a single master node connected via high-speed networking to child nodes. The master node parcels out each piece of the computing problem to child nodes and then typically handles compilation of the results. These systems usually also run some sort of scheduler that fits job requirements to available hardware based on job profiles and accessibility rights of the submitting user(s). (http://en.wikipedia.org/wiki/High-performance_computing)

Chapter 2

Infiniband   A high-speed switching technology typically used by high-performance computing clusters for control and data exchange between nodes. Infiniband is a more flexible offshoot of the fibre channel technology that was originally targeted for storage area networks. (http://en.wikipedia.org/wiki/Infiniband)

Blue Hawaii   An IBM SP2 supercomputer at the University of Hawai'i Department of Information and Computer Sciences. It is also noteworthy that Blue Hawaii was the grandson of the chess-playing supercomputer Deep Blue, which beat Chess Master Garry Kasparov. (http://en.wikipedia.org/wiki/Garry_Kasparov)

SCP (Secure Copy)/sFTP (Secure File Transfer Protocol)/SSH (Secure Shell)   Methods of securely transferring data between computers. All these systems are typically installed as part of a suite of programs collectively called SSH and have the ability to create secure connections using various encryption methodologies. These programs are significant in that other programs can utilize the SSH suite to achieve secure communications to other machines. (http://en.wikipedia.org/wiki/Ssh)

IBM's OS-VM   OS-VM is but One of a long heritage of operating system innovations from IBM, although it's debatable whether IBM or some other firm was the first to offer the concept of virtual machines hosted under some sort of master operating system. Often used to segregate confidential computing from prying eyes, OS-VM was also commonly used by service bureaus to separate customers from each other. (http://en.wikipedia.org/wiki/VM_%28operating_system%29)

Moore's law A popular observational theory that the number of transistors that can be place inexpensively onto a chip will double every two years. This theory has been at the heart of the argument over the industry's ability to have enough computing power to deal with the bloat being caused by higher- and higher-level languages. The common excuse from programming teams is that it's cheaper to get the product to market than to spend additional time on code optimization. (http://en.wikipedia.org/wiki/Moore%27s_law)

Content Management Systems Normally referred to a Web-based system that presents dynamically built Web pages based on configuration information typically stored in some sort of SQL database. The key to these systems is their ability to customize what is presented on the fly, and in many cases customize what is presented to the user based on profiles set up by the administrator. These systems also typically have some sort of work flow capability and in many cases collaboration tools of some sort. (http://en.wikipedia.org/wiki/Content_management_system)

Service Bureau A term historically applied to companies that provided mainframes for rent, it is now used to describe a great number of services-for-hire organizations. A good example is in payroll or taxes, for which these service bureaus provide surge capability for companies that are unwilling or unable to handle the surge internally. (http://en.wikipedia.org/wiki/Service_bureau)

Chapter 3

Carrier Sense Multiple Access First created by Norman Abramson during the AlohaNET project, this methodology set up one of the first network protocols and had nodes listen before they transmitted (that's the carrier sense portion), with everyone hearing at the same time (that's multiple access portion), which became the foundation for Ethernet when Robert Metcalf of Xerox added collision detection, taking an academic research project and turning it into a commercial product. (http://en.wikipedia.org/wiki/ALOHANET; http://en.wikipedia.org/wiki/Carrier_sense_multiple_access)

Microsoft .NET Programming Environment A programming framework and abstraction layer that reduces the need for system-level programming for new applications. The framework provides libraries and modules that the programmer can utilize to access system functions, graphics, network input/output, etc. The concept is to remove the necessity for programmers to worry about writing low-level code to manipulate and access hardware and system functions. That is, for example, instead of needing to write several thousand instructions to describe in minute detail how to open a garage door, you could just issue a command to your driving program to "open-garage-door." These types of environments greatly speed application development and in many ways reduce potential bugs in the code. (http://en.wikipedia.org/wiki/.NET_Framework)

PHP   A hypertext markup language abstraction layer, a scripting language that provides ways to utilizing common functions by invoking a PHP command instead of needing to write lengthy and complex custom code for every program. The acronym PHP originally stood for Personal Home Page. (http://en.wikipedia.org/wiki/Php)

Python   A high-level programming language that can also be considered an abstraction layer. Python is another in a long line of open-source scripting languages developed to allow for quick development with less coding. (http://en.wikipedia.org/wiki/Python_%28programming_language%29)

Ruby on Rails   A modern Web scripting language that provides modeling functionality in an attempt to increase the amount of self-evident documentation embedded in the code. This abstraction layer has become very popular with Software-as-a-Service) providers. (http://en.wikipedia.org/wiki/Ruby_on_rails)

Adobe AIR   A programmatic abstraction layer that integrates Flash as an integral part of the language and provides a runtime environment that allows for development of Web-based products nearly identical to traditional thick programs on client machines. Also known as Adobe Integrated Runtime. (http://en.wikipedia.org/wiki/Adobe_air)

Type 1 Hypervisor   A virtualization environment installed onto bare metal or directly on the hardware platform. The current state of the art has not eliminated a base operating system completely, but it has stripped the environment down to a point where the hypervisor has unparalleled control over the hardware abstraction layer. By getting the general-use operating system out of the way, type 1 systems also tend to give significantly better performance than type 2 systems. (http://en.wikipedia.org/wiki/Hypervisor)

Type 2 Hypervisors   A virtualization environment installed onto a host operating system as a user or system space application. An added advantage is that now the hypervisor is running as a normal user instead of being a privileged superuser. A very common application is for a "safe" workstation environment that is purposely protected from attack. (http://en.wikipedia.org/wiki/Hypervisor)

Hyperthreading   A proprietary Intel technology used to improve parallelization of computations (doing multiple tasks at once) performed on PC microprocessors. For each processor core that is physically present, the operating system addresses two virtual processors and shares the workload between them when possible. (http://en.wikipedia.org/wiki/Hyperthreading)

IP-KVM (IP Keyboard-Video-Mouse)   A device that allows a single keyboard+monitor+mouse to be switched and shared between multiple computer systems. The IP portion indicates remote access capability over the Internet, typically with a Web browser augmented with some sort of browser plug-in. (http://en.wikipedia.org/wiki/KVM_switch)

Argonne National Laboratory   A massive government research facility managed by the University of Chicago that is dedicated to research. The Math and Computer Science Directorate (MCS) there has been responsible for the development of a great number of open-source projects with a high concentration in the field of supercomputing. (http://en.wikipedia.org/wiki/Argonne_National_Laboratory)

NISPOM (National Industrial Security Program Operating Manual)   The rulebook that provides guidelines for the handling of classified materials for government contractors. Chapter 8 of this manual deals specifically with the auditing and review requirements of computing devices used in a classified environment. (http://en.wikipedia.org/wiki/NISPOM)

Health Insurance Portability and Accountability Act (HIPAA)   A federal law that seeks to create a greater level of accountability in the health industry with regard to patient confidentiality. While a great number of computer industry devices tout HIPAA compliance, it should be noted that nowhere in the act or the applicable regulations are specific pieces of technology mentioned. Only goals are stated; implementation is up to the organization. Organizations do, however, have to be able to prove how they have been compliant. (http://en.wikipedia.org/wiki/HIPAA)

Sarbanes-Oxley Act of 2002   A U.S. federal law named for its principal sponsors, also known as the Public Company Accounting Reform and Investor Protection Act and the Corporate and Auditing Accountability and Responsibility Act, and commonly called Sarbanes-Oxley, Sarbox, or SOX. Enacted in reaction to a number of major corporate bankruptcies and accounting scandals, the legislation set new or enhanced standards for all U.S. public company boards, management, and public accounting firms. It does not apply to privately held companies. Debate continues about the effectiveness of the act. Supporters say it has helped restore public confidence in big business by strengthening controls of accounting practices; opponents say it has reduced America's competitive edge in global markets and created an overly complex regulatory environment. (http://en.wikipedia.org/wiki/Sarbox)

Wang Laboratories   A technology company founded in 1951 by Dr. An Wang and Dr. G. Y. Chu. It originally built complex financial calculators and later entered the computer industry. Known for its word processors, this forward-thinking corporation literally set the standard for modern word processing, and its VS (virtual system) operating system provided a level of access control to data that was unparalleled at the time. (http://en.wikipedia.org/wiki/Wang_Laboratories)

SalesForce   A pioneer in Software as a Service, whose customer relations management (CRM) system set the standard for CRM worldwide. (http://en.wikipedia.org/wiki/Salesforce)

Customer Relations Management (CRM)   A strategy for managing a company's interactions with customers and sales prospects. It involves using technology to organize, automate, and synchronize business processes. Sometimes belittled by being called "contact management," CRM goes quite a bit further in how it handles and cross-references the relationship between an organization and its customers. Common uses are for coordination and record keeping for both inside and outside sales forces, and most commonly for call centers. Some very sophisticated systems harvest the call accounting record information for each phone call, providing the operators with background information, purchase history, internal comments on subjects to avoid, etc. (http://en.wikipedia.org/wiki/Customer_relationship_management)

Chapter 4

WebEx   A Web-based service purchased by Cisco that provides the ability for a large number of clients to view desktop applications simultaneously. This type of system has become wildly popular with sales and marketing professionals, allowing for remote "live demos" that let them reach a dramatically larger audience in a shorter amount of time. It has also become extremely attractive to technical support organizations, because the technology also allows tech support engineers to "take over" the screens of customers, allowing them to solve problems much more quickly. (http://en.wikipedia.org/wiki/Webex)

NetMeeting   One of the least-known pieces of software included by Microsoft Corporation since it started shipping Windows 95, this H.323 (video conferencing standard) application provided video conferencing, shared applications, and white boards to users. However, the complexity of getting H.323 applications to work correctly through firewalls eventually spelled its doom, and it was dropped from the software list after Windows XP. Interestingly, the H.323 standard has grown in popularity, but on dedicated systems put out by corporations such as Polycom and Tandberg. (http://en.wikipedia.org/wiki/Netmeeting)

SSL-VPN (Secure Sockets Layer–Virtual Private Network)   Previous (IP-SEC) VPN implementations required a complex arrangement of encryption keys and handshaking that, while an Internet standard, was far from simple to set up. SSL-VPN leverages existing encryption and key exchange technology already inside every Web browser to create a secure link without a complex setup procedure. In addition, some implementations can be run from USB flash drives, and upon log-out will remove all history entries related to the session—in theory, leaving no footprints behind. (http://en.wikipedia.org/wiki/Secure_Sockets_Layer_virtual_private_network)

Flex   A programming abstraction layer for the creation of Rich Internet Applications (RIA) that integrates the Adobe Flash multimedia language. (http://en.wikipedia.org/wiki/Adobe_Flex)

AJAX   A programming abstraction layer designed specifically to provide for a greater level of interactivity to/from the Web server and the client. While the name is defined as asynchronous Javascript and XML, it does not require programming in either. (http://en.wikipedia.org/wiki/AJAX)

PERL   A general-purpose scripting language originally developed by Larry Wall at NAS, which has become one of the most popular systems administrator scripting tools used worldwide. (http://en.wikipedia.org/wiki/PERL)

Code Generators   A slightly dated term referring to any type of application that could accept some sort of human-oriented language (high-level language) and translate to or generate a more specific computer-oriented language. (http://en.wikipedia.org/wiki/Code_generator)

Assembler Language   Sometimes considered to be the first computer language, this programming language is infamous for being extremely difficult to master, but because it is so closely linked to the base machine language, it is capable of doing just about anything the computer is capable of doing. More simply put, there isn't anything you can't do in Assembler, which is also why it is closely controlled by many system administrators. Because Assembler translates to relatively few machine-language operands (the most basic actions a computer CPU can do), it is also considered one of the fastest computer languages in existence. (http://en.wikipedia.org/wiki/Assembly_language#Assembler)

C Programming Language   Originally created at Bell Laboratories by Dennis Ritchie, C is known for being extremely concise but also prone to mistakes due to its reliance on context and symbols. The old story about a single parenthesis being out of place causing the failure of an early missile launch may not refer to C, but it could have, because of C's heavy reliance on the placement of parentheses plaement. (http://en.wikipedia.org/wiki/C_programming_language)

SPSS   Originally called the Statistics Package for the Social Sciences, SPSS was one of the first data analytics packages designed specifically to relieve researchers from tedious coding in order to do common statistical analysis. Now called PASW (Predictive Analytics SoftWare), this system was purchased by IBM in 2009. (http://en.wikipedia.org/wiki/Spss)

SAS   An acronym for the Statistical Analysis System, SAS has grown into a popular system for data manipulation and has a worldwide following. Maintained by the SAS Institute in Carey, North Carolina, this system has morphed from an advanced statistical analysis tool to an extremely popular mainframe data mining tool. (http://en.wikipedia.org/wiki/SAS_System)

Embedded Computing/Systems   Typically employing small single- or few-function devices, embedded computing is a discipline that typically requires programming in a low-level language such as C to control hardware functions. Almost any modern electronic device now contains embedded programming; this discipline's normal product is called firmware and is permanently or nearly permanently burned onto semiconductors/chips. Software that controls a single-function device is typically also called firmware. (http://en.wikipedia.org/wiki/Embedded_computing)

High-Level Programming Languages   The opposite of low-level programming languages. Lest we be circular, "low" refers to how close a language is to the native computer machine language, and "high" refers to its closeness to human languages. Examples of high-level languages include CoBOL, FORTRAN, Java, and BASIC, in which a single high-level language statement eventually becomes many to several thousand machine-language instructions. (http://en.wikipedia.org/wiki/High_level_programming_languages)

FORTRAN   A blended word based on its original purpose, which was Formula Translation. This language is notable in that it was one of the first half-dozen computer languages to be developed and continues to be popular for scientific inquiry due to its power to manipulate and work on numbers. It is also one of the more popular languages on modern supercomputers. (http://en.wikipedia.org/wiki/FORTRAN)

COBOL   Dating back to work by Grace Hopper for the U.S. Navy in 1959, the COmmon Business Oriented Language remained the standard for business computing well past the turn of the century. The COBOL 2002 standard includes support for object-oriented programming and other modern language features. (http://en.wikipedia.org/wiki/Cobol)

PL1 Programming Language One was designed for the scientific community and has its strengths in recursive analysis and its ability to represent complex mathematical functions. (http://en.wikipedia.org/wiki/Pl1)

LISP Named for its strength in List Processing, this language has become the darling of the artificial intelligence world and is infamous among programmers everywhere for its liberal use of nested parentheses. (http://en.wikipedia.org/wiki/LISP)

APL Named after a book called *A Programming Language,* this high-level language is infamous for its use of Greek letters. Because it concentrates on mathematical manipulation, the Greek characters were necessary as a well-known shorthand for mathematical functions and constants. Old-time programmers almost always thought of this language when someone would say that it was "Greek to them." (http://en.wikipedia.org/wiki/APL_%28programming_language%29)

SNOBOL String Oriented Symbolic Language, Noted as one of the first high-level programming languages that was able to do complex string manipulation (i.e., characters instead of just numbers). This language made possible huge amounts of research on human languages and their incredibly complex nuances. (http://en.wikipedia.org/wiki/Snobol)

BASIC Beginner's All-Purpose Symbolic Instruction Code, a high-level language notable for being one of the first interpreted computer languages, in which instructions were translated to an intermediate low-level language as soon as the instruction was entered. The entire program was not executed until a "run" command was issued. This was also typically the first programming language taught in many university computer science programs, and it was very popular as a result of its default inclusion with early microcomputers. The compiled version (instructions were typed into a text file and then run through another program to translate it into machine language, the result being an "executable" that could be run by anyone, without needing the original compiler) of BASIC was also the very first compiled programming language for *any* microcomputer. It was developed by then-Lt. Commander Gordon Eubanks of the U.S. Navy Polaris submarine fleet. Notably, it was partially written under the polar ice caps while Eubanks was on patrol. (http://en.wikipedia.org/wiki/BASIC)

IBM Programmer's Library Collection An artifact from when mainframes ruled business computing, this collection of books was considered the ultimate authority on syntax and methodologies for IBM programming languages. Typically, these horribly expensive documentation sets were put out in common areas on racks for community use. Third-party programming books did not appear until much later. A more commonly known series on supercomputer programming topics is called the IBM Red Book series. (http://en.wikipedia. org/wiki/IBM_Redbooks)

DMZ   Traditionally an acronym for demilitarized zone, DMZ in our context refers to a separate zone on a firewall normally dedicated for servers. This zone allows a special set of firewall rules to be applied for high levels of protection for traffic inbound from the outside world, but lower levels for access from a trusted area. (http://en.wikipedia.org/wiki/DMZ_%28computing%29)

SAP   One of the massive business software vendors of the world, SAP was originally part of IBM and was later spun off. In our context, we mention their products due to the extremely high price tags typically encountered and the level of complexity in setting up the environment. We use them as an example of a good candidate for virtual machine image test drive systems. (http://en. wikipedia.org/wiki/SAP_AG)

Unified Communications   A trend that seems to have grown out of the extended capabilities typically found in instant messaging products, *unified* refers to how multiple communications methods can be unified into a single client or suite. In the case of Microsoft, the UC offerings are threaded through nearly the entire Office suite to provide both communications and presence (presence = user status) in context (e.g., ok to forward telephone calls *only* for members of your workgroup, but for no one else when user status changes to "in meeting." (http://en.wikipedia.org/wiki/Unified_communications)

InteropNET   The large-scale demonstration network built by a volunteer engineering team in support of the Interop trade show. Unique in the world in that the InteropNET was originally set up as a testing arena for network equipment engineering teams for as-yet-unannounced products. This volunteer team is responsible for a large number of the Internet standards called RFCs (request for comments).

NTFS   New Technology File System, a spinoff from a joint project by IBM and Microsoft. The OS/2 operating system also included a new file system that provided for a greater degree of reliability and storage capability. Further developed by Microsoft as part of the NT operating system, the NTFS has been part of the Microsoft operating system product line since NT version 1.0. When used in context of this book, it should be noted that NTFS dramatically increased the maximum file and volume size available to the operating system in addition to adding advanced journaling and other features to increase speed and reliability for storage systems. (http://en.wikipedia.org/wiki/NTFS)

FAT/DOS   File Allocation Table, while now used mostly to describe a volume formatting method, actually refers to a special file that contained information about how files were stored on a direct-access storage device. Dating back to the CPM operating system from Digital Research Corporation, the FAT file system dates back to the earliest general-purpose microcomputers. In our context, FAT illustrates a volume formatting method that was easily transferrable but also limited in storage capability. (http://en.wikipedia.org/wiki/File_Allocation_Table)

Hot Versus Warm Versus Cold Virtual Server Images   The gist is that the temperature of backups, virtual server images, or databases is in direct relationship to the frequency of synchronization. *Hot* means direct synchronization with no data loss, since the updates are constant. *Warm* means periodic but frequent updates, and *cold* means that only the initial setup is done and no updates are done until needed. Very similar in concept to hot/warm/cold data processing sites. (http://en.wikipedia.org/wiki/Hot_site)

Asterisk/TrixBox   An open-source software project that implemented a Private Branch Exchange (PBX: office telephone system). TrixBox refers to a divergence from the original Asterisk project; this version is more appliance in nature and as a result dramatically easier to set up and maintain. The drawback is that you lose some of the customizability found in the original project offering. (http://en.wikipedia.org/wiki/Asterisk_PBX)

Hardig/Anvil Road Cases   Various brands of durable equipment cases have made it to market; Hardig is well known in the scientific world and Anvil is better known in the music world. Simply put, these semicustomized cases protect delicate electronic equipment from damage when they are taken "on the road" and must be packed into transportation, loaded and unloaded multiple times, and in general are subjected to a large amount of abuse. (http://en.wikipedia.org/wiki/Road_cases)

Chapter 5

Active Directory (AD)   A Microsoft implementation of a potentially large-scale user identity and authentication system modeled after the X.500 directory model proposed by the International Standards Organization. Key to this system is its tightly woven integration into the Windows operating system to provide rich identity information while providing a user/device authentication system that can be distributed across a very large organization. (http://en.wikipedia.org/wiki/Active_directory)

Network Throughput   Commonly confused with bandwidth, throughput is more involved with sustained ability to transmit different types of data over sustained periods. While a typical Ethernet link might be theoretically capable of providing 1000 megabits per second, the real throughput is typically much less due to transmission overhead, traffic congestion, and a myriad of other factors. (http://en.wikipedia.org/wiki/Measuring_network_throughput)

Jitter   In the context of Voice-over-IP, jitter refers to uneven delays between data packets that typically show up as stuttering in sound quality or worse. (http://en.wikipedia.org/wiki/Jitter)

Latency   In the context of networking, latency refers to the amount of time to get data from one endpoint to another. In terms of Voice-over-IP, latency is most often felt as delay from when a person starts speaking to when that sound is heard at the other end. (http://en.wikipedia.org/wiki/Latency_%28audio%29)

SlashDot   A technology-oriented webzine with a huge following of readers. This massive reader base posts notices about Web pages they find important, and in some cases this post could potentially drive millions of readers to that site. In our context, being "slashdot'ed" means that the number of hits to a website has risen astronomically due to a story posted about it on the SlashDot news site. (http://en.wikipedia.org/wiki/Slashdot)

Round Robin Distributions   When used in the context of load balancing, round robin refers to how Web requests are divided up among servers. Each request is taken in order and distributed to the next server in line. With weighted round robin distribution, certain devices in the load-balanced array are capable of handling either greater or lesser amounts of load than the others. Weighting is used to adjust the amount of load put on those servers. (http://en.wikipedia.org/wiki/Round_robin_DNS)

Gaussian Distributions   A statistical model, also called a normal distribution, in which probabilities of occurrence tend to center around the mean value. When used to talk about networking traffic or load balancing, the connotation is that the device is trying to model more accurately how networking traffic occurs in real life. (http://en.wikipedia.org/wiki/Gaussian_distribution)

OpenView (HP OpenView)   A network and network resource management console application put out by Hewlett Packard that has become one of the best support management console tools on the market. Support in this case means that the network equipment manufacturer has created specialized equipment description programs that give OpenView access to features that provide for control and monitoring of equipment details. (http://en.wikipedia.org/wiki/Hp_Openview)

Unicenter (aka CA Unicenter) Similar in intent to HP OpenView, Unicenter is more of a suite of programs whose intent is to provide end-to-end IT management. Going beyond just equipment monitoring, Unicenter encompasses troubleticketing, change management, and other needs. Unicenter and OpenView seem to be the "big boys" in the IT management market right now. (http://en.wikipedia.org/wiki/CA_Unicenter)

Microsoft PowerShell A command-line interface for Microsoft Windows operating systems that is an effort to provide advanced scripting capability for Windows. While some might compare it to shells such as BASH under the Linux operating system, PowerShell commands can be executed by various programming/scripting environments while still being controllable via the Windows security model. (http://en.wikipedia.org/wiki/Windows_PowerShell)

Data Mashup Tools Greatly misunderstood, the overall concept of data mashup is one of conversion and manipulation of data in an ad-hoc basis. A good example is how some data sources use a full name, while others separate first name and last name into separate database fields. Thus, in order to migrate data from the first example to the second, something needs to combine the firstname and lastname fields to produce the fullname field in the second example. Another example is where one database stores only a Zipcode, but the second really wants a "state" field. A data mashup tool can do a lookup on the Zipcode to populate the state field in the results. (http://en.wikipedia.org/wiki/Apatar)

"Bot Armies" or "Zombie Armies" or "Botnets" Botnet armies are a highly illegal activity in which someone takes advantage of various operating system or application weaknesses to install programs (worms, virus, etc.) onto the vulnerable machine. These Trojan applications allow the "bot herder" to remotely execute programs for illegal purposes. Spam is sometimes sent via these zombie armies, as well as denial of service attacks and a multitude of other activities in which large numbers of data sources are necessary. In many cases the actual owners of the zombies are unaware that someone else is using their computing facility and that their lack of willingness to update and secure their computer is a reason why there is so much spam in the world. (http://en.wikipedia.org/wiki/Botnets)

Value-Added Resellers (VARs) The concept here is that a VAR does considerably more than just sell computers or IT products. In this context, a VAR can provide customization of the environment up to and including custom programming so that the IT infrastructure better meets the needs of the customer. A good example is VARs that specialize in the legal or medical market and have extensive knowledge of the special needs of those types of operations. (http://en.wikipedia.org/wiki/Value-added_reseller)

eDirectory (Novell eDirectory)   A rival to Microsoft's Active Directory, the Novell solution came out of its Netware Directory Service (NDS), which predates the Microsoft solution. Noteworthy is that the eDirectory solution does not require any specific operating system (though different versions exist for Windows versus Linux), as Active Directory does. (http://en.wikipedia.org/wiki/EDirectory)

LDAP (Lightweight Directory Access Protocol)   Yet another implementation of the X.500 directory model, LDAP has its strongest support with Unix/Linux operating systems. OpenLDAP is an open-source implementation offered for a large number of operating systems with an equally large number of add-ons available to help with the complexity of the system. (http://en.wikipedia.org/wiki/Lightweight_Directory_Access_Protocol)

Identity Management (IDM)   IDM is a topic that drew quite a bit of attention early after the year 2000 but has since been absorbed into the functions of most operating systems and security auditing systems. The concept is to have a single authoritative source of authentication information in an organization that is further extended to provide human-oriented directory information (personal info, digital rights management, etc.) to create self-provisioning white pages and Web portals. (http://www.infoworld.com/d/security-central/identity-management-challenge-506)

Security Event Management (SEM)   These systems seek to be the single authority for access management in the entire organization and, while they are extremely ambitious, the SEM movement is analogous to folks like the "green party" in any political race: They wanted to be the center of the universe but ended up settling for adding their political plank to the winning party. SEM functions are now commonplace in just about all the major network infrastructure systems as well as operating systems. (http://www.infoworld.com/d/security-central/security-event-managers-rule-roost-300)

Verifone   Another fine Hawaiian company founded by an ex-GTE Hawaiian Telephone engineer. Karl Chang proposed a simple data device that could read the magnetic stripes on credit cards for the purpose of automating the credit card validation process. Verifone's success created a huge market, leading to the credit validation clearing houses currently in vogue on the Internet. (http://en.wikipedia.org/wiki/Verifone)

RSA Corporation   Founded by three MIT mathematicians, RSA has become the leader in third-party dual-key encryption technology used throughout the IT industry. Their ground-breaking work on dual-key encryption has made modern secure browsers possible. (http://en.wikipedia.org/wiki/Rsa)

Dr. Wesley Peterson   The founder of the University of Hawai'i Department of Information and Computer Sciences, Dr. Peterson is known for his work on the mathematical representation of data for the error correction of data transmissions and is considered the father of the CRC (Cyclical Redundancy Check) used throughout the data communications industry. Awarded the Japan Award for Technology by the emperor of Japan, Dr. Peterson passed away on May 6, 2009, fulfilling his wish to pass away while teaching. (http://en.wikipedia.org/wiki/Wesley_Peterson)

Chapter 6

Geographic Load Balancing   Similar in concept to traditional load balancing, the geographic portion describes how the system is able to do a reverse lookup on source Internet addresses and, through domain name service (DNS) lookup, redirect the request to a server geographically closer to them. This reduces transit charges and also increases the perceived speed of the Web page display. (http://en.wikipedia.org/wiki/Load_balancing_%28computing%29)

Application Programming Interface (API)   This collection of computer code is definitely one of the most-used abstraction layers in the computer industry today. The base concept is to create a collection of programs that have well-defined inputs and outputs and can be utilized over and over again to access specialized hardware or software. A good analogy is the automobile dashboard, wheel, and pedals, which form a well-known interface easily understood by the general public. Using this interface, drivers can operate their vehicles without having to know anything about the primitives of the car (how the fuel injection actually works, etc.). APIs do the same and also sometimes hide what might be proprietary methodology from prying eyes. (http://en.wikipedia.org/wiki/API)

Jetsons View of the World   The *Jetsons* animated cartoon portrayed a future world that wasn't quite perfect; they had flying cars, but those cars often broke down just like the ground-based cars of today. The concept is that the grass might be greener on the other side of the century, but you still have to mow it. We want those fancy widgets, but just because it's new and modern doesn't mean it will solve all your problems. (http://en.wikipedia.org/wiki/The_Jetsons)

Cache/Caching/Cached   The concept of caching in terms of the networking industry is to move portions of data stored on slower media (such as disks) onto faster media (such as memory) in order to greatly increase the speed at which data can be retrieved. (http://en.wikipedia.org/wiki/Caching)

Relational DataBase Management System (RDBMS)   The concept of a relational database was proposed by C. J. Codd, a well-known computer scientist of the 1960s and 1970s). Dr. Codd proposed the storage of data in table format with related data, but without undue duplication. His proposal of normalization sought to create a system of data storage tables with the least amount of data duplication. The management system can be supposed as a system that can help facilitate de-duplication, while also providing for manipulation of the actual database for maintenance purposes. (http://en.wikipedia.org/wiki/RDBMS)

Netbooks   Smaller, less expensive laptop computers, the concept behind the Netbook was to strip a laptop down to essentials, providing for a lightweight computing platform that has at the center of its function applications that utilize the Internet. In the context of this book, we're proposing that Netbooks are morphing into Internet Netbooks, which are connected to some sort of Internet connection full-time, allowing the device to utilize cloud computing to do the "heavy lifting" on certain applications. (http://en.wikipedia.org/wiki/Netbook)

Network Attached Storage (NAS)   As opposed to a file server based on a general-purpose operating system such as Linux or Windows, the NAS system is a much smaller device that original offered only file storage capabilities. While that original limitation is long gone, the concept remains that the NAS is a smaller, less expensive, and easier-to-manage networked file storage device. (http://en.wikipedia.org/wiki/Network_attached_storage)

Universal Plug and Play (UPnP)   An attempt to provide auto-configuration services to consumer network devices, this network protocol assumes a significant level of trust to allow for administrator-level control of your networking devices. It does, however, allow for compatible devices to exchange setup needs with each other, providing for dramatic short-cuts in configuration, when it works. (http://en.wikipedia.org/wiki/UPnP)

ZigBee   An ad-hoc (peer-to-peer) wireless networking technology governed by the ZigBee Alliance. The concept is that a self-organizing and self-healing wireless network is a good match for home automation systems. One of the authors worked with some of the original ZigBee creators during a joint research project deploying environmental sensors in Kilauea Crater at the Volcanoes National Park. The MIT project proposed an extremely cheap but durable system that was eventually spun off as Ember Corporation. Zigbee is a favorite for several proposed wireless energy-monitoring systems being considered by several energy-producing utilities. (http://en.wikipedia.org/wiki/Zigbee)

Chapter 7

Backhoe Fade A comical but very real event in the world of data communications, when construction fails to check for utility placement before digging. The term backhoe fade refers to the data connectivity fading to nothing as a backhoe rips up the communications cables. (http://en.wikipedia.org/wiki/Backhoe_fade#Backhoe_fade)

Network Demarcation Point Originally used to describe the point in a home telephone system where the phone company's responsibility ended and the consumer's started. The data communication industry uses it to indicate a similar location where the data service provider "drops off" the connection on the customer premises. (http://en.wikipedia.org/wiki/Demarcation_point)

Network Address Translation (NAT) A process whereby a networking device translates the network packet addresses in such a way that a large number of network devices "behind" said device all look to be coming from a single "outside" network address. This address-saving device could possibly also be one of the reasons why IPv6 adoption has been so slow in the Western world. If such devices use only a single address, then the need to uproot Western networks and renumber them using the long and complex IPv6 is considered less necessary. (http://en.wikipedia.org/wiki/Network_address_translation)

Slammer Worm (SQL Slammer Worm) Sometime around 5:30 UTC on January 25, 2003, this computer malware started an attack on any exposed network SQL server-enabled computer system. The resulting denial-of-service event nearly brought the entire Internet down from the resulting flood of traffic. (http://en.wikipedia.org/wiki/SQL_slammer_%28computer_worm%29)

Access Control Lists (ACLs) Also known as Access Control Scripts, these lists of decision logic control access to and from network devices, like routers. Through the careful manipulation of ACLs, network engineers are able to "filter out" malware/unwanted traffic. (http://en.wikipedia.org/wiki/Access_control_lists)

Border Gateway Protocol (BGP) Considered the master language of the Internet, this network routing protocol is how routers control the cross-connect pathways between different Internet domains. Poorly implemented, BGP misconfigurations could potentially create just as much damage as a denial-of-service attack. (http://en.wikipedia.org/wiki/Bgp)

Plone A public-domain content management system based on Zope, which is itself based on Python. Plone is a massive abstraction layer that provides dynamic content with little or no programming necessary. (http://en.wikipedia.org/wiki/Plone_%28software%29)

Free Cooling   This concept refers to where the outside ambient temperature is low enough so that building cooling towers no longer need to use energy to compress a refrigerant. (http://en.wikipedia.org/wiki/Free_cooling)

IP/TV   Created by Karl Auerbach, this network protocol provided a way to reliably and economically transmit high-quality video across the inherently unreliable Internet. (http://en.wikipedia.org/wiki/IPTV)

Promiscuous Mode   A configuration mode in modern Ethernet switches under which all the data transmitted on certain ports are duplicated on another. It is typically called SPANS (Cisco terminology) or port mirroring in Ethernet switches. Although it is not limited to switches, the term basically means to turn off the native filtering system implemented on most Ethernet devices to filter out traffic that is not specifically addressed to itself. A network interface card put into promiscuous mode will allow an application such as Wireshark/Sniffer/Observer to look at 100% of the packets being transmitted on the network. (http://en.wikipedia.org/wiki/Promiscuous_mode)

Network Tap   Typically, a physical device designed to electrically or optically duplicate data from one physical network link onto another link for purposes of network analysis. (http://en.wikipedia.org/wiki/Network_tap)

Windows Management Instrumentation (WMI)   A network and programmatic interface found in the Windows operating system that allows for remote queries of system information based on the remote user rights set up by the system administrator. (http://en.wikipedia.org/wiki/Windows_Management_Instrumentation)

Flowchart   Considered obsolete by many, the concept of a flowchart is to represent the logic of an operation graphically. Regardless of whether it's software or hardware, decisions in how a workflow is handled can be diagrammed through simple geometric shapes. Its general advantage is that it can be clearly understood without prior knowledge of a programming language. (http://en.wikipedia.org/wiki/Flowchart)

Chapter 8

License Dongle   In the never-ending war against software piracy, some vendors have begun putting the software-activation keys onto some sort of external device plugged into either a USB or parallel port on the back of the machine. You can freely copy the media, and install it all you want, but the software is useless unless you have that physical license key. (http://en.wikipedia.org/wiki/Copy_protection)

Activation or License Server   Some software vendors allow for a separate server to be set up that handles handing out activation or license keys to other devices. The key to this is the end-user license agreement, which includes a caveat that revolves around the simultaneous number of users allowed rather than the number of installs. So, in an environment such as VMWare or Windows Hypervisor, where servers come and go constantly, the activation server provides for a way to hand out licenses to stay legal, but without having to hard-code a license key to a specific machine. (http://en.wikipedia.org/wiki/License_server)

Blog-o-Sphere or Blogosphere   A fairly derogatory description of the collection of blogs and the fact that blogs are for the most part transitory in nature and for the most part without peer review. The main point is that the number and types of blog on the Internet is nearly unquantifiable, since new blogs pop up for nearly every potential opinion on any topic you can imagine. (http://en.wikipedia.org/wiki/Blogosphere)

Remote Control Utilities   Software solutions (Remote Desktop, VNC, GoToMyPC, etc.) that allow for a remote computer to take over a local computer using the Internet. The advantage is that applications are running locally and do not have to transfer data files over potentially slow wide-area network links; only the keystrokes, video, and mouse movements are transmitted from remote to local. Some systems provide for encrypted log-ins, and some provide for large amounts of data compression of the video stream to allow for higher resolution over slow connections. (http://en.wikipedia.org/wiki/Remote_Desktop_Protocol)

Ring 0   Like medieval armor, the protection in a modern computer operating system is made up of layers arranged in rings around the most sensitive piece, in this case the kernel. The closer you get to the kernel, the more sensitive the operations are and the higher the potential for a program to crash an entire computer. When describing driver programs (programs that provide an interface to a piece of hardware), you hear a lot about ring zero versus user space. (http://en.wikipedia.org/wiki/Ring_%28computer_security%29)

Advanced Network Computing Laboratory (ANCL)   Founded in 1996 by Brian Chee, ANCL was created with the intent of providing a neutral network equipment test facility for the expressed purpose of providing competitive product reviews for technology magazines. Originally with Internet Week, it was later attached to InfoWorld after Internet Week closed its doors. ANCL's secondary purpose is to provide real-world experience to computer science and engineering students through reviews, community service projects, and participation on the Interop tradeshow networking team. (http://www.ancl.hawaii.edu)

Service Processors (SP)   Small computers that piggyback on modern servers to provide environmental control and information to system managers. The concept is that this smaller computer will stay powered up regardless of the status of the main machine, and the service processor will be the actual authority for power control. So, pushing the power button really only sends signal to the service processor requesting power up. Modern service processors provide for programmatic access through protocol standards such as IPMI, drac, iLo, and others. A service processor aggregation appliance, such as those offered by Avocent, acts as a middleman reading the various flavors of service processor while presenting the data to the systems manager in a unified manner. (http://en.wikipedia.org/wiki/Ipmi)

VMDK and VHD   Two flavors of virtual hard disk formats, VMDK for VMWare and VHD for Microsoft Hypervisor. While containing the entire virtual machine, these files also contain virtualization connection information describing the types of disk, input/output, video, RAM, and other system-specific information. In most cases you can copy the single file and get the entire machine. If you use system snapshots, each snapshot freezes the system configuration in time, which allows you to "roll back" changes. However, snapshots are typically used for temporary situations, and in most cases their existence prevents single file backups or other virtual hosting parameters. (http://en.wikipedia.org/wiki/VMDK)

Monolithic Versus Virtualized Servers   Mono, meaning single, alludes to a stand-alone server that is the only thing using a single physical computer. This term is an attempt to more easily differentiate stand-alone servers from their virtualized cousins. (http://en.wikipedia.org/wiki/Monolithic)

Security Identifier (SID)   Created as part of the system generation process, each SID is designed to be a unique identifier as part of the Microsoft security systems. These unique identifiers are used by the security system instead of human-assigned identifiers that may accidentally become duplicated. The SID is extremely important in the virtualized world, and if you copy a system image into a VM host, the very first thing you are asked is whether you want to have the VM host assign a new set of SIDs to the new system. Duplicated SIDs can have potentially disastrous side affects. (http://en.wikipedia.org/wiki/Security_Identifier)

Duty Cycle   While normally used to describe power equipment, the concept of duty cycle is used to describe how long a piece of equipment may operate before requiring a rest or cool-down period. Shredders are a good example; for every, say, 20 minutes of operation, it must be allowed to cool down for 120 minutes. In the context of this book, we use duty cycle to describe the percentage of a day that a server can be used to its fullest capability. So a typical workstation might be a 25% duty cycle device where its normal workday coincides with a human workday. Going too much longer than this could reduce the overall reliability of the system. Purpose-built servers (100% duty cycle) typically have electronic components on their motherboards spread farther apart and/or have cooling channels to direct airflow across key components, something not normally provided on most workstations. (http://en.wikipedia.org/wiki/Duty_cycle)

N+1 This concept is used to describe several types of equipment, but in this book we've used it to describe power supplies. The concept is that if your system requires two power supplies to meet the needs of the system, the plus-one portion means that a third power supply is operational in the machine to take over should one of the primary power supplies fail. The "plus" factor describes the number of spares that are automatically available. (http://en.wikipedia.org/wiki/N%2B1_Redundancy)

iSCSI A networking protocol designed to allow for the creation of storage area networks using commodity Ethernet switches instead of dramatically more expensive fiber channel switches. Consisting of a target (disk array) and initiators (the server that is using the array), this system typically also allows for connections using some sort of user profile to limit what each initiator can access. (http://en.wikipedia.org/wiki/ISCSI)

Fibre Channel (FC) A local-area network transport protocol used primarily for connecting storage arrays to servers. This system was originally created by IBM to replace the huge complex disk system connection cables while also allowing for greater flexibility, however the predecessor to Fibre Channel was adopted rather than the proprietary IBM HIPPI system. Although it is a networking protocol, it is not compatible with the more common Ethernet, and must be connected using dedicated Fibre Channel switches. (http://en.wikipedia.org/wiki/Fibre_Channel)

Logical Unit Number (LUN) While used in quite a few contexts in the computing industry, this book uses it in the context of storage arrays. In this case the logical unit number is an identifier for pieces of the storage array made available for use in the storage area network. It is the LUN that is connected to the virtualization system. (http://en.wikipedia.org/wiki/Logical_Unit_Number)

Block Level (Storage Blocks) A block in the context of a data storage system refers to the smallest piece of data that can be read/written to that system. Through block size manipulation, systems administrators can optimize disk throughput. For example, if a database system typically has a record of 450 bytes, throughput can be maximized by using a 512-byte block size. So, in

theory, an entire record can be read or written using a single block. (http://en.
wikipedia.org/wiki/Storage_block)

Chapter 9

Network Access Control (NAC)   NAC is an evolving concept that started
with several competing standards. One of the most common is called 802.1x
and requires a special piece of software on each client called a supplicant. The
idea is that only when users present valid credentials is their traffic allowed even
to enter the network. It can be applied to both wired and wireless networks,
and in many cases 802.1x or one of the other competing standards has become
a common optional piece for most enterprise-grade network switches. (http://
en.wikipedia.org/wiki/Network_access_control)

Intrusion Detection Systems (IDS)   The ability to open up every single
packet that flies by, inspect it not only for worms and virus, but also compare it
to attack signatures. IDS has been the moving target of network security systems
for the better part of a decade and is in our opinion one of the major reasons why
firewalls keep getting bigger and bigger. With some attacks taking hundreds or
thousands of packets, we can compare it to knowing what a thousand-piece
jigsaw puzzle looks like after putting together only perhaps a half-dozen pieces.
(http://en.wikipedia.org/wiki/Intrusion_Detection_System)

Intrusion Prevention Systems (IPS)   If intrusion detection systems are the
burglar alarm, the intrusion prevention systems are your armed guards. Once an
intrusion has been determined, filters are slammed into place that should negate
the attack. Modern UTM firewall appliances (all-in-one boxes) tend to have
both integrated into the device. Such systems alleviate the need to manually
put into place large numbers of specialized access rules to deal with transitory
attacks. (http://en.wikipedia.org/wiki/Intrusion_prevention_system)

Unified Threat Management (UTM)   The so called all-in-one approach is
how the firewall industry is responding to the small to medium-sized business
market. The concept that a simple port blocking firewall is enough for small
business has gone the way of the dodo since so many attacks exploit openings
in the firewalls to break into vulnerable Web servers and other such Internet
services offered by business servers today. These UTMs instead allow for
Internet services to be offered up to the Internet, but still provide the ability to
inspect the access to see if malware is attempting to slip in. (http://en.wikipedia.
org/wiki/Unified_Threat_Management)

Algorithms   This often-misspelled term refers to formulas or methodologies
and is often used to describe how a computer program achieves its results. In

many cases, the algorithm is a set of English-language descriptions (or whatever your native language may be) describing how to do a process in a step-by-step fashion. There is a common saying in the computer industry that programmers must become casual experts in a great number of industries, since you must first learn how to do a process by hand if you expect to be able to automate the process. (http://en.wikipedia.org/wiki/Algorithms)

Chapter 10

Simple Object Access Protocol (SOAP)   Described as a simpler way to harvest information off websites, the concept is that each field on a web Page has a unique identifier, and through the SOAP protocol can ask the Web server to deliver the data in those specific fields. The idea is to provide a way to deliver access to data publically without opening potential security holes by giving direct network access to the database. (http://en.wikipedia.org/wiki/SOAP)

Common Gateway Interface (CGI)   One of the early methods by which websites can execute other programs to yield results outside the capabilities of existing Web servers. A good example is AutoCAD, which has a collection of special programs inserted into a Web server that can be called from within Web pages. It in turn accepts information on what CAD model you'd like to see in three dimensions and it then renders that portion of the model for display with a Web browser. This functionality is definitely outside the current capabilities of Web servers, but CGI provides a way to extend website capabilities more easily. (http://en.wikipedia.org/wiki/Common_Gateway_Interface)

Berkeley Open Infrastructure for Network Computing (BOINC)   The BOINC toolkit is a result of the success of grid computing projects such as SETI@home and Folding@home and offers users a toolkit approach for creating their own grid applications. (http://en.wikipedia.org/wiki/Boinc)

Aracibo, Puerto Rico   This city in Puerto Rico is best known as the location of the world's largest radio telescope, which is operated by Cornell University. Because of its huge dish inset into the ground and its massive receptor array suspended on cables over the disk, the Aracibo Radio Observatory has been featured in a number of science fiction movies. (http://en.wikipedia.org/wiki/Arecibo_Observatory)

CompuServe Information Services (CIS)   The first large-scale online information system, CompuServe went far beyond what simple bulletin boards (dial-up systems for posting notes, email, and announcements) were capable of at the time. CompuServe was the first service that provided links into specialized data services, methods for online ordering of merchandise, and other services that are now commonplace on the Internet. All of this was done over one of the world's largest dial-up modem pools, spread across the globe. (http://en.wikipedia.org/wiki/Compuserve)

Windows Terminal Server   This add-on to the Windows Server operating system provides remote access to the server and in addition allows remote users to run applications and do server functions in a virtual desktop environment. Similar in function to what was provided on older time-share computers, the remote desktop environment has become one of the most popular ways to do remote systems management, and a way to run large applications at the server instead of over potentially slow remote connections. (http://en.wikipedia.org/wiki/Windows_Terminal_Server)

Smart Card   Identical in size to a typical credit card, the smart card has circuitry inside the card that can do limited processing and storage. Typically used to hold user credentials, the smart card has some sort of electrical contact on one face of the card so that electrical connections can be made once the card is inserted into an appropriate reader. The smart card has been adopted by Microsoft for all its identification badges and is used to provide an extra layer of security for access to corporate communications infrastructure. It should be noted that smart card support has existed in the Windows operating system since the very early days of Windows. (http://en.wikipedia.org/wiki/Smart_card)

Bitmap   The overall concept is one of turning bits on and off to make a picture. By combining bits in various color layers, computers are able to combine the colors to create a more realistic color representation on the computer screen or printer. The disadvantage of bitmap technology is that resolution and picture integrity are lost or compromised as the image is enlarged. (http://en.wikipedia.org/wiki/Bitmap)

PeopleSoft   One of the leaders in human resource management information systems, this corporation has expanded their offerings to also encompass customer relations management. It is mentioned in this book as an example of a popular HR system that in many cases has become the authority for information about an employee. (http://en.wikipedia.org/wiki/Peoplesoft)

Clipper Chip   A hardware-based encryption system proposed by the U.S. government as a method of providing strong encryption to the computer industry. Because of controversy surrounding rumored "back doors" in the chip designed specifically for use by law enforcement; the programmed died within a couple of years. (http://en.wikipedia.org/wiki/Clipper_chip)

Thin Client/Thin Computer   The concept is to strip down a general-purpose operating system to provide only the platform and essential services for specific functions. The surge of thin clients would have computer systems with little or no local storage that would boot from Flash storage devices and provide only the ability to print, browse the Web, and set up virtual private networks. The intent is to provide the richness of a Web browser but with security and simplicity harking back to the days of "dumb terminals." (http://en.wikipedia.org/wiki/Thin_client)

Minitel   A French videotext system similar in function to CompuServe, which was intended to provide advanced communications services to French telecom customers. This was at the time the only nationally supported communications system that had as its intent the wish to provide what the Internet today provides. (http://en.wikipedia.org/wiki/Minitel)

Index